# THE PLEASURES
# OF
# THE PAST

ALSO BY DAVID CANNADINE

*Lords and Landlords: The Aristocracy and the Towns, 1774–1967*
*Rituals of Royalty: Power and Ceremonial in Traditional Societies* (editor)
*Patricians, Power and Politics in Nineteenth-Century Towns* (editor)
*Exploring the Urban Past: Essays in Urban History by H. J. Dyos* (editor)

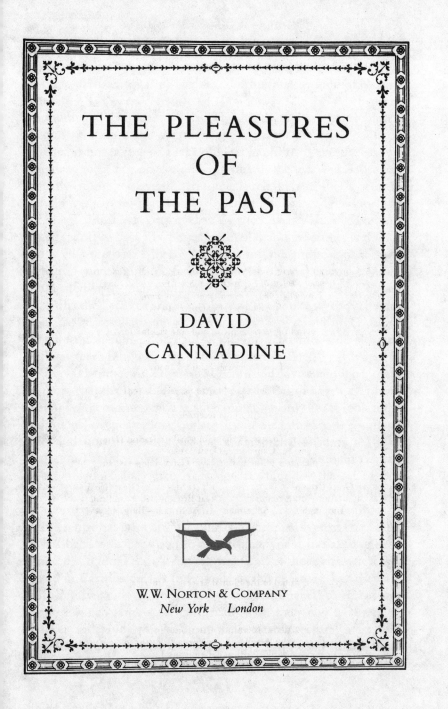

# THE PLEASURES
# OF
# THE PAST

## DAVID
## CANNADINE

W. W. NORTON & COMPANY
New York   London

First American Edition, 1989

First published as a Norton paperback 1991

Library of Congress Cataloging-in-Publication Data
Cannadine, David, 1950–
The pleasures of the past / David Cannadine.—1st ed.
p.   cm.
1. Great Britain—Civilization—20th century.   2. Great Britain—
Civilization—19th century.   3. Great Britain—Kings and rulers—
Biography.   4. Statesmen—Great Britain—Biography.
5. Historiography.   I. Title.
DA566.4.C25   1989
941.08—dc20          89-8537
CIP

Printed in the United States of America

ISBN 0-393-30749-2

W.W. Norton & Company, Inc.
500 Fifth Avenue, New York, N.Y. 10110
W.W. Norton & Company Ltd
10 Coptic Street, London WC1A 1PU

2 3 4 5 6 7 8 9 0

FOR MARGO

# CONTENTS

CONTENTS

## PART FOUR: GENERALITY

## PART FIVE: BIOGRAPHY

Illustrations appear on page 120, and between pages 130 and 131.

# PREFACE

I hope this book is as much pleasure to read as it has been to write. The essays and reviews collected here have been produced in idle moments between 1981 and 1987. With differing degrees of presumptuousness and expertise, they range across political, economic, social, urban and cultural history. But they are all in some way concerned with the history of modern Britain, and with the state of modern British history. As such, their perspective is unapologetically trans-Atlantic: some pieces were written in Princeton, New Haven and New York; some in Cambridge, Birmingham and London; and not a few were pondered and drafted in mid air.

Of course, there is a large element of randomness in the books that come one's way for such extended review. Nevertheless, a variety of themes stand out and recur: the cult of the national heritage and of the country house, the increasingly critical attitude of writers on the monarchy, the decay of Victorian cities and the problems of urban blight, the first serious studies of the post-war Conservative governments, and the diversities and doubts which characterize the contemporary historical scene. And behind all this lies the particular and pervasive climate of opinion current in Thatcher's England and Reagan's America, which has deeply influenced both the type and the content of British history produced during the present decade.

Inevitably, writing reviews of this kind is as hazardous an enterprise as it is enjoyable. Some tight-lipped colleagues disapprove of exuberant prose, and dismiss the concern to reach a broad, non-professional audience as little more than self-indulgent exhibitionism. And it would be absurd to suppose that all the authors of the books discussed here have read these reviews with unequivocal delight. But I hope these occasional essays convey something of the relevance and the interest, the excitement and the breadth, the pleasure and the fun, which characterize – or should characterize – history in general, and modern British history in particular. The fact that history is difficult, demanding and important is no reason for making it dull, or for taking it (or its practitioners) too seriously.

I am very much indebted to the editors of the *London Review of Books*, the *New York Review of Books*, *The Times Literary Supplement*, *New Statesman and Society*, *Encounter* and *History*, in whose journals these pieces first appeared, for permission to reprint them here. I am especially grateful to Karl Miller, who first gave me the opportunity and the space to write such pieces, and to those friends and colleagues who have urged me to bring them together in this way. Without Michael Shaw, Stuart Proffitt and the staff of Collins, they would never have appeared in this form. And without Linda Colley, they would never have appeared at all. I hope they do not feel they have too much to answer for.

D.N.C.                                                         *13 September, 1988*
Christ's College,
Cambridge

# PART ONE

# ROYALTY

# The House of Windsor

On 29 July 1981, a high society wedding took place in a large and well-known London church, between two members of the English upper classes. The groom was a well-meaning man in his early thirties, who came from a good family with unusually extensive continental connections. He had been educated at Cambridge University and had served in the Royal Navy. He had discreetly sown his wild oats, and had finally found an appropriate and acceptable wife, to his parents' great relief. The bride was thirteen years his junior, and her pedigree was unimpeachably aristocratic. Her beauty was more renowned than her brains, her virginity had been publicly vouched for by her uncle, and her fertility had been privately verified by her gynaecologist. The wedding itself was faultlessly planned and impeccably executed: the groom's family turned out in formidable array; the bride's parents, although divorced, appeared together for the occasion; there was a large congregation of well-wishers and admirers; an august clergyman officiated at the service; and the honeymoon was spent on a cruise.

Marriages like these, involving people rather like these, take place all the time in the smart London churches and fashionable country parishes of England. Generally, they attract little attention; but this was no ordinary upper-class wedding. For the man in question was Charles Philip Arthur George Mountbatten-Windsor, Prince of Wales and heir to the throne of England. And his bride was Lady Diana Frances Spencer, who was suddenly transformed, Cinderella-like, from being the daughter of an otherwise obscure aristocrat into a fairytale princess and future queen. It was a wedding such as dreams are made of, and nearly a billion people, one-eighth of the earth's total population, chose to watch it on their television screens, thereby providing the largest audience ever to observe a single event in the whole of human history. Never has there been such emphatic corroboration of Walter Bagehot's famous dictum: 'a princely marriage is the brilliant edition of a universal fact, and as such it rivets mankind.'

Yet this celebrated aphorism, which was actually quoted on the day by the Archbishop of Canterbury, is less universally valid than its undoubted appropriateness in this case might imply. In Britain itself, most nineteenth-century royal weddings were family affairs rather than public spectacles, and the marriage of an earlier Prince of Wales in 1863 – which actually occasioned Bagehot's remark – was in fact a decidedly lacklustre occasion. And in the twentieth century, the majority of surviving monarchies have evolved a ceremonial style so low-key and understated that their weddings, funerals and coronations are rarely the subject of international concern. So, *pace* Bagehot, the world-wide interest in the pageants and personalities of the British monarchy is of relatively recent origin and without parallel in any other royal house today. How, then, can we explain the survival and efflorescence of this one single European monarchy, when almost every other dynasty has either disappeared completely, or abandoned all but a shadow of its ancient royal pretensions?

It is this question which John Pearson addresses and answers in his fascinating and healthily sceptical book.[1] As he rightly points out, the pomp and popularity we now associate with the British monarchy are both in fact relatively recent developments. In the seventeenth century, the English were the pioneers of republican endeavour and parliamentary sovereignty, executing one king, and throwing out another. In the eighteenth century, they imported the Hanoverians, a dull and obscure German dynasty, who were looked down on by the great grandees of the realm and were rarely popular or beloved. Nor were Victoria and Albert much better: dutiful and high-minded, they seemed more German than English; they antagonized the ultra-patriot Lord Palmerston; and such triumphs as Albert's Great Exhibition were distinctly short-lived. As the supreme believers in progress and improvement, the early Victorians were more interested in demystifying monarchy than in venerating it, and they regarded the flummery of its ceremonial as alien to the rational spirit of the age. Indeed, after the death of Albert in 1861, the royal reputation reached its nadir, and there were widespread demands for another British republic.

Accordingly, it was only during the last quarter of the nineteenth century that the British monarchy came to assume its essentially modern form. The reasons for this development are complex, and may have had less to do with the personalities of the monarchs themselves than with the social turbulence, democratic politics, imperial rivalries and international tensions which characterized the period, and in the consequent rediscovery and conscious manipulation of the irrational element in national life. For whatever reason, from the late 1880s, the hitherto unpopular and reclusive 'Widow at Windsor' found herself reincarnated as the mother figure of the world's greatest empire, the most venerated woman on earth, more an icon and a symbol than a real human being. Her Golden Jubilee of 1887, and her Diamond Jubilee ten years later, were unprecedented instances of splendid ceremonial and personal apotheosis; her death and funeral were genuinely global events; and she bequeathed to her successor a monarchy fundamentally transformed. Most of its 'ancient traditions' are thus no older than the Statue of Liberty, and some are a good deal more recent.

These were the beginnings of a revived and rejuvenated British monarchy which survived with only minor interruptions until the early 1950s. Edward VII enjoyed grand ceremonial with a gusto his mother had never displayed. George V was decent and dutiful, and added middle-class morality to majestic spectacle. Edward VIII briefly threatened both the probity and the pageantry of this royal regime, but his infatuation with Mrs Simpson meant he was conveniently removed. And George VI repeated his father's formula once more: simple yet sacred, mundane but magical. Other thrones fell in the aftermath of war and revolution, but when Queen Elizabeth II was crowned amidst universal rejoicing and widespread television coverage in 1953, the British monarchy seemed more secure than ever. Almost nothing was really known about the personalities of the people concerned; yet that was an integral part of their mystique and appeal.

But from the mid 1950s, this formula began to fail, as the much-trumpeted 'New Elizabethan Age' fell rather flat. As the British Empire disintegrated, great power status disappeared, and domestic attitudes began to change, it was no longer clear precisely what role the monarchy should fill, as it came to seem increasingly remote and out of touch. During the late 1950s, critics like John Grigg and Malcolm Muggeridge likened the Queen to a priggish and prissy schoolgirl, surrounded by crusty and snobbish courtiers, and John Osborne attacked the whole institution of monarchy as 'the gold filling in a mouth full of decay'. The weddings of Princess Margaret, the Duke of Kent and Princess Alexandra failed to rekindle the euphoria of the Coronation, and in the 1960s, the era of 'swinging London' and Harold Wilson's 'white-hot' technological revolution, the monarchy seemed increasingly irrelevant, anachronistic and accident-prone. Even Prince Philip feared that it – and he – might soon become museum pieces.

But this did not happen, and Pearson's account of the steps taken to avoid this fate is the most original part of the book. In the late 1960s, when Prince Charles reached the age to enter public life, a deliberate and highly successful attempt was made to re-launch the monarchy. In part, this involved the adapting and updating of ceremonial: Prince Charles's public investiture as Prince of Wales at Caernarvon Castle was the first royal pageant to be conceived and planned throughout as a television spectacular. But even more innovative was the decision to present the members of the royal family, no longer as public icons, but as people and personalities in their own right, by breaking the taboos against showing extemporaneous royal conversations and informal royal activities. Accordingly, Prince Charles was interviewed on radio and television, and talked engagingly and spontaneously about himself and his role. And a major television film, *Royal Family*, gave the first real glimpse of the Queen and her relations as fallible if fabulous people. Shown in 140 countries, it was an instant success: the monarchy might have lost the allure that brought it sentimental deference, but it had become instead an object of unrivalled public curiosity.

Thus, Pearson argues, the curtain rose on the most compulsive and original soap opera in the world, which combines scandal and splendour, personality and pageantry, in a way which neither *Dallas* nor *Dynasty* can rival, and which has been running with remarkable success ever since. On the one hand, the impeccably planned television spectacles continue, each attracting a greater audience than the one before: the Queen's Silver Jubilee, Lord Mountbatten's funeral, the wedding of the Prince and Princess of Wales. But alongside this public theatricality is set the back-stage drama of royal private lives. Is all well between Princess Anne and her husband, Mark Phillips? Will Prince Michael of Kent be allowed to marry a divorced Catholic? Who will Prince Andrew's next girlfriend be? Is the Princess of Wales anorexic? As middle-class morality has changed, so these daily happenings in the lives of the royal family have become more fascinating, not less, and the media, once so discreet, have become much more revealing. As Walter Bagehot might have put it when Princess Margaret's marriage to Lord Snowdon broke down: 'a princely divorce is the brilliant edition of a universal fact, and as such it rivets mankind.'

As a description of the undulating contours of royal renown, Pearson's account seems, historically, entirely convincing. But as he also shows, neither the transformation of the British monarchy at the end of the nineteenth century, nor its successful re-launching in the second half of the twentieth, has happened by accident. The magic of monarchy requires magicians to manufacture and manipulate it, and his book is much concerned to find out exactly who they were and are. In the first phase of royal efflorescence, much of the responsibility lay with blue-blooded impresarios like Lord Esher and the Duke of Norfolk, who brought a new professionalism and sense of theatre into the planning and staging of royal pageants. They were assisted by the journalists and press lords who, from the 1880s, took a far more well-disposed attitude towards the monarchy than had been fashionable in the earlier years of Victoria's reign, and showed remarkable – and largely self-imposed – discretion at the time of the abdication. And they in turn were supported by Sir John Reith's British Broadcasting Corporation, which deliberately projected the most favourable image of the monarchy, in its broadcasts of great state occasions, its coverage of royal visits and events, and its transmission of the King's Christmas message to the Empire.

By the late 1950s, however, one symptom of the monarchy's increasing isolation was its inability to keep up with recent developments in the media, whether sensationalist journalism or serious television, and it was only in the late 1960s that the decision was taken to re-launch the monarchy by exploiting, rather than resisting, them. The first equerry assigned to Prince Charles, David Checketts, also sat on the board of one of London's smartest public relations companies, and it was he who coached the prince on how best to appear before the cameras. In 1968, a new press secretary, William Hestletine, was appointed by Buckingham Palace, and his handling of the media was noticeably more adroit and less hostile than that of his predecessor. And Richard Cawston, the producer of *Royal Family*, took the greatest trouble to ensure that his film presented the monarchy in the most relaxed, engaging and acceptable way. Indeed, so successful were these three men in promoting and projecting this new, human face of royalty, that no one at the time noticed what was going on, or that the most ancient of British institutions was now being effectively 'marketed like a packet of detergent'.

But this is not the only influence which Pearson sees as being significant in the making of the modern British monarchy. Of equal importance in establishing its image has been the contribution of a succession of formidable women. Historically, of course, monarchy is a quintessentially male enterprise: as priest or magician, warrior or warlord, lawmaker or governor, it is the man who is in charge, while his wife is expected to do little more than look beautiful and produce children. But as the modern British monarchy has evolved, it has been divested of most of its historical functions, and so its macho and mystical male roles have been much attenuated. A British monarch is no longer a god or a priest, he only makes laws in the most formal of senses, and although he wears a uniform and appears on horseback, he does not take charge of the armed services, either in peace or war. Significantly, the Hanoverians were the last British royal dynasty to be dominated by the males of the family. Since then, the men may sometimes have reigned, but it is the women – whether as queen regnant or queen consort – who have really set the tone.

This new style of matriarchal monarchy was begun by Queen Victoria, whose husband Albert merely discovered the impotence of being earnest, and died young and unfulfilled, while she went on to old age and apotheosis. Edward VII lived most of his life in his mother's shadow, reigned only briefly, and was outlived by his wife. George V was brought up to venerate his grandmother, and, for all his hectoring manner, was a far less robust personality than his consort Queen Mary. Even Edward VIII ran almost true to type, since he always had affairs with married women, and in Wallis Simpson found the ideal mother figure. George VI was very much the creation of his mother, Queen Mary, and his wife, Queen Elizabeth, and it is she who remains the monarchy's presiding matriarch today. Meanwhile, Prince Philip has made even less impact on events than Prince Albert, while Prince Charles is completely outshone by the dominant female presence: his grandmother seems immortal and beyond criticism; his mother seems set to bar his way to the throne for the rest of the century; and his wife is far more glamorous and sought after than he is.

Seen in this perspective, the notion of 'the merry wives of Windsor' takes on an altogether new meaning: for it is their ideal of decency and dutifulness which has been successfully imposed on the royal males, while those with initiative or ambition, glamour or personality, cleverness or opinions, have been ruthlessly suppressed. George V and George VI conformed exactly to the preferred type, and Prince Charles shows every sign of doing so as well. Edward VIII did not, and had to abdicate, and the same was true of Lord Snowdon, who merely got divorced. Not surprisingly, many of the Windsor women strongly disapproved of Lord Mountbatten, the only royal male in recent years who resolutely refused to conform, successfully carved out his own career, and actually got away with it. But with this conspicuous exception, the Windsor men have been effectively prevented from fulfilling any real male role, except one. Once they have done their bit towards perpetuating the royal line, there is virtually nothing left for them to do.

Yet oddly enough, the British monarchy is as much a monument to male chauvinism as it is to male castration, since all these dominant women have been extremely unemancipated, 'always gracious, always feminine'. One reason why Princess Margaret and Princess Anne get such a bad press is that they resolutely refuse to conform to this stereotype, the one because she lives an eventful private life, the other because she is tough, competitive and swears at journalists. And the tyranny of the double standard made it almost impossible for Prince Charles to find a suitable bride, since most of the available women were either too intelligent, or were blighted by what was euphemistically called 'a past'. By contrast, Lady Diana's great merit was that she was 'the absolute antithesis of the modern, self-assertive, liberated girl'. And, although it has been impossible to maintain this view in the case of Sarah Ferguson, the circumlocutions to which the British press has resorted only show how much the ideal type of royal woman remains totally unemancipated – and the more powerful within the family as a result.

In analysing these recent royal revivals, Pearson is both stronger and more interesting on the supply rather than the demand side: the entrepreneurs and image makers, the men in charge of the media, and the women in charge of the men. But this is only half of the answer, since even the best salesman in the world needs to be sure there is an audience, and the most sophisticated marketing techniques cannot create one if it is just not there. So how is the continuing demand for the British monarchy to be explained? After all, the country over which these people reign is less important now than at any time in its modern history; the monarchs themselves wield less effective power than Queen Victoria did even in her dotage; and as Pearson himself admits, by presenting the royal family as individuals rather than as icons, this new marketing technique merely exposes them for what they really are, namely 'a group of rather ordinary people, none of them unusually intelligent or witty or accomplished or remarkable'. So why exactly do they appeal so much?

In the case of Britain itself, it is distressingly clear that the royal family has thrived in recent years as the all-purpose antidote to international decline, economic decay and social unrest. As the circumstances of British life become more dreary, the pomp of monarchy becomes all the more magical. But in addition, it is held to bolster Britain's battered self-esteem overseas, where it can also be presented as a unique national possession, one of the few remaining assets for which the country is still genuinely the envy and cynosure of the world. But why, in turn, is this so? The Americans revolted against monarchy over two hundred years ago; the loyalty of Commonwealth countries is inexorably weakening, both to Britain and to the Queen; and what possible relevance can the Windsor saga have to the nations of republican Europe or the third world today?

But that very question may itself provide part of the answer: for what makes the monarchy compulsive reading and viewing for so much of the world is that it is irresistibly irrelevant. It is not the British monarchy as *monarchy* that the world is interested in, but the British monarchy as harmless entertainment. In one guise, it is like a soap opera, but better: nature does not imitate art, it surpasses it. The personalities are more plausible, the houses more lavish, and the spectacles far more splendid, than anything the Ewings or the Carringtons can devise. But in another guise, it is like the real world of power, politics and propaganda, but nicer: impotently dignified rather than threateningly efficient. Compared with the personality cults of Lenin and Stalin, Hitler and Mussolini, Gadaffi and Reagan, the British royal family offers more decency, greater glamour, and is mercifully free from the risk that its actions will bring about another world war. As one courtier put it at the time of the last royal wedding, 'We're in the happiness business.'

But there are real dangers in this, especially for Britain itself. To begin with, as Pearson admits, this degree of exposure to the media inevitably trivialises the institution of monarchy, by showing how much of the lives of those connected with it are concerned with *being*, and how little of their time is spent in *doing*. It is not so much that the Princess of Wales is an empress with no clothes, but that, on the contrary, wearing clothes is just about the only thing that she actually does do. Moreover, it is surely dangerous for a nation in Britain's current condition to be quite so proud of this essentially ornamental and anachronistic institution. Romance and escapism are all very well, but it may be the case that these very attitudes – which the monarchy engenders, legitimates and depends on – impede any serious attempt to modernize a society which is desperately in need of such treatment. And to equate British self-esteem with the fact that the Windsor soap opera tops the world television ratings is ultimately to demean and diminish a once-great nation.

The real problem with the monarchy – and Pearson's book illustrates it rather than addresses it – is that it is so successful in preventing any real discussion of whether Britain is better off with it, or without it. By constantly dwelling on both the trivia and the tinsel, the media give the impression that the continued existence of the royal family is absolutely indispensable to Britain's national well being, and it allows almost no space to the consideration of the alternative, republican case which was more freely discussed in the seventeenth and the nineteenth centuries than it is now. Indeed, it is taken for granted that anyone entertaining such views is either demented or unpatriotic, or both. And in the same way, the royal ceremonial is value-laden, visual rhetoric, in which the medium is indeed the message, and the message is that no alternative system should possibly be considered. As a result, the very idea that there might be other constitutional arrangements than a monarchy is, for most people in Britain, literally unthinkable; and the fact that this is so, and that even a sceptical and irreverent writer like Pearson obviously thinks so, is the ultimate demonstration of just how successful the monarchy's media manipulation has become.

★

And so the royal road show continues serenely on its way. On 23 July this year, another high society wedding will take place in another well-known London church, between two more members of the English upper classes. He is a sailor who fought for Britain in the Falklands, she is of a good family and has worked for a Mayfair graphics firm. The wedding itself has been faultlessly planned, and will no doubt be impeccably executed: the ceremonial will be incomparably splendid, the world will watch and wonder, spines will tingle, eyes will be moist, and disbelief will be willingly suspended once again. But before we lose all sense of perspective and proportion, a case should at least be made for the wilful reassertion of some incredulity. The pomp will take care of itself; what we really need is a little more circumspection.

(1986)

NOTE:
1. John Pearson, *The Ultimate Family: The Selling of the House of Windsor* (London, 1986).

# 2

# Prince Albert

Western monarchy is not merely, as Max Weber observed, institutionalized charisma: it is institutionalized male chauvinism as well. Whether priest or magician, philosopher or warrior, sovereigns are expected to be men, and in most cases they are. The Kingdom of Heaven is ruled by a God not a Goddess, and the Kingdom of the Jungle by a lion not a lioness (or by Tarzan not by Jane). In some countries, the Salic law made it impossible for women to accede to the throne, and even where it did not, women have always been severely disadvantaged in the succession stakes. If a king's first child is a son, he is *ipso facto* heir apparent, and will accede automatically; but if the child is a daughter, she is merely heir presumptive, and will only accede if no son is subsequently born. A king is by definition king regnant, and his consort is therefore queen; but the husband of a queen regnant is not therefore king. And so, with inexorable if superficially paradoxical logic, it is always better to be the woman playing the role of the man (with correspondingly increased scope as queen regnant) than to be the man playing the role of the woman (with much diminished opportunities as prince consort). Kings usually reign, and queens occasionally rule: but gender always governs.

So being the husband of a regnant queen is even more of a non-job than being vice-president of the United States. To be so close to the presidency as to be only a heartbeat away from the White House is one thing; to be so near to the throne yet with no prospect of ever occupying it is quite another. And, since queens regnant are understandably unusual in Western history, their consorts are even rarer, and most inevitably live and die obscure. How many people, for instance, can name the husbands of

Catherine the Great and Maria Theresa? Or know the male consorts of English regnant queens since the sixteenth century? Queen Elizabeth I preferred to execute her favourites rather than marry them; Queen Anne's husband, Prince George of Denmark, was no more significant a figure in his day than Mr Thatcher is in ours. Then there was Prince Albert; now there is the Duke of Edinburgh, whom the Queen has never created Prince Consort; and, since King Charles III and King William V are ready and waiting to reign, there will probably not be another male consort to a British regnant queen until the second half of the twenty-first century at the earliest.

Only because Albert is in competition with such pygmies does he appear a giant. For he was never a major figure in his own right. Like all male consorts, he had the wrong job for his sex, or the wrong sex for his job, and he was additionally hampered by being dead and gone at forty-two. Queen Victoria lived for twenty years before she married him, and reigned for another forty after he died. His period of influence – their time of married bliss – was a mere two decades, far too short a span for achieving much in public life, compared with figures like Palmerston, Gladstone, or the Queen herself, who were on the stage of history for sixty years and more. And yet, as Mrs Thatcher selectively celebrates Victorian values, Albertian attitudes resurface too. The 165th anniversary of his birth, and the 123rd anniversary of his death, are not immediately obvious dates for commemoration. But in England during the last few months there has been a mild outbreak of orchestrated Alberto-mania. He has been the subject of an elaborate and much-publicized exhibition in London; there have been Albert weekends, Albert lectures, and Albert concerts; and he has even found himself acclaimed as 'a man comparable to Thomas Jefferson'.[1]

As this fanciful and flattering comparison implies, the quest for the historical Albert is far from easy, and far from finished. He possessed such an elusive personality, and appeared in so many different guises, that one biography is never adequate, and all biographies are never enough. There is, to begin with, Albert in life; the flesh-and-blood being, who was adored by the Queen but regarded with hostility or indifference by most of her subjects for most of his life. Then there is Albert in death: the sculptured statue and sepulchred saint, glimpsed tremulously through a veritable Niagara of Victorian (or, rather, Victoria's) tears. And there is Albert in myth: the constitutional paragon who, with a prescience only visible in hindsight, steered the silly and adolescent Queen away from the snares and follies of political partisanship into the righteous paths of detachment and impartiality by preaching the gospel of Walter Bagehot before he had even written it. One difficulty with most biographies of Albert is that they are never completely clear which of these three subjects they are concerned with. Another is that they do not consider other, and perhaps more fruitful, ways of evaluating him. The three most recent studies of the Prince Consort well illustrate both the strengths and the shortcomings of the biographical method of writing royal history.

Robert Rhodes James's life of Albert is presented as a personal and political portrait of the man in his times.[2] Like the Prince's previous biographers, he is ultimately defeated in his quest for the real, inner Albert, because most of his personal papers were destroyed. But he does present him (and also, on occasion, his wife) as a more credible human being, more flawed yet also more attractive, than he has ever appeared before. He shows, for instance, how the Prince's upbringing in Germany, in the shadows of his profligate and promiscuous father and elder brother, left him in constant fear of family scandal. He gives an impressive account of the young Albert's rigorous education, at The Rosenau and at Bonn University. He offers a candidly critical catalogue of the young Victoria's failings: she was prejudiced, emotional, intolerant, unintellectual, artless, unimaginative, ungrateful, cold, and arrogant. He paints a tender and moving picture of their storm-clouds-and-sunshine marriage, one of the great romances of history. And he provides the most detailed description yet of the upbringing and education of their eldest son, the Prince of Wales, an episode from which neither Albert nor Victoria emerges with much credit.

Rhodes James also illustrates well the problems that the Prince Consort faced as a man trying to do a woman's job, when what he really wanted was a male role. At the time of Albert's wedding, his uncle, King Leopold of the Belgians, warned the British prime minister Lord Melbourne that 'the position of a husband of a Queen, who reigns in her own right, is a position of the greatest difficulty for *any person* and at *any time*', and in his early years Albert certainly found it to be so. Victoria, who was understandably intimidated by his trained and powerful intellect, tried to keep him at a distance, by hiding behind Melbourne and Baroness Lehzen, her governess. He was forced to have his household chosen for him by the Queen and her prime minister; she explicitly stated that he must play no part in politics; and she banned him from being present at her audiences with ministers. His arms were quartered with the royal arms in the inferior position, as if he was a woman; he was not given a British peerage; and he was only formally created Prince Consort in 1857. When he protested that their honeymoon at Windsor was too short, she replied imperiously, 'You forget, my dearest love, that I am the sovereign, and that business can stop and wait for nothing.' As Albert summarized it despondently, 'I am only the husband, not the master, in the house.'

For a man of his gifts, training, and ambitions, this was highly frustrating. But the demise of the Melbourne ministry, the departure of Lehzen, and the fact that throughout the 1840s Victoria was pregnant almost as much as she was regnant, enabled Albert to establish himself as her indispensable guide and confidential adviser, working with his desk beside hers, drafting her official letters, and seeing ministers, either in her company or on his own. All this is well enough known, but Rhodes James goes much further than any previous biographer in showing the awesome ambitions which Albert entertained, not for himself personally, but for the monarchy as an institution. Far from training Victoria to be an impartial and impotent sovereign, as is still popularly supposed, Albert's 'dominant purpose was not to reduce, but significantly to *increase*, the real power and influence of the Crown'. Hence his highly publicized and partisan support of Peel, who believed in executive government as strongly as he did, and his equally emphatic hostility to Palmerston, not only on account of his wayward morals, but also because he sought to deny Albert's claim to a major part in the making and conduct of foreign policy. For the Prince Consort, the crown should occupy a central, creative part in the work of running the country: its duty and purpose were no less than to 'watch and control government'. Clearly Albert was playing for very high stakes indeed.

But, of course, it never really worked. As Rhodes James rightly notes, Albert was intent upon 'the maximum of political influence with the minimum of criticism', something which any seasoned politician would have told him was impossible. From the very start, he received a bad press, and throughout his life influential journals like *Punch* and *The Times* remained hostile. At the time of the wedding he was pilloried as a poor and lowly foreigner on the make. He made no friends, never understood the English character, and remained, on his own admission, 'a true German'. He was too intellectual, too cosmopolitan, too earnest, too bourgeois, to establish a rapport with the public. He never really grasped English party politics, and overrated his position vis-à-vis the crown, and Victoria's position vis-à-vis her ministers. He suffered for supporting Peel too strongly, and his opposition to Palmerston, 'the minister of England', only made his patriotism seem even more suspect. He meddled too much, delegated too little, and worked too hard, given his weak physical frame. He cried too easily as a boy, tired too easily as a man, and died too easily as a prince. Unlike Victoria, he lacked the will to live. When the going got tough, she got harder, but he got softer; and in the end he got so soft that he dissolved completely.

Such is Rhodes James's Albert: convincing yet incomplete. The book is curiously uneven in its coverage, giving too much space to the young Prince, and far too little to the 1850s, the decade which, Rhodes James suggests, saw Albert's influence at its greatest. Yet it is hard to be sure of this, especially when it appears that the author has not consulted the numerous and weighty papers of the leading politicians of the time. The result is not merely a rather claustrophobic account, excessively dependent on the royal archives, but one that makes it impossible to assess Albert's real importance in the political life of the country. *He* may have thought he was influential; but what did the politicians think? The book also suffers because the author has clearly not absorbed much of the recent work on the 1840s and 1850s: a biography that cites such antique authorities as H.A.L. Fisher, A. C. Benson, and Justin McCarthy can hardly be said to be at the cutting edge of modern historical scholarship. The prose is occasionally orotund to the point of flatulence; the lack of genealogical tables makes Albert's ancestors and relatives hard to place; and the citations to the royal archives are so vague as to be all but useless to scholars.

More fundamentally, the three major claims that Rhodes James advances on behalf of Albert are contradicted by much of the evidence he actually presents. He suggests, for instance, that the Prince Consort was 'the most astute and ambitious political of his age'. But this is mere hyperbole: all too often, Albert was wrong in judgment, mistaken in understanding, and defeated in manoeuvre. And to claim that he had 'to deal with men of power whose knowledge, experience, and intelligence were often inferior to his' ignores both his own youth and naiveté and the heavyweight accomplishments of men like Peel, Palmerston, Russell, and Derby. Secondly, Rhodes James argues that Albert 'established the principles of political neutrality', of 'genuine impartiality', and brought the monarchy much popularity as a result. Yet much of the novelty of his book derives from the overwhelming amount of material he deploys that points in the opposite direction. Finally, he frequently describes Albert as England's answer to Jefferson. But one has only to compare Osborne with Monticello to see the difference between an earnest bourgeois plodder and an inspired Enlightenment genius.

To make such invidious comparisons only does Albert harm: for while he was no Jefferson, he was, more modestly, an uncommonly gifted prince. That fact emerges with impressive conviction from Hermione Hobhouse's study, which nicely complements Rhodes James's book.[3] As a biographer and member of Parliament, he is naturally strongest on politics and personalities; as a former secretary of the Victorian Society and author of a major study of Thomas Cubitt, she is much more interested in 'Prince Albert's work for education, art and science.' Her well-illustrated and extensively researched book is ostensibly the catalogue to the Albert Exhibition at the Royal College of Art in London, which has recently closed. But in fact it is a major study in its own right: the fullest and most sympathetic account of Albert's multifarious activities that we are ever likely to get. Without doubt, Albert was the most compassionate, gifted, versatile, intellectual, and well-educated figure that the British royal family has either produced or recruited during the last two hundred years. Of course, the competition is not strong; but the Prince Consort's range of activities, concern for the poor, delight in the company of intellectuals, and genuine interest in the arts and sciences were certainly of an unsurpassed high order.

Like that of the exhibition, the purpose of Hobhouse's book is to convey 'the full range of Albert's contribution to British national life'. And so it does. He was instrumental in the buying and building of Osborne and Balmoral; he suggested a new suite of entertaining rooms at Buckingham Palace, as well as the Mall frontage; and he nearly (but, alas, not quite) made the drains run on time at Windsor. He composed songs and sacred music, and was a competent sketcher and etcher; he patronized Winterhalter and Landseer and collected early German and Italian paintings. He ran model farms at Windsor and Balmoral, and exhibited his livestock at shows throughout the country. He rode to hounds with skill and verve, and was a competent shot. He believed in better housing for the workers, better education at Cambridge University (of which he was chancellor), and better weapons for the army. He was president or chairman of innumerable societies; he chaired one Royal Commission charged with the decoration of the Houses of Parliament; and he chaired another that planned the Great Exhibition of 1851. And all this was only in his spare time, in those odd moments of respite from the treadmill of public engagements and official correspondence.

As a picture of a gifted and humane man, driven by duty and

conscience to do good works, Hobhouse's book is vividly convincing. Once again, however, the real Albert, the man himself, is suffocated beneath the weight of worthy endeavour. And, although the author's mastery of Victorian culture and artifacts is predictably impressive, she is less sure-footed when she writes of Albert the politician. Certainly, her claim that the Prince Consort's 'greatest contribution to the history of England was indubitably the way in which he established the idea of a monarchy above party politics' is not borne out in Rhodes James's book (even though in some moods he also thinks it is). Above all, it still remains unclear just how important Albert's contribution to English life really was. Of course it was many-sided; but was it really significant? His interest in working-class housing, for instance, made little real impact; his army reforms were at best 'discreet but significant', and at worst, as in the case of his design of new headgear, merely a nuisance; the Royal Commission responsible for the decoration of the Palace of Westminster was hardly a success; and 'Albertopolis', the South Kensington complex of museums and colleges, is more a monument to him than of him. Even the Great Exhibition was far from being a single-handed, Albertian triumph: it was not his idea in the first place; the Crystal Palace was Paxton's creation; and Albert's conception of the exhibition as a monument to peace and internationalism was not how it was seen by the mass of the people.

For all his earnest and ambitious versatility, Albert was never really popular in life and despite the title of Darby and Smith's fascinating and well-produced book, it is not clear that he was ever really popular in death, either.[4] Of course, there was an immediate outpouring of spontaneous and guilty grief – guilt because Albert's qualities had so rarely been acclaimed in life, and grief because the Victorians grieved easily and publicly, especially over untimely death. But more measured commemoration of Albert was lukewarm, limited, and unsuccessful. Only twenty-five statues to him were put up throughout Britain and the empire, and they were no better at capturing the real Albert than any of his subsequent biographers have been. He was depicted as a soldier despite the fact that he was a man of peace; in medieval costume even though he was in many ways a quintessentially contemporary person; as a religious figure, when faith meant little to him; and floundering beneath yards of robes and decorations, although his life was characterized by earnestness and simplicity. In some towns, commemorative schemes were held up or abandoned through lack of money, and in others, where monuments took the more utilitarian form of institutes, hospitals, clocks, fountains, and almshouses, the association with Albert was soon completely forgotten.

Considering the pathos of his early death, the Victorians' addiction to heroes, and their incorrigible inclination towards sentimentality, it is really the *lack* of a cult of the Prince that is most impressive. But if the British people refused to make him a saint, the Queen certainly did. She clung to her grief with reclusive and lifelong tenacity; she surrounded Albert's sacred memory with the full panoply of relics, shrines, and holy days; she wanted all future kings of England to be called Albert for ever and ever, amen; and she commissioned numerous statues, busts, and paintings. But even her more public projects – at Frogmore, in the Albert Memorial Chapel at Windsor, and the Albert Memorial itself at Kensington – were not entirely successful. There were constant wrangles over money, designs, and architects; there was much architectural criticism of Frogmore and the Albert Memorial. None of these schemes was completed until the 1870s; and they never became places of popular pilgrimage. Indeed, by the time of her own apotheosis at her Golden and Diamond Jubilees, Albert had long since been forgotten. She may have made a saint out of him; but it was the British people who made a saint out of her.

Oddly enough, then, the result of all this positive interest in the Prince Consort is largely negative so far as his reputation is concerned. Beyond question, he was, as he set out to be, a 'good and useful man', and each of these books eloquently illustrates that in one way or another. But, like most biographers, these authors advance additional claims for the importance of their subject's life, the significance of his death, and the magnitude of his achievements, which are contradicted by much of the evidence they present. For, *pace* Rhodes James, Albert was no Jefferson; *pace* Hobhouse, he was not the architect of constitutional monarchy; *pace* Darby and Smith, there was no posthumous cult; and *pace* everybody, he was never really popular. Significantly, it has proved no easier to establish a cult of Albert in the 1980s than it did in the 1860s: the exhibition devoted to his life and work which has recently closed in London 'spectacularly failed to interest the British public', and lost its sponsors a great deal of money.

The common failing of all biographers of Albert is that, sooner or later, they never can resist the temptation to present him as the precursor of the modern British monarchy when in fact, as the public's indifference to him today only serves to show, he was a world away from the impotent and glamorous soap opera it has since become. What we really need are some nonbiographical studies of Albert, which get his life and works in a more rigorous and realistic historical perspective, showing that he was more the end of an old style of monarchy than he was the beginning of a new. For in more ways than one, Albert left no legacy at all: he was the end of the line. There were no successors to the 1851 exhibition's spirit of peace and internationalism. He left the Queen with no textbook training in the trade of impartial sovereign. The education he devised for his son was rejected, which was perhaps just as well, for by the time he acceded to the throne, the job was so much diminished that such an intellectual training was quite unnecessary. By contrast, the role that Albert had wanted for the monarchy was fundamental, rather than ornamental, and most developments since his death would have caused him displeasure and regret. For he was more interested in emulating William III than in anticipating someone like the Duke of Edinburgh. Victoria may have been the first constitutional monarch; but Albert was the last philosopher king.

(1984)

NOTES:
1. Royal College of Art, 'Prince Albert: His Life and Work', November 1983 to March 1984.

2. Robert Rhodes James, *Prince Albert: A Biography* (London, 1983).
3. Hermione Hobhouse, *Prince Albert: His Life and Work* (London, 1983).
4. Elisabeth Darby and Nicola Smith, *The Cult of the Prince Consort* (London, 1983).

# Queen Victoria

The last British monarchs who gave their names to their times were Queen Victoria and King Edward VII. But whereas the word 'Edwardian' merely defined a decade, the adjective 'Victorian' conjured up an age – when God was an Englishman, when Britannia ruled the waves, and when the pound was indeed a sterling currency. And presiding over this era of providential and predestined progress was the Queen-Empress herself, whose life became the essence and the embodiment of her times. At her Golden and Diamond Jubilees, she was rapturously acclaimed as the bourgeois Gloriana, the fairy queen of a gas-lit realm, whose reign had marked and moulded an era of unprecedented national improvement and unrivalled imperial expansion. And, appropriately enough, nothing became the Victorian age like the ending of it: no woman in history has ever been mourned by so many people as the 'great white queen'; and after her death, the British were never so certain of themselves or of their destiny again.

For the age did not long survive the passing of its eponymous empress. The Edwardian era was a flash, hedonistic reaction against Victorian primness, and in the holocaust of the First World War, the old and easy nineteenth-century certainties vanished for ever. In the cynical and disillusioned years which followed, the Victorians were roundly derided as vulgar, philistine, hypocritical and middle class, most memorably by Lytton Strachey, whose stilettoed studies of Cardinal Manning, Florence Nightingale, Thomas Arnold and General Gordon left their reputations in tatters. And, since 1945, the professional historians have remorselessly exposed the contradictions which lay at the very heart of the Victorian era – of poverty and squalor in the midst of plenty and prosperity, of anti-industrial values which gradually throttled an ostensibly commercial society, of aristocractic power which resourcefully thwarted the advent of democracy, and of economic and international anxieties which were the darker side of the cult of empire.

But until very recently, the Queen herself has effectively escaped this sceptical and scholarly scrutiny. While the Victorian age now seems so diverse and contradictory that the phrase itself has been virtually robbed of all meaning, and while her reign merely endows it with a nominal unity of tone and time which substantively it may never have possessed, the Queen herself remains *regina intacta*. The destruction of most of her papers and the discretion of most of her courtiers meant that many secrets went with her to the grave. The carefully vetted publication of selections from her letters and extracts from her journals between 1907 and 1932 only enhanced the popular picture of a woman formidable, tragic, yet winning. Even Lytton Strachey was overwhelmed by the most eminent Victorian of them all, and despite the occasional Bloomsbury barbs, composed an adulatory biography which remains a classic of its kind. And the scholarly revolution in Victorian studies since 1945 has likewise failed to dethrone the Queen: in Elizabeth Longford's sensitive and well-disposed biography, she still shines forth, resolved to be good, and on the whole succeeding.

This widening gap between our enhanced understanding of the Victorian era and our unchanging perception of the Victorian queen, is easily explained. In part, it is because academic scholars and royal biographers tend to plough their separate furrows. No British sovereign since George I has received a full-scale study from a professional historian. Instead, most recent royal biographers have been gifted amateurs, who excel at the stylish evocation of a personality, but who are largely oblivious to broader historical trends and meanings, and are often unaware of most recent scholarly developments. But in addition, the very nature of the monarchy as an hereditary institution, and the conditions governing access to its archives, necessarily means that most royal biographies are excessively deferential and discreet, and are more concerned to sustain the mythology and mystique of the institution than they are to question or examine it. Imagine the difficulties involved in writing a life of Abraham Lincoln if Ronald Reagan was his great grandson.

But in 1987, the year of the hundredth anniversary of the Queen's Golden Jubilee, it is surely high time that some deliberate attempt was made to bridge this widening gap between the Victorian monarch and the Victorian age. At first glance, Stanley Weintraub's book does nothing of the kind, but merely repeats and reworks the well-known biographical themes of headstrong schoolgirl, devoted wife, desolate widow and apotheosized symbol, while leaving the broader historical context both vague and incomplete.[1] The accounts of the central political episodes of the reign, from the Bedchamber Crisis to Home Rule, say nothing that is new, and the old myth that Albert created an impartial monarchy 'above party' is repeated yet again. More generally, we are portentously informed that, during the course of her reign, Victoria 'became England', but this un-doubted transformation is left an unexplained anthropomorphic miracle.

But what redeems this book, and makes it a major contribution to royal biography despite its undeniable historical limitations, is that it does indeed offer a more candid, critical and convincing interpretation of the Queen herself, by using diaries, journals and letters that have recently become available, and by probing more carefully and less coyly into the medical details of royal living. For in all the best senses, this is indeed an intimate portrait, more concerned with courtly intrigue than with party politics, more interested in doctors and physicians than in cabinet ministers, and more preoccupied with sex, pregnancies and bereavements than with wars, elections and Acts of Parliament. And this subordi-nation of the public to the private, the political to the personal, not only provides much new detail about the monarch and her court: it also suggests that it was these very basic facts of life, of 'birth, copulation and death', which actually mattered most to the Queen. Victoria, on this reading, was much more the mother of her children than the mother of her people, not so much a national icon as a brass-tacks queen.

She was born in 1819, and within a year both her father (the indebted Duke of Kent) and her grandfather (the insane King George III) had died. Her mother was a minor German princess, who was penniless and friendless, and whose only asset was her daughter who might – but only might – one day become Queen of England. Victoria's early years were thus lived out against a background at once lonely and insecure, as her mother sought to barter her daughter's uncertain succession prospects for an increased parliamentary grant, as the remaining sons of George III tried vainly to beget rival claimants, and as courtiers and governesses squabbled and intrigued for mastery of the child. But in 1837 she duly acceded to the throne, where her early years were far from happy: she was subject to fits of depression, sick headaches, nausea and listlessness; her infatuation with the prime minister Lord Melbourne was clearly a search for the father figure she had never known; and her ill-judged behaviour over the Bedchamber Crisis and the Flora Hastings affair displayed to the world her naiveté and lack of judgment.

In 1840, she entered into an arranged match with Prince Albert. He was a minor German princeling who could not possibly expect to do better; and she, although Queen of England, was short, plain and inclined to be plump. Although they came to love each other with strong physical passion, the dominant theme of this second phase of Victoria's life was that in twenty years of marriage, she produced nine children. One consequence was that she had little time, energy or inclination for politics, and it was this which enabled Albert to step in and become the uncrowned king. Another was that as she became more fat and more plain, and as the Prince, too, aged rapidly, they increasingly indulged their sensual urges by acquiring such unVictorian artifacts as nude paintings and sculptures. But above all, it seems clear that Victoria hated pregnancy, hated childbirth, hated babies and hated children. Despite the image – carefully projected in the paintings of Landseer and Winterhalter – of a cosy, *gemütlich*, bourgeois family, the Queen showed little warmth of feeling for her off-spring, and it is hardly surprising that most became unhappy or delinquent or both.

During the third phase of her life, from 1861 to 1888, birth and copulation came to an abrupt end, and death established its pre-eminence in her life. Her mother and her husband died within six months of each other, in Albert's case probably from stomach cancer which may have afflicted him for four years. In 1871 the Queen herself became dangerously ill with a severe throat in-flammation and an underarm abscess, and in the same year, the Prince of Wales nearly succumbed to typhoid. The first of her daughters died in 1878 and the first of her sons in 1884. Four years later, her son-in-law, who had reigned for only ninety-nine days as the German Emperor, died of cancer of the throat. Victoria, meanwhile, abandoned herself to an orgy of grief so extreme and so reclusive that politicians found her almost impossible to deal with. Only Albert's nightshirt and John Brown's arms offered her consolation and, with the precedents of Hanoverian madness in mind, there were fears for her sanity. But she retained her reason, and manipulated her children more unscrupulously than ever, ridding herself of those whom she disliked, and doing her utmost to prevent the departure of those she did not wish to lose.

By the last phase of her reign, the Queen had become very fat, rather ugly, semi-invalid and half blind. Understandably, she was by now obsessed with her health, and when she travelled she took with her, in addition to her servants, courtiers and available members of her family, a vast medical retinue of surgeons, physicians, oculists and apothecaries. But her children and grandchildren continued to die like leaves falling off an autumn tree. The only demise which gave relief bordering upon satisfac-tion was that of the Duke of Clarence, from pneumonia, in 1892. As the eldest son of the Prince of Wales, he was in direct line of succession to the throne. But he was backward, uneducable, bisexual and reputedly afflicted with gonorrhoea. Fortunately, after his timely death, his fiancée, Princess May of Teck, was persuaded to transfer her affections to his younger brother George, and the couple were duly married. How much of these machinations the Queen actually knew is unclear, for by then her health was conspicuously failing. She rarely spoke to her courtiers, and had to have letters read out to her. Almost every day of her year was by now the anniversary of a family death, to which she finally added her own in January 1901, succumbing to a combination of insomnia, nutritional deficiency, and several minor strokes.

The woman who emerges from the medical details of these pages is both less agreeable and more plausible than the icon of contemporary jubilees or the paragon of subsequent biographers. In general, she was callous, insensitive, obstinate, outspoken, capricious and bigoted (not for nothing is the book's epigraph a quotation from the Red Queen in *Alice Through the Looking Glass*). But in particular, this biography is the first to demonstrate the full extent of her quite inordinate selfishness. No one was ever allowed to inconvenience her, and nothing could stand in the way of her regular migrations to Windsor, Osborne and Balmoral. Successive governments were grandly informed that political crises and general elections must not take place at times she deemed unacceptable, and busy and overworked ministers were frequently obliged to travel long distances by land and sea to transact what was often the most trivial of business with her. Her treatment of people as varied as Lady Flora Hastings, Lord Derby and Mr Gladstone was quite inexcusable; when staying at Inverary Castle, she once refused to allow the Duke and Duchess of Argyll to dine with her at their own table; and she became so possessive of her long-suffering courtiers that she regarded any decision to marry or to leave as a personal affront which she rarely forgave.

Underlying this was the bizarre and unreal nature of court life. For the cardinal principle was that the Queen must be obeyed, and it was this 'long unchecked habit of self-indulgence' which effectively transformed the monarch into a monster and her courtiers into sycophantic cyphers. No topic could be raised in conversation except by the Queen, and no one dared give her an opinion which she did not wish to hear, or tell her a truth she did not desire to know. The result was a court regimen at once tyrannical and tedious, unbearable and unreal. Royal children, court retainers and members of the household were incarcerated for weeks in the seclusion of Osborne, the mausoleum of Windsor, and the chill and the snow of Balmoral. Although they often did not see the Queen for days, they were not allowed to lead independent lives, but always had to be at her beck and call. Lacking the inner resources to occupy their minds and their time, the men took up chain-smoking to relieve the boredom, while John Brown drank and the Munshi philandered. No wonder so many became obsessed with their health: there was little else to do.

This combination of temperament and environment inevitably meant that the Queen's political views were reactionary in the extreme. She hated London, never read a newspaper, and knew next to nothing of the lives of most of her subjects. She opposed factory legislation, army reform and the introduction of examinations into the civil service. She disapproved of improved education for the working classes – especially women – because it might give them aspirations beyond their station. She constantly supported royal and reactionary regimes abroad, doing all she could to frustrate Palmerston's more liberal policy, and she loathed the Irish and did her utmost to thwart Gladstone's more enlightened initiatives. In politics as in everything else, she was congenitally incapable of seeing any viewpoint other than her own, dismissing those with whom she disagreed as agitators, radicals, socialists and communists, who sought to overturn the God-given order of society. In most books, these views are breezily excused as further evidence of the Queen's 'character': but we can now see them for what they really were, namely upper-class paranoia of an advanced kind, which was to erupt with such violence in England between 1910 and 1914.

Although Weintraub himself makes no real attempt to integrate this new version of the Victorian Queen into our overall picture of the Victorian age, he has certainly provided ample material with which others might try. For we can now locate the Queen much more precisely within her own world, not as the vague incarnation of her age as a whole, but as the powerful embodiment of its most

conservative characteristics and reactionary elements. In a civilization often acclaimed as improving and progressive, the Queen –
along with many others – was resolutely opposed to such developments. In a country frequently described as rational, capitalist and
democratic, the monarchy remained – along with many others – a
secretive, unaccountable, self-perpetuating and arguably corrupt
institution. Indeed, by the end of Victoria's reign, the gap between
the popular perception and the private reality of the royal family
had probably never been wider.

Accordingly, we can now begin to appreciate the real extent to
which the monarchy both gratified and promoted the craving for
escapism, fantasy and make-believe which was in fact so marked a
feature of Victorian life. We hear much about Albert's concern for
business and technology (as in the Great Exhibition). But the
anti-industrial values which the Queen and Prince projected – by
their pastoral cult of Osborne and Balmoral, by their general lack
of interest in the wealth-creating process, and by their snobbish
and conservative hostility to self-improvement – seem to have
been a great deal more powerful. Those who believe that
nineteenth-century Britain witnessed the destruction of the industrial spirit might begin their search for the culprit at the very top of
the tree. In the same way, there is clearly some close connection, in
the late nineteenth century, between the decline of Britain's
international position, the self-conscious expansion of empire,
and the revived cult of the monarchy. The fact that the last
hundred years have simultaneously seen the emasculation of the
British lion and the apotheosis of the British crown is surely more
than mere coincidence.

Now it may be objected that such speculation runs far ahead of
the evidence; that it depends on the uncritical acceptance of a
highly critical and unusual view of Queen Victoria; and that this in
turn relies far too much on medical evidence which needs the most
careful handling and interpretation. But while these caveats must
undoubtedly be borne in mind, they are hardly overwhelming
objections. For this book convincingly establishes that the royal
court was indeed a brass-tacks world, where the elemental facts of
birth and death, the undisciplined eccentricities of temperament,

and the clashes of personality and the crises of family life, themselves provided the mainspring to the action. And the result is a more candid and nuanced picture of the Queen which enables us to situate her in her age in a way that has hitherto not been possible. We can no more understand her without it than we can comprehend it without her.

(1987)

NOTE:
1. Stanley Weintraub, *Victoria: Biography of a Queen* (London, 1987).

# King George V

George V has been as fortunate in his biographers as any monarch could be. Not for him the lachrymose sentimentality which, at the Queen's behest and with her all-too-active co-operation, Theodore Martin lavished on the Prince Consort; still less the 'feline skill' of Sidney Lee who, disregarding the advice of Edward VII, 'Stick to Shakespeare, Mr Lee, there's money in Shakespeare', produced a double-decker biography of his late majesty; least of all the flippant irreverences of Lytton Strachey's *Queen Victoria*, which caused George V to erupt with rage. On the contrary, the monarch whom the present Queen delighted to call 'Grandpapa England' received the very epitome of grave, tasteful and well-regarded biography. John Gore chronicled the inner man, his tastes, hobbies and friendships; and Harold Nicolson described his public life and times. Nicolson's book in particular did as much to confirm George's reputation as a good king as it did to confirm his own reputation as a good writer, and established a model for royal biography successfully followed by Lady Longford on Queen Victoria, Sir Philip Magnus on Edward VII, Lady Donaldson on Edward VIII, James Pope-Hennessy on Queen Mary and Sir John Wheeler-Bennett on George VI.

Now the wheel has come full circle, and we are back to George V again. Is there any need for this? If plain history does not repeat itself, is there any reason why royal biography should? In this case at least, the answer is an emphatic yes. When Gore and Nicolson wrote, George V's widow was still alive, one son was King as George VI, and another was ex-King as Duke of Windsor. Not

surprisingly, their books were masterpieces of tact and discretion
– qualities necessary in a courtier, but inhibiting in a biographer.
Although he was given full access to the relevant papers, Nicolson
was explicitly instructed to omit things and incidents which were
discreditable, to avoid descending to personalities, to produce the
history of an institution rather than the biography of a person, and
to submit the finished product to the Palace for approval. 'The
Royal Family,' Nicolson rightly observed, 'feel their myth is a
piece of gossamer, and must not be blown upon.'

Nor was he exactly a sympathetic biographer. He had no mystic
feeling for the monarchy, regarding it 'merely as a useful institution'. He thought George V, a 'dull individual' who 'lacked
charm', while his own intellectual pretensions, Labour Party
loyalties and homosexual proclivities would hardly have endeared
him to the late King. George V disliked intellectuals ('I am not a
professor like my grandfather'), detested Socialists ('His language
about the Labour Party was as violent as ever', Neville Chamberlain recorded in 1923), and abhorred homosexuals ('I thought
people like that shot themselves'). On the other hand, he adored
collecting stamps, which Nicolson dismissed as 'mere scraps of
paper', and he was devoted to York Cottage, Sandringham,
which Nicolson derided as 'a horrid little house', worse than an
unseemly villa in Surbiton. 'For seventeen years,' Nicolson dis-
paragingly recorded in his diary while working on the King's early
married life, 'he did nothing at all but kill animals and stick in
stamps.' But taste and tact came to the rescue, as these astringent
sentiments were clothed in the orotund platitudes of the official
life: 'These years succeeded each other with placid similitude. He
lived the life of a privileged country gentleman, unostentatious,
comparatively retired, almost obscure.'

Nicolson's loyal and royal life was thus more a triumph of will
than of empathy, of tact rather than tolerance. And although it was
received with great acclaim as the first word on the subject, in the
nature of things it could scarcely be the last. By contrast, Kenneth
Rose's superb biography will surely stand as the best and most
interesting study of George V that we are ever likely to get.[1] There
is much greater understanding by the author of his subject, and the

public and private lives are brought together with great skill and advantage. As a work of art, it is outstanding: beautifully proportioned, elegantly written, and abounding in memorable phrases, scintillating anecdotes and splendid set-pieces. As a piece of scholarship, it is equally impressive, deploying material drawn from fifty archive collections to illuminate the King's reign and personality far more vividly than Gore and Nicolson were able to do. And, as befits the well-connected writer of the 'Albany' column in the *Sunday Telegraph*, these researches are enlivened by recollections of the crowned and the coroneted, beginning with the Queen Mother, the Emperor Hirohito, the King of Norway and the late Lord Mountbatten, and only then descending to mere peers and commoners.

The George V who emerges from a first reading of these golden pages is instantly recognizable as the familiar figure created by Gore and Nicolson: the symbolic king, standing for stability and continuity in a rapidly dissolving world; the human King, who brought an inspired common sense and kindliness to his work and reign; the family King, with a devoted wife and brood of children; the tolerant King, devoid of the prejudices of class, colour or race; the sailor King, whose sporting activities endeared him to many of his subjects; the imperial King, who journeyed to India to crown himself at his own Durbar; the patriot King, who embodied wartime fortitude at a time of unprecedented national trial; the constitutional King, who took the lead, with scrupulous propriety, in seeking an Irish settlement in 1914 and 1922 and a National Government in 1931; the impartial King, who gave a considerate, uncondescending welcome to the first Labour Government; the fatherly King, who made moving broadcasts at Christmas and enjoyed deserved if unsought apotheosis at the time of his Silver Jubilee; and the much-loved King, of whom it was said at his passing; 'the sunset of his death tinged the whole world's sky'.

If this was all the book had to say, it would be tempting to conclude that tact and discretion had triumphed again; that courtly civilities had once more prevailed over biographical candour; and that the royal gossamer still remains unruffled by the wind. But only the most cursory reading by myopic and fervent monarchists could sustain such an unappreciative conclusion. For on closer inspection, the book appears in a totally different light. Courtly, tactful and well-disposed though it undoubtedly is, it is also a remarkably candid and frequently critical account, which presents George V far less favourably than the pages of Gore and Nicolson. Whether Kenneth Rose is entirely happy and comfortable with this is not altogether clear; but time and again, the evidence he presents subjects the royal gossamer to some healthy and sceptical gusts. Ironically, perhaps, a more well-disposed author seems to have produced a less well-disposed book.

Take, for instance, Rose's account of the late nineteenth-century royal family in which the future George V was brought up, which marshals an array of personalities so eccentric and bizarre that they could only have flourished in the hot-house atmosphere of a royal court. There was the ageing Queen, still in her widow's weeds, and still insisting that all Albert's male descendants must bear his name until the end of time; the future Edward VII, a cosmopolitan roué, successively ensnared in the Mordaunt divorce cause and the Tranby Croft card scandal; and the ravishing Princess Alexandra, who smothered her children in excessively mawkish and possessive affection, and retained to her death the mind of an adolescent. Then, among the younger contingent, there was George's elder brother, Prince Albert Victor, Duke of Clarence, congenitally listless, almost illiterate, vacant and effete. For a time, he and George shared the same girl in St John's Wood. 'She is a ripper', George recorded. Some, of course, felt the same about Clarence. His intended consort was Princess May of Teck, a royal in a million, who it was hoped would pull him together. On his premature (and extremely fortunate) demise, she married Prince George instead.

The rest of his life was a succession of such fantasy worlds. Both Alexandra and her daughter Victoria were highly jealous of May, and spitefully conspired against her until the end of their days. And, as marriage heightened the tensions of family life, so accession enhanced the tyrannical trivialities of the Court. In George's court (all courts?), endless hours were lavished on matters of dress and protocol, precedence and honours, even in the darkest days of the war. Should the King ride into Delhi on a horse or an elephant? Could the Governor-General of Canada have an embossed red crown on his official stationery? When Churchill was First Lord of the Admiralty, George successfully dissuaded him from calling a ship HMS *Pitt*, because the name was 'neither euphonious nor dignified', and the men might invent 'nicknames of ill-conditioned words rhyming with it'. And opulence and privilege only enhanced this sense of unreality. There were servants by the hundred, courtiers by the score. At Balmoral, a small dinner would be six courses, with a minimum of eight footmen and five pipers in attendance. And when the King left to travel south by train, there were seventeen reserve engines waiting along the route from Ballater to London, all with steam up, in case the royal locomotive should break down.

Even Kenneth Rose's patience is worn thin by such 'persistent mummery' and George V, who endured, and came to love, this unreal and suffocating atmosphere, was much affected by it. His formal education was limited, and was effectively over by the age of twelve. To the end of his life, he wrote with painful slowness; he always had trouble with his spelling; he was indifferent to science, culture and the arts; and he spoke no foreign language with even halting fluency. He was sent into the navy, which made him both homesick and seasick, and reinforced his mental indigence, his impatience with qualifications and subtleties, his mistrust of imagination and intuition, and his obsession with dress and deportment. By his late teens, he was less well-educated than the average public schoolboy; he had few friends of his own age; and he hated London society and foreign travel. He shouted at servants, swore a good deal, and rarely smiled. After his marriage, he stagnated at Sandringham, where (as Nicolson observed) he slaughtered birds by the thousand and stuck in stamps. As Rose candidly admits, in 1910 few could regard his accession 'with enthusiasm or even confidence'.

Nor did he get off to a good start as king. As Prince of Wales, he had needlessly antagonized his father's Liberal ministers by trumpeting his disapproval of them like a loud, stupid, overgrown schoolboy. He thought Asquith 'not quite a gentleman' (which was true, but hurtful, and hardly to the point), described Lloyd George as 'that damned fellow', and found Churchill little better. With good reason, the Liberal Government viewed his accession with alarm: there were real and justified doubts about his discretion, his competence and his impartiality; he formed his opinions of politicians too much on the basis of class-bound likes and dislikes; and he identified himself too closely with Conservative prejudice and aristocratic excess. At a time when Asquith was wrestling with the crisis over the House of Lords, with a Conservative Party obstructive to the point of irresponsibility, with Irish Home Rulers insistent on a settlement, and with Ulster Unionists on the brink of rebellion, the new incumbent of the throne was at best an added irritant, implausibly accusing Churchill of being a socialist, and obstructively opposing the return of Fisher to the Admiralty.

This is a much less flattering picture than that painted by George V's official biographers, and Rose's account of the King in the war is equally critical. Of course, his duty, patriotism and dedication were beyond doubt, but not everyone knew that, and there were blunders. He was slow in ordering the removal of the German Emperor's Garter banner from St George's Chapel, and hasty in changing the royal family name to Windsor (though he did thereby provoke one of the Kaiser's few jokes, which was that he looked forward to the next performance of that well-known opera, 'The Merry Wives of Saxe-Coburg-Gotha'). Taking the pledge made the Court look ridiculous; visiting the ships made the King seasick; and on one visit to his troops he was painfully thrown from his horse. On the eve of the Passchendaele offensive, the Court's main concern was whether or not women workers in munitions factories should remove their gloves when presented to the Queen. In the latter stages of the war, the King supported Haig and his strategy with inflexible stubbornness; he opposed the removal of that Blimpish nonentity Robertson as CIGS; and he was reluctant to recognize that Lloyd George was the only man who could win the war. His only successful initiative was in overturning the views of his ministers by insisting that the Tsar (his cousin) should be denied asylum in Britain. But even that shrewdly selfish move did not altogether allay the growing mood of republicanism (about which it would have been instructive to hear more).

In many ways, then, the King did not have a good war as a constitutional monarch. Rose's treatment of his remaining peacetime years offers fewer new insights, some but not all of which modify the traditional picture. It still remains unclear whether, in 1924, the King chose Baldwin in preference to Curzon as Prime Minister because the latter was a peer or because he was Curzon. The descriptions of the King's handling of the first Labour administration and of the formation of the National Government largely confirm Nicolson's account, but during the General Strike, at least in some moods, the King was clearly more belligerent than Nicolson leads us to believe. It is impossible to be clear whether he abhorred the dictators or not; he rebuked the Mahatma with the memorable words, 'Remember, Mr Gandhi, I won't have any attacks on my Empire'; and he seems to have left no lasting mark on foreign policy. Of all his prime ministers, he liked MacDonald the best, which hardly inspires confidence in his political judgment.

Most politicians, in fact, found George V very difficult to deal with. His obsessions with the trivia of courtly life meant that he rebuked ministers who were working twenty hours a day to win the war because they were wearing the wrong hats. At official meetings, they were treated to a lengthy and often stentorian royal monologue, usually ill-ordered and thought-out, which permitted them no time for a question or comment. Asquith thought a royal audience on a par with having a tooth out; Churchill felt the King's comments on naval policy were stupid and silly; Curzon called him 'the little man'; Fisher dubbed the King and his Queen 'futile and fertile'. Lloyd George, at his most charitable, thought the King 'a jolly chap', yet felt that there was 'not much inside his head'. But then, as Arthur Balfour asked him, 'whatever would you do if you had a ruler who had brains?' The condescension was unkind, but the criticisms were not without their substance.

It is not quite clear whether Kenneth Rose is happy with the direction in which this evidence leads. In an effort to turn the tables on the King's critics, he subjects the politicians to a sustained onslaught of pejorative adjectives, harsher than those which the ministers used about the King. Asquith is supine, silent, complacent, immobile, dilatory and self-indulgent. Churchill is insensitive, tactless, wilful and impossible. Bonar Law is unamiable, curt, dour, abrasive and disrespectful. Lloyd George is nonchalant, graceless and spiteful. Fisher is venomous, Baldwin is slothful, Balfour is irresolute. And the Webbs, who so criticized MacDonald for selling out to the Establishment, are lambasted for their cruelly doctrinaire minds, and for being too self-impaled upon their rectitude to have any fun. There is, no doubt, some truth in these disparaging descriptions. But such sustained belittling of so many public personages smacks slightly of special pleading on behalf of the King. And in any case, pointing up the faults in them in no sense diminishes the shortcomings they found in him.

When it comes to discussing the King as a man, Rose tries even harder to rebut familiar criticisms, when in fact he largely substantiates them. For instance, he suggests that there is 'much evidence' to 'disprove' the 'hurtful legend' that George V was a harsh father, and devotes several sledge-hammer pages to refuting the oft-quoted statement attributed to George V that he was afraid of his father and, by God, his children would be afraid of him. But even if that statement is suspect the circumstances it summarises are not. When young, one of the King's sons was ill-treated, another had his digestion ruined for life, and all were forced to wear splints to prevent them being knock-kneed. They were lamentably ill-educated, and all showed signs of nervous tension which stemmed from parental scolding and distance. Queen Mary was remote and cold, and was pitifully blind to her shortcomings as a mother. The King was anxious, overbearing, exacting, heavy-handed, stern and unreasonable. He cursed and criticized too much, and enthused and encouraged too little. He made no effort to understand his eldest son, whom he constantly took to task over trivial matters of dress and deportment. As father of his people, George might have been an unexpected success; as a father of his children, he was little short of disastrous.

Nor was his record much better as a husband. Rose assures us that George's married life was 'idyllic', and that 'no couple more epitomized the virtues of a Christian marriage' than did the King and Queen. That he loved her and was aware of how much he owed her is plain; that he was utterly faithful seems equally beyond doubt. But, as Mr Rose admits elsewhere, the reality of the Queen's position was one of 'dignified slavery'. She was obliged to wear old-fashioned clothes because the King liked her that way; to endure the tedium of shooting at Balmoral because that was his wish; to curb her youthful high spirits in the graver atmosphere of his Court; and to neglect her interest in the arts because he did not share it. They did not find it easy to talk to each other with feeling or intimacy, and the King frequently shouted at her. As Rose admits, the Queen's servitude (which he implausibly describes as 'self-imposed') was 'absolute'. Only after the King's death did she really blossom. This may have been an 'idyllic' marriage for him: it is hard to see how it was for her.

By the time he reaches the King's well-known insensitivity to aesthetic matters, even Rose's mellifluous patience is wearing a little thin, as he unconvincingly condemns the 'disdain of the sophisticated' (surely Mr Rose is sophisticated?), with their 'little whinnies of despair' at the King's lack of culture. But the disdain and the despair seem all too apt. George V 'did not care' for *King Lear*, and had never heard of Thomas Hardy. He thought *Fidelio* 'damned dull' and believed Turner was 'mad', waved his stick at a Cézanne and, on seeing the French Impressionists in the Tate Gallery Extension, trumpeted to the Queen: 'Here's something to make you laugh, May.' Nor is the King's boorishness excused by arguing that Queen Mary's own cultural interests were less broad than is popularly supposed. In near despair, Mr Rose bravely concludes that 'some of the King's subjects were doubtless disappointed by their sovereign's near indifference to the fine arts; many more were heartened by his patronage of sport.' But to praise the King for slaughtering thousands of birds a day hardly acquits him on the count of philistinism.

Of course, it would be highly anachronistic to condemn George V by the exalted latterday standards of Dr Spock and the Women's Movement, to say nothing of Animal Liberation and Gay Rights. But it is difficult to resist the more measured conclusion that, as a constitutional monarch, George V was often difficult, irritating or just plain wrong, and that as an individual he was at best a lovable ogre. And this in turn makes it impossible to accept the fundamental argument of Mr Rose's book, that the King himself deserves the credit for the survival of the monarchy because the nation 'recognized virtue in a humble heart'. Beyond doubt, there is some truth in this, but it is not the whole of it, and it is not the major part of it. The most powerful explanations for the survival of the monarchy during the reign of George V are probably sheer good luck, and the sustained endeavours of others on its behalf. If, for instance, Britain had lost the First World War, the monarchy would surely have gone, along with much else. It would have been condemned as the apex of a discredited social and political system; the German blood of the King and Queen would have been a fatal disadvantage; and the King's support of Haig and obstruction of Lloyd George would only have increased the force of the criticism. As Lloyd George later put it, 'I owe him nothing. He owes his throne to me.'

For the rest of his reign, the survival and efficient functioning of the monarchy depended largely on those loyal, patient and resourceful officials who made up for his shortcomings, protected him from himself, and safeguarded him from the world. Without his ever-vigilant private secretaries, who drafted and handled all his official correspondence, it is difficult to see how a monarch of such limited, untrained intellect could actually have coped. Indiscreet servants and courtiers, who repeated the King's more inane or ill-advised remarks, were dismissed; and high society, although individually critical of the King, was corporately discreet. The generous coverage in the press, about which the King didn't give a damn, was partly the result of deliberate endeavours by Wigram, his private secretary, and partly a consequence of what the papers chose to print. The Christmas broadcasts and the Silver Jubilee celebrations, which did so much to bring the King popularity at the end of his reign, were dreamed up in Whitehall. Above all, much of the popularity of the monarchy in George V's time is to be explained, not in terms of Grandpapa England, but by the sensationally successful tours and appearances undertaken by the Prince of Wales. Faced with most of these circumstances and developments, George was more often than not passive, uncomprehending and even unco-operative. It would be too harsh to say that the British monarchy survived despite him rather than because of him, but the amount of credit which he personally deserves is probably not all that much.

On the basis of the evidence he deploys, it is hard to believe that Mr Rose would dissent from this view. Indeed, the most intriguing and baffling aspect of this book is not its subject, who is made far more real and credible than ever before, but its author. What, exactly, does he make of all this? In his prologue, he quotes approvingly Violet Markham's words: 'In the end, it is character not cleverness that counts; goodness and simplicity, not analytical subtlety and the power to spin verbal webs.' But it cannot be said that this quite masterly book lends much support to such a view – partly because, without Mr Rose's cleverness, analytical subtlety and power to spin verbal webs, the King's character, goodness and simplicity would shine forth less luminously than in fact they do, and partly because, even allowing for all of this, they shine forth less brightly and more intermittently than they did in the pages of Gore and Nicolson. So what, precisely, is this book all about? Did it begin as another well-disposed work of tact and discretion in which, to the author's embarrassment, these courtly attitudes have been remorselessly overwhelmed by the weight of contrary evidence? Or was it conceived as a work of sceptical re-evaluation, brilliantly disguised to resemble the earlier, admiring studies, so as to get past watchful royal eyes? It is hard to be sure. Has George V again been fortunate in his biographer? Or is his luck beginning to run out?

(1983)

NOTE:
1. Kenneth Rose, *King George V* (London, 1983).

# The Duke of Windsor

'The choice before ex-kings', Herbert Morrison remarked in 1937 on the occasion of the Windsors' characteristically ill-advised visit to Nazi Germany, 'is either to fade out of the public eye or be a nuisance.' It has generally been assumed that the Duke – the most famous, bemused and embittered ex-king of the twentieth century, who gave up an empire for the woman he loved, and who never ceased to regret his sacrifice even as he relished his surrender – came in the second of these categories. And, since it is even easier to hit a man when he is dead than when he is down, tilting at Windsor has recently become a popular sport. Some of the jousting has been in dubious taste, with lances forged in malice, aimed in hatred, and wielded in spite. But others, more interested in history than in hearsay, have landed some shrewd blows on their target. Chief among these Windsor-wallopers has been Frances Donaldson, whose much-acclaimed biography under-mined many of the legends which lingered from his time as Prince of Wales, substantiated most of the criticisms levelled against him as King Edward VIII, and painted a pathetic picture of his later years as Duke of Windsor, a 'weary, wayward, wandering ghost', shuffling with rootless opulence from resort to resort, getting 'more tanned and more tired'.

Recently, however, the ailing Duchess's friend and lawyer, Maitre Blum, has decided to launch a counter-offensive against those ascendant assailants. None of Windsor's critics, the argument runs, has tried to see events from his point of view – not surpris-ingly since none of them has been allowed access to his papers. Even Lady Donaldson wrote of Edward VIII from the outside, as others saw him, rather than from the inside, as he saw others. In order to put the record straight, as she sees it, Maitre Blum has invited the lawyer-historian Michael Bloch to be the Duke's champion, and has given him extensive access to the Windsor archive. His first piece of ducal defence – dedicated to Maitre Blum, 'guide, pupil-master and friend', and pointedly describing the Windsors as 'Their Royal Highnesses' – is an account of the Duke's war years, covering his military service in France, his journey to Spain and departure from Europe, and his time as Governor of the Bahamas.[1] The result is a riveting peep into the minds and feelings of the Duke and Duchess, a horrifying picture of misery and unhappiness, and an impassioned plea that justice be done to the Duke in death which, Bloch feels, was so shamefully denied him in life.

Bloch's thesis is as simple as his tactics: the best way to defend the Windsors is to prosecute their traducers – the Establishment in general and the Court in particular. Throughout the war, Bloch argues, Windsor only desired to serve his country: this was a magnanimous gesture meant with all the sincerity of a loyal and royal citizen. But, he suggests, at a time when all men of talent and goodwill should have pulled together, and when the great perils of war should have banished interest in lesser matters, the Windsors were the object of a shabby and shameful vendetta conducted by 'those at Court and in other high places'. Against them they directed an 'unremitting campaign of ostracism, spite and calumny', characterized by 'secret instructions', 'punishment', 'intrigues', 'hostility', 'persecutions', 'madness', 'silence and ice'. 'They were', he continues, 'determined that, come what may, the Duke's war years, covering his military service in France, his recover any work, influence or honour.' So he was cast out into the cold and kept under constant restraint and scrutiny, while back home the British public were 'subtly indoctrinated' to see the Windsors only as a 'spoilt, sly and sybaritic couple deserving of little consideration'.

With all the singlemindedness of a committed advocate, Bloch selects the evidence to support this view. The Windsors' wedding, he notes, was 'boycotted' by the Palace: the only present from the

King was the 'terrible insult' of denying Windsor's wife the title Her Royal Highness. The military job given to the Duke in France during the period of the 'phoney war' was a mean attempt to ensure that his talents were not appropriately used. The Governorship of the Bahamas ('a grave of reputations') was a 'bizarre' appointment, the 'pettiest and most difficult' in the British Empire, which condemned Windsor to frustration and exile far from the country he desired to serve. Even there, persecution followed, as 'amazing' instructions went out from the Palace that the Duchess was not to be curtseyed to, and 'extraordinary' attempts were made to prevent the Windsors from visiting the United States, for fear that the Duke would outshine George VI there in popularity. In fact, Bloch argues, Windsor did 'excellently' as Governor: his administration was 'the best the Bahamas had had in recent times'. But such was the abiding hostility to him in official circles that the post which he deserved and would have carried off brilliantly – that of roving Ambassador in the United States – was never proffered. All that came his way after the Bahamas was the equally humiliating offer of governing Bermuda.

That the Windsors believed all this cannot be doubted. They devoted a large part of their memoirs to articulating their embittered hurt, and were still talking about it when Kenneth Harris interviewed them for television in 1970. But this book is the first to reveal the true extent of their pain, anguish and suffering. Wallis saw the Bahamas as the 'St Helena of 1940', where her husband, 'the naughty boy', was 'dumped solely by family jealousy' and 'the Palace vendetta'. 'Even the war can't stop the family hatred,' she cried. 'They will never stop murdering the Duke of Windsor. It is his own family who are against him.' And Windsor took the same view, railing against 'the chronic insult to my wife', which meant 'hitting at me where I was most vulnerable', and protesting at 'the mean and petty humiliations', the 'virulence of the campaign that official England launched against me'. 'Ever since,' he wrote to George VI, 'I returned to England in 1939 to offer my services and you continued to persecute me, I must frankly admit that I have become very bitter indeed.' Spurned by his own flesh and blood, the 'semi-Royal family' as he now described them, he felt especially ill treated by the 'belligerence' and 'insults' of the King, by Queen Elizabeth's resolute opposition to his return, and by the 'icy-cold' hostility of Queen Mary.

No one reading this book can possibly question the sincerity of these sentiments. But while it establishes beyond any reasonable doubt the depth and extent of the Windsors' misery and bitterness, it does not demonstrate that Windsor was correct in his analysis of why he was treated in the way he was. It is one thing to say that Windsor *thought* there was a campaign against him; it is quite another to show that it *actually existed*. And, since this book rests so heavily on Windsor's papers, it is by definition unable to offer much in the way of evidence or proof. Bloch's difficulty is that he is caught between the historian's loyalty to his evidence (which suggests one interpretation), and the lawyer's loyalty to his client (which suggests another). 'What I have done', he explained to the *Standard*, 'is to express the Duke's point of view. I am in the position of a lawyer asked to present the case for the defence.' But presenting the Duke's point of view and making the case for the defence are not necessarily the same thing. And neither is the same as laying 'out the facts and the evidence for them with particular comprehensiveness and regard for accuracy', which is what, in his preface, he claims he is doing.

But is he? At the outset, Bloch makes no attempt to consider Windsor's reputation when the war broke out. By then, his record as an ex-king was no better than it had been as a constitutional monarch. As Edward VIII he had never really understood his constitutional position; he refused to abide by the advice which his private secretaries tendered him; he did not take his public and ceremonial duties as seriously as he should have done; he was careless and inattentive in dealing with state papers; his political sympathies were certainly pro-German and perhaps pro-Nazi; he was reckless and adolescently indiscreet in his private life; and he kept his family (and especially the anxiety-ridden Duke of York) inexcusably in the dark until the very last moment over the abdication. Nor had he done much better in his first months as

Duke of Windsor. He pestered George VI with daily phone calls, tactlessly presuming to advise him how to do a job which he himself had thrown up; and the visit he and Wallis made to Germany despite advice to the contrary (a trip which even Bloch coyly admits was 'disastrous'), resulted in photographs of Windsor shaking hands with Hitler and (so it seemed) giving the Nazi salute. Under these circumstances, the politest thing that could be said about the Duke in war time was that he was a risk: he could not be relied upon. Without this perspective, which Bloch neither provides nor considers, it is impossible to understand the treatment which Windsor received at the hands of the Establishment. It was not so much they who had made life difficult for him, but he who had made life difficult for them.

Under these circumstances, it is hardly surprising that there were many people in high places who distrusted him in 1939. But Bloch will have none of this, resorting as he does to the well-known device of supposing that all critics of his hero – whether as King or Duke – were either foolish or wicked or both. Thus Baldwin, whose role in the abdication was far less malevolently conspiratorial than Edward's apologists will allow, is dismissed as 'tedious'. In contrast to Wallis, Queen Mary is implausibly pilloried for 'that determined desire to be Queen' which she had so 'vigorously demonstrated by her rapid change of fiancé in the early 1890s'. Edward's two private secretaries, who gave him scrupulously proper constitutional advice, are similarly written off: Lascelles for possessing a 'poisonously prejudiced' ear, and Hardinge for his 'questionable loyalty.' In the Bahamas, Etienne Duputch, whose newspaper was frequently critical of Windsor, is summed up as 'highly opinionated', 'outspoken to the point of rashness', whose attacks 'verged on the intemperate or the personal'. And Beaverbrook, having abandoned in the war his earlier support for the Duke, is described as being, in 1942, 'just about the worst person to whom he could have turned for help'. Most revealingly, 'Fruity' Metcalfe, who stood by Edward in the darkest times of his life, and whose highly critical letters were used by Frances Donaldson to such good effect, is written off as 'bombastic', 'wild and furious', 'earthy and explosive', and 'given to eccentric outbursts'. The fact that such people's opinions of Windsor counted for something, and might even have had some substance to them, is not even considered. On the other hand, Diana Mosley's biography of the Duchess, which it would be polite to call banal and more accurate to describe as blinkered, is thought to be 'delightful'.

Thus Bloch goes about his business, carefully painting a one-sided picture. The same is true of his analysis of Churchill's wartime attitude towards the Duke, a laboured attempt to avoid reaching the obvious conclusion suggested by the evidence. It is, of course, true that Churchill, like Beaverbrook, had supported Windsor in 1936: but that was largely for tactical reasons, in the hope of embarrassing Baldwin. Later, as is well known, both he and Beaverbook came to see the folly of their ways, and to realize that Windsor was not up to much. So, although Churchill continued to treat the Duke with the utmost personal courtesy, he was not prepared to take the risk of offering him more exposed or more important employment. But Windsor could only see this as further evidence of a Palace conspiracy. 'I used to have your support', he told Churchill in July 1940, 'until you reached the supreme power of Prime Minister, since when you seem to have subscribed to the Court's hostile attitude towards me.' And Bloch reiterates this irritated reaction as if it were historical fact. 'Churchill depended', he writes, 'for the oft-imperilled supremacy of his position on the personal support of the King and Queen, and part of the price was that they should always have the last word when it came to deciding the Duke of Windsor's fate.' But this is, to say the least, a fanciful view, for which no substantiating evidence is offered. The idea that Churchill, at the head of his wartime coalition, was so vulnerable that only the support of George VI and Queen Elizabeth stood between him and defeat suggests a relationship between monarch and minister which Walpole and the elder Pitt, let alone Disraeli or Gladstone, would have had difficulty in recognizing.

Several other important episodes receive equally partial and partisan treatment. Bloch's book opens with an account of the Duke's forty-fifth birthday party in Paris in June 1939, but neglects to note that the celebrations began with a party given by the German Ambassador, Count von Welczech, who welcomed the Duke and Duchess with the Nazi salute. We are told of the Duke's international broadcast from Verdun on 7 May 1939, appealing to the Americans in particular for world peace; but no mention is made of the fact that it coincided with the visit of the King and Queen to the United States and Canada, thereby making it an extraordinarily ill-judged venture. The episodes concerning the sending of a plane to France in September 1939 to take the Windsors home, and Windsor's reputed abandonment of Metcalfe in Paris in June 1940, are too lightly glossed over for comfort. Most worryingly, Bloch quotes from the diary of Sir Ronald Storrs for 14 July 1940, reporting a conversation with Lord Lloyd, the Colonial Secretary, who said that 'the Windsor appointment in the Bahamas is the King's own idea, to keep him at all costs out of England'. 'Here', Bloch announces triumphantly, 'all is revealed.' But it most certainly is not. For three days later, Storrs records further gossip about Windsor. 'I don't care', the Duke is reported as saying, 'who wins the war: I am more than half a German myself.' It was, as Storrs rightly remarked, 'a dreadful saying even to pass on'. So dreadful, in fact, that Bloch does not pass it on at all. To say, under such circumstances, that 'the Duke was always alive to the dangers of indiscretion', is hardly consistent with the evidence.

By such methods, Bloch tries to show that the world really did correspond to Windsor's mistaken preception of it. But it is an uphill and unconvincing struggle. And the same is true of his treatment of specific episodes of Windsor's Bahamas governorship. He shows, for example, how insulted Windsor was at being sent there; but there were perfectly valid official reasons why this appointment should have been made. Where, in the Second World War, could so conspicuous a figure, with strongly suspected pro-Nazi sympathies, be safely put? He must be got out of Europe because (as in Spain in the summer of 1940) there might be German plots to kidnap him; and, for the same reason, he must be kept out of Asia or Africa. His military training was insufficient for a service job (where again, in any case, he would be too much of a risk), and his understanding of constitutional propriety was too limited, and his commitment to the war effort too suspect, for him to be entrusted with an Embassy. Since the dominions had protested against Wallis as Queen, they were hardly likely to welcome her as the consort of a governor-general. That effectively ruled out most things, except a job in the New World; and even there, the options were limited. There were no suitable posts in the USA or Canada, and South America was, again, too much of a security risk. All that remained were the British colonies in the western hemisphere, of which the Bahamas was about the most appropriate. As Bloch observes when describing the Duke's predecessors, the governorship was 'a post to be filled by an incompetent and eccentric official who could not be got rid of on account of his personal connections'. The fact that Windsor fitted these requirements exactly does not seem to have occurred to him.

The charge that the British government further sought to humiliate the Duke by preventing him from meeting Roosevelt in the autumn of 1940 is equally hard to substantiate. On the contrary, there were perfectly good reasons why the government 'was not anxious in any way to encourage' a 'meeting between the Duke of Windsor and the President'. For all of 1940 and most of 1941, the United States was publicly neutral. There was a strong isolationist lobby, and the German, Italian and Irish minorities had to be handled with the greatest care. During the winter of 1940–1, while the lend-lease negotiations were in progress, it was imperative that nothing should be said to give the impression that Britain's will to win was flagging, or to arouse anti-British feeling there. Under these circumstances, the last thing the British wanted was to have Windsor shooting off his mouth to the American President or the American people. Of course, Roosevelt wanted to meet Windsor: like most upper-class Americans he was fascinated by British royalty. But he was never an easy ally to handle, and the fear that he might get hold of the wrong end of the stick from the Duke was understandably real. To suggest, as Bloch does, that the British government were prepared to run the risk of upsetting the President by keeping him and Windsor apart merely in continuation of the supposed Palace vendetta against him, is to show as limited an understanding of the realities of war and diplomacy as did the Duke himself.

As Governor of the Bahamas, Windsor clearly did better than his greatest detractors have argued, although he did not do as well as this apologia suggests. They entertained lavishly; they were good at ceremonial functions; he showed real interest in promoting the economic development of the islands; and he seems to have handled the riots of 1942 with firmness and success. But against this, they were tactless in their dealings with the press; he made several major errors of judgment, as over the Oakes murder case; he associated with suspect and unsavoury characters like Wenner-Gren; and the opulence of their living and their travelling attracted adverse publicity from the isolationist press in America. Above all, they made it abundantly plain that they hated the Bahamas ('this dump', 'this lousy little island'), and that they regarded the appointment as an insult ('we loathe the job', 'we both hate it') rather than as a challenge or a duty. Men like Churchill, shouldering the crushing burden of war fifteen hours a day, seven days a week, can hardly have been sympathetic to Windsor whimpering on his tropical island for a holiday. There may have been termites invading Government House; but bombs were falling on Buckingham Palace. All told, a realistic appraisal would be that Windsor had done just well enough for another government job, but had not deserved promotion. And that, in the form of the Governorship of Bermuda, is exactly what he was offered. But he turned it down, assuming that it was meant as further humiliation.

For he always had his eye set on larger and quite unrealistic prizes. In 1942 he wrote grandly that 'it might be considered unwise and inopportune to attempt to force the displacement of certain holders of such appointments as Ambassador or Governor-General at the present time', which makes clear his continuing expectation that such rearrangements would be made some time later. More particularly, from 1944 to 1952, he cherished the idea that he might be appointed roving ambassador to the United States. But no such job was forthcoming, from Labour, Conservative or Coalition governments, and Windsor took it as another slight, even though the reasons for refusal were both obvious and telling. Bloch assures us that the Duke could 'have done great things' for Anglo-American relations; but precisely how is not specified. Windsor made it clear that he would handle any such job 'my own way'; but the last time he had done that was as King – not exactly an encouraging precedent. Never in his life did he learn tact or discretion or the need to abide by his ministers' advice: as King, these were fatal disadvantages; as ambassador they were crippling disqualifications. In any case, the job would have necessitated extensive and itinerant entertaining, which would have required a large staff and perhaps two houses. It could hardly have cost the Exchequer less than £100,000 a year, and would probably have cost a great deal more. The idea that, in embattled, war-weary, austerity-ridden Britain, Foreign Secretaries like Eden or Bevin could have gone to Parliament to ask for such funds to finance Windsor on the North American cocktail circuit is, perhaps, a little far fetched.

So, despite the author's laboured efforts and partisan advocacy, the man who emerges from this book remains the easily recognizable figure more acutely described by Frances Donaldson – proud, paranoid, and rather pathetic. Like George III, another unhappy but more dutiful monarch, Windsor was unable to distinguish between himself as a man and his office as King, between his position as a private citizen and his role as a member of the royal family. When, as King, he was given scrupulously proper constitutional advice which he did not like, he assumed it was motivated by personal spite – as in 1936, when Hardinge, his private secretary, sent him a memorandum pointing out that his friendship with Mrs Simpson was bringing the monarchy into disrepute, to which his only response was: 'They had struck at the very roots of my pride.' In the same way, as ex-King in the period covered by this book, he interpreted official decisions made from the broad perspective of war and high policy as if they were exclusively part of a vendetta against him: as when, in 1940, the government tried to get him back from Spain to England, but all he could do was to try to make his return conditional upon the government meeting his demands about his wife's title. 'David's pride was engaged', Wallis later wrote of that episode. Indeed, throughout his adult life, it always was.

Edward's difficulty was that he was too proud to be a success, as a constitutional monarch or as an ex-King. For he never realized that, like all other members of the Establishment from the highest to the lowest, he, too, was constrained by rules, some of which he would ignore or break at his peril, some of which could not be broken at all, even by the King. The rules themselves may have been right or wrong, sensible or stuffy, honest or hypocritical. But they were *there* and, as a King and a member of the royal family, he could no more break them with impunity than could the humblest member of his household. So, he never grasped that the trade-off of abdication was only – and *could* only be – that he became free to marry Wallis. But it did not, *could* not, make her any more acceptable a member of the royal family at that time. She was still a twice-divorced woman, and no amount of abdication on Edward's part could wipe that particular slate clean, and transform her into a Lady Di-like paragon. The Church of England's disapproval of divorce at that time was absolute and, in the 1930s, the royal family was expected to conform to its teaching more completely than it is today. That teaching may have been harsh, intolerant and anachronistic (it certainly seems so now), and it may have been given by prelates like Cosmo Lang, who seemed more full of cant and humbug than charity and compassion. But everyone, especially the monarch and royal family, was trapped by these rules. That was not vendetta; it was, simply, how things were.

From this, everything else flowed with the inexorability of the Nile in full flood. If Wallis was twice divorced, she could not be Queen, and she could not be a Royal Duchess because she could not, officially, be married according to the rites of the Church of England (except by a renegade and exhibitionist vicar who was promptly disowned by his bishop). So, whatever personal views other members of the royal family had in the matter, they could not attend the wedding, even if they had wanted to. It was not a boycott; they, too, had no choice. Likewise, it is hard to see how

George VI could have made Wallis 'Her Royal Highness' when the church of which he was titular head did not recognize the marriage. And in any case, she was twice divorced, while Edward's previous lovers (all of whom he had ultimately dropped abruptly) had always been married women. The union might not last; she might not be the only Duchess of Windsor; how many more might there be? In the same way, the 'humiliating and distressing' instructions that went out to the Bahamas that she was not to be curtseyed to necessarily followed from all that had gone before. This is not to defend either the existence or the substance of such rules; but Windsor laid up for himself great unhappiness by being so proud and so foolish as to suppose that he could flout them. That may have been his wish; but neither as monarch nor as ex-King was it his option.

Thereafter, as this book shows, Windsor made himself even more unhappy by believing that he was denied further employment because of the Palace vendetta against him, when it seems much more likely that this was because there was no job for which he was suitable. Later in the war, Windsor wanted an 'appointment worthy of my experience', but presumed he would not get it because 'family jealousy would oppose any suggestion' of such a job. Once more, it is Windsor's inability to distinguish between the private and the public, the personal and the official, which stands out. For the real explanation was obvious, even if Windsor was too proud to see it. Despite all the talk of the Duke's 'talents' and 'great gifts' which were 'so wretchedly underused', it is not at all clear what they actually were, and the Duke's apologists are always deafeningly silent in suggesting precisely what, in the post-war world, he could have done by way of an official job. An embassy? A governor-generalship? A military command? Quite correctly, in 1940, these appointments were ruled out, and Windsor's behaviour thereafter only demonstrated the wisdom of that decision. Having ceased to be King, Windsor could only be given employment by the state on the basis of his merits and his record and, in 1945 as in 1940, they were not very good. When competing in the post-war marketplace for grand Establishment jobs with such pillars of state as Slim, Alexander or Mountbatten, it is hardly surprising that all Windsor got was the offer of Bermuda. But the force of this argument would have been so wounding to his pride that he preferred to explain his lack of an official job in terms of others' malevolence rather than his unfittedness.

By the end of this book, it seems clear, Windsor's pride was melting into acute paranoia – delusions of grandeur, on the one hand (especially about the type of job to which he was entitled and the obeisance which was his wife's due); and delusions of persecution, on the other (especially in supposing that he was denied 'suitable' employment by the Court and the Establishment for no better reason than personal spite). Of course, it is not beyond the bounds of possibility that the Establishment in general and the Court in particular were motivated by spite, malice, pettiness, as Windsor believed. Certainly Queen Elizabeth regretted that her husband had to shoulder the burden Edward cast aside, and Queen Mary regarded Wallis as an 'adventuress' who had brought 'humiliation' on the family. But many a mother disapproves of the woman her son marries and, as that general formulation of this particular instance suggests, families are as much the matrix of affection as they are the crucibles of conflict. That Queen Mary, Queen Elizabeth and King George VI all disapproved of Windsor for quitting his job and letting down the family seems clear. But it seems equally likely that Queen Mary retained real affection for her son, just as George VI did for his brother, and that both of them genuinely regretted the way in which events had unfolded, for Edward as much as for themselves. Bloch's characterization of the royal family's attitude seems unconvincingly crude.

Moreover, it is without documentary support, since only one letter is quoted from the royal archives, and the relevant Cabinet papers will not be available until 2036. Of course, this lack of evidence does not by itself exonerate the Court or the Establishment. 'They' may have covered their tracks very well; much may never have been written down; letters may have been destroyed; and many central figures have undoubtedly taken their secrets with them to the grave. All that can be said at the moment, on the basis of the evidence available, is that the Establishment's treatment of Windsor seems well explained and entirely justified on the grounds of official policy and government prudence, which neither Windsor nor his wife could understand or admit. Quite simply, the Duke was a bad risk, and a nation involved in a war to the death could not be too careful. Undeniably, Windsor's view is well put here: the hurt, the anguish, the bitterness sear across every page. But the evocation of a state of mind is not a defence of the person who experienced it. To write the biography of a paranoid almost exclusively from his own papers necessarily results in the tortured reasoning, the special pleading and the selective use of evidence which are all displayed here. At the time of the abdication, Queen Mary wrote to Windsor in 1938: 'You did not seem able to take in any point of view but your own.' That is why he was an unsuccessful King; it is also why this is an unconvincing book. Like Windsor, the author protests too much.

(1982)

NOTE:
1. Michael Bloch, *The Duke of Windsor's War* (London, 1982).

# Lord Mountbatten

Admiral of the Fleet the Earl Mountbatten of Burma was the most honoured Englishman of his generation. By the time the IRA assassinated him in August 1979, he had amassed a collection of titles and decorations, orders and medals, so extensive and so remarkable that when he wore them on full-dress, ceremonial occasions, he looked more like a Ruritanian relic than a man who had done the state some service well into the age of the atomic bomb and the Polaris submarine. To most foreign observers, and even to some natives, the British honours system is an *ancien régime* anachronism of incomprehensible complexity and questionable worth. But to Mountbatten, it was the staff and stuff of life. For while most British politicians, civil servants and military men reluctantly settle for the occasional decoration, Mountbatten collected his titles and orders as a philatelist collects stamps – remorselessly, singlemindedly and voraciously. 'In honour bound' was not just his family motto: it was also the direction of his life's ambition, and the summation of his life's achievements.

To Mountbatten's many admirers – who ranged from Barbara Cartland and Noel Coward to Clement Attlee and Harold Macmillan, and of whom the most ardent was, undoubtedly, himself – these honours were both deserved and appropriate. In the first place, he was very royal: Queen Victoria was his great-grandmother, the last Czar was his uncle, the future King Edward VIII was his best man, Prince Philip was his nephew, and Prince Charles his 'honorary grandson'. In the second place, he was very charismatic: exceptionally good looking, married to the richest and most beautiful heiress of her generation, a brilliant leader, and a formidable operator and committee man. And in the third place, he was very successful: in peace and war, as a military man and as a proconsul, he held a succession of important appointments, which he discharged with brilliance and aplomb. Seen in this light, Mountbatten was an authentic twentieth-century hero, the last warrior prince, whose entry was the longest in Britain's *Who's Who*, with the exception of Winston Churchill himself.

Yet to his critics – and there were many, and they grew in number with the years – these honours were ill-gotten gains, which concealed failures of judgment and shortcomings of character more than they rewarded real achievement. For all his charm and style, Mountbatten's marriage was never particularly happy, and since his death *Private Eye* has alleged that he was a practising homosexual. To many Americans like General Stilwell, his wartime deputy in south-east Asia, he was a posturing playboy, a gingerbread admiral, who was inordinately vain and insufferably self-obsessed. To conservative imperialists like Lord Beaverbrook, he was completely untrustworthy: a radical chic poseur, who implausibly espoused socialist principles despite his rank and riches, and who went to India as Viceroy only to throw away the jewel in the crown. To military men like Admiral Cunningham and Field Marshals Alanbrooke and Hull, he was an unscrupulous and irresponsible opportunist, whose own ideas were rarely good, and whose good ideas were rarely his own. And even the royal family occasionally resented his high- and heavy-handed interference: Prince Philip and Prince Charles may have venerated him to excess, but the Queen, the Queen Mother and Princess Margaret seem to have been much less enamoured.

Of course, all great men by definition have their critics; but all men who have their critics are not by definition great. Which was Mountbatten: a flawed hero or an heroic flop? And why was he both so honoured yet so disliked? Philip Ziegler's massive and masterly official biography is the first attempt to answer these questions without Mountbatten himself looking on.[1] Even so, it cannot have been an easy task. The Mountbatten archive is enormous; both of his daughters are still alive; almost every major world figure seems to have had dealings with him; and many of the matters in which he was involved remain controversial or classified or both. Yet despite these daunting difficulties, Ziegler has produced an outstanding book – beautifully written, admirably proportioned, and striking just the right balance between the life and the times. It is also quite remarkably fairminded, doing full justice to Mountbatten's virtues and accomplishments, while never losing sight of his faults and failings. The result, as Ziegler admits, is a book which would have caused its subject 'much pain and dismay'. Put another way, this means that at each stage in his career, it becomes clear why Mountbatten had not only his admirers, but also his critics.

His father was Prince Louis of Battenberg, a minor German princeling, who came to England to pursue a naval career, and did so with such success that he reached the summit of the senior service as First Sea Lord by 1912. But when war broke out, violent outbursts of anti-German feeling forced him to resign his post, to renounce his royal titles, to change his name from Battenberg to Mountbatten, and to begin life anew and unemployed as the first Marquess of Milford Haven. His second son, who had been born in 1900 as His Serene Highness, Prince Louis of Battenberg, and who was at that time a cadet at the Royal Naval College, Osborne, became, accordingly, Lord Louis Mountbatten: the younger son of a peer instead of the younger son of a prince. But he also became many other things as well. During his early years, Mountbatten had lived the comfortable existence of minor royalty, had been a solid but not outstanding schoolboy, and had shown no real promise of future distinction. But his father's downfall, which was the most traumatic experience of his life, abruptly changed all that, and drove him to atone for this family humiliation by getting to the very top of the naval profession himself. Like Churchill, much of Mountbatten's inordinate ambition derived from the burning desire to vindicate his father's unjustly slighted reputation. Fame was the spur because shame was the spur.

To this end, Mountbatten ruthlessly exploited his royal connections to further his own career. In the closing stages of the war, he got himself appointed a midshipman on Admiral Beatty's flagship, and in the early days of peace, he accompanied the Prince of Wales on his sensationally successful tours to India and the antipodes. For equally self-interested reasons, he married Edwina Ashley, the granddaughter of the millionaire financier Sir Ernest Cassel. Sociologically, the match was perfect: she had wealth; he had status; they both had ambition. Matrimonially, it was less successful: he had some affairs; she had a great many; they were emotionally quite incompatible. Not, Ziegler insists, because Mountbatten was homosexual: there is no evidence for that. But rather because Mountbatten was more interested in work than sex, whereas with Edwina it was very much the other way round. Indeed the fact that he did not excel in the bedroom may only have sharpened his already voracious appetite for worldly success. He may have been one of the bright young things of the 'twenties and 'thirties by night and at weekends; but during the daytime, he worked hard to establish himself as a promising naval officer, he excelled in the unheroic world of wireless communications, and he earned a deserved reputation as a gifted and flamboyant leader of men.

During the Second World War, he advanced inexorably, not just despite, but almost because, of some spectacular setbacks. In the period of the phony war, he commanded the destroyer HMS *Kelly*, and dashed about the North Sea and the Mediterranean, doing little except getting his ship sunk off Crete; but Noel Coward publicized his deeds in his film *In Which We Serve*, and he was taken up by Churchill as a man of audacity after his own heart. In 1941, he was put in charge of Combined Operations, which mounted raids on the continent by integrated units of naval, army and air force personnel. Eventually, this bore fruit in the D-Day landing; but before that, little of substance was achieved, and the raid on Dieppe, which was very much Mountbatten's brainchild, went catastrophically wrong. Yet Churchill continued to believe in him, and in 1943 made him Supreme Allied Commander in South-East Asia, where the British war effort was bogged down in more than just the monsoon. Mountbatten raised the morale of his men, brought them much-needed publicity, and was noticeably sympathetic towards the nationalist movements in Burma, Malaya, Indonesia and Indo-China in the aftermath of

Victory. Militarily, his achievements seem rather less conspicuous: his headquarters were in Ceylon, 2,000 miles from the front line; his strategic conceptions were uninspired; and his relations with his immediate subordinates were far from untroubled.

Nevertheless, by this stage in his career, Mountbatten's rise to stardom was unstoppable. His progressive views, his experience east of Suez, and his close links with the King-Emperor himself, made him the ideal man for ending British Rule in India in 1947. The will to govern had gone; the machinery of government was breaking down; the incumbent Viceroy, Lord Wavell, had run out of ideas; there was growing sectarian violence between Muslims and Hindus; and the political initiative was increasingly passing to non-British hands. By fixing a definite date for independence in the very near future, the British government briefly recaptured the initiative, and Attlee sent Mountbatten to scuttle the Raj as decently and decorously as possible. He established close and cordial relations with Gandhi and Nehru (with whom Edwina had a long-lasting affair); he concocted a scheme for partition which the Hindus, the Muslims, the British government and most of the princes were prepared to accept; and he drove it through with a combination of ruthlessness and charm. But once again, it was not quite the triumph Mountbatten claimed: he rushed independence through with almost frenzied speed; he failed to conciliate Jinnah or to hold the balance impartially between India and Pakistan; he did not solve the problems of Hyderabad and Kashmir; and there were the terrible massacres in the aftermath of partition in which perhaps half a million died.

Having sunk the Raj to his own and the Labour government's satisfaction, Mountbatten could have had virtually any job for the asking; but he was determined to return to the navy and, after a succession of routine, high-level posts, at the Admiralty and in the Mediterranean, as well as some concerted and unsubtle lobbying, he finally achieved his lifelong ambition of becoming First Sea Lord in 1955. By then, severe defence spending cuts meant the navy was contracting and morale was low. Mountbatten at once instituted a ruthless programme of retrenchment and rationalization; he set up a committee to outline future policy in an attempt to ward off further cuts: and he lobbied hard in Whitehall for guided missile destroyers, aircraft carriers and Polaris submarines. He opposed Eden's policy over Suez, blaming the Prime Minister for his catastrophic misjudgment of Nasser, and for his inept mishandling of world opinion. Shortly after Eden's resignation, Mountbatten became Chief of the Defence Staff and, with the backing of Harold Macmillan, began to amalgamate the separate armed services departments into a new and centralized Ministry of Defence. More heretically, he was among the first to recognize that the notion of an independent British deterrent was no longer realistic, and he offended entrenched opinion on both sides of the Atlantic by his (unsuccessful) opposition to the global build-up of nuclear weapons.

After such a long and flamboyant career as Lord High Everything Else, Mountbatten's retirement was, predictably, far from unobtrusive. He had always preferred action to repose, and the death of his wife in 1960 merely strengthened his distaste for being alone. He was made Governor of the Isle of Wight and Colonel of the Life Guards, and immediately bought a new set of uniforms to celebrate. He chaired a royal commission on prison security, was nearly sent to Rhodesia to deal with Ian Smith, and continued his campaign for multilateral disarmament. He made a television series about the twentieth century, and called it his life and times; he was much involved in royal affairs, from arranging for the return of the Duke of Windsor's papers to grooming Prince Charles for his future responsibilities; and he devoted considerable time and thought to the planning of his ceremonial funeral. It was, in the end, fully as splendid as he intended: the governments he had served and the monarchs he had counselled turned out in force; the men he had commanded and the nations he had freed sent their representatives; his medals and decorations were publicly paraded for the last time; in death, as in life, he was the centre of attention.

Whether he was ever anything more than that is, however, rather more difficult to decide. For after reading this biography, two important questions remain. What, exactly, does Ziegler make of Mountbatten? And what, on the basis of the evidence he presents, should *we* make of him? The answer to the first question seems clear; 'remember', Ziegler tells us, 'in spite of everything, he was a great man'. His record may not have been quite as outstanding as he himself believed, but it remains remarkable, even so. In all the major tasks of his life – Combined Operations, South-East Asia, India, as First Sea Lord and Chief of the Defence Staff – it is Ziegler's considered conclusion that most men would have failed where Mountbatten succeeded, and that no man would have succeeded where Mountbatten failed. Not surprisingly, then, many of his critics were motivated by little more than envy – of a man who had been given so much, but had himself achieved even more. On the whole, the British prefer their royalty to be ornamental and impotent rather than ornamental and important.

Yet for all this well-disposed argumentation, there is much in this book to support rather than to silence Mountbatten's critics. He wanted to be thought a great captain, but was never an outstanding sailor; the *Kelly* spent almost as much time in dry dock as afloat; and he never commanded a fleet in a major naval engagement. The disaster of Dieppe cast a permanent shadow over his time at Combined Operations; as Supreme Commander, he was never really tested as Eisenhower was in Europe and MacArthur was in the Pacific; and as Viceroy, he gave away an India torn and divided. He wanted to be the man who re-organized Britain's armed services in the post-war world, but he failed to overcome conservative military opposition, and he left his last post disliked and distrusted by most of his colleagues. In short, there was about almost everything Mountbatten did an element of the makeshift, the insubstantial, the incomplete and the disingenuous, a disquieting gap between the promise and the performance, the image and the reality, which no amount of bragging and bravura on his part could ever quite conceal. And when Ziegler writes, in his last sentence, that Mountbatten 'flared brilliantly across the face of the twentieth century', it rather sounds as though he concedes as much himself.

The division of opinion between Mountbatten's admirers and

his critics thus remains unresolved, and it is easy to see why. For what is missing in this biography is the very same perspective that Mountbatten's contemporary detractors also lacked, namely a broader historical sense of just what it was that he was really doing. Depicting him as a man of action, whose career was a veritable cavalcade of prizes and honours, makes splendid biography, but it leaves out consideration of the very real constraints which set the bounds both to what Mountbatten could do, and to how well he could do it. When he was born, Queen Victoria was on the throne, Britannia ruled the waves, the British Empire was the largest the world had ever known, and the pound was worth not only twenty shillings but also five dollars. When he died, Mrs Thatcher was at Downing Street, the Royal Navy was but a shadow of its former self, the British Empire had disintegrated into the Commonwealth, and the pound was only worth one hundred pence or less than two dollars. It was these circumstances of an inexorably declining Britain which provided the background to Mountbatten's life, and the yardstick by which his achievements must be judged.

National decline is, by definition, a very difficult thing to accept or to handle, and the British have found it no easier than any other nation to come to terms with it. Indeed many people, especially the politicians and military who were among Mountbatten's foremost critics, would not, or could not, recognize that it was happening at all. Winston Churchill, for instance, never quite forgave Mountbatten for 'giving away' India, and grandiloquently refused to preside over the dissolution of the British Empire. But someone had to, and Mountbatten did. Most members of the royal family are employed to open things: to lay foundation stones or launch ships. But Mountbatten was quite brilliant at the much more difficult and important job of *closing things down*: not just, or most significantly, the Japanese Empire; but, more crucially, the independent deterrent, the autonomous armed services, the Royal Navy and the Raj. As such he was the pioneering and pre-eminent *de*-imperialist, who was followed, in the next quarter century, by many other morticians of empire, who sought, sometimes unavailingly, to pull down the flag and to hand over power with dignity and decency: men like Templar in Malaya, Foot in Cyprus, Trevelyan in Aden, and Soames in Southern Rhodesia.

By the end of the Second World War, Mountbatten had come to realize very clearly – and very early – that it was useless to ignore or to regret the decline of Britain as a world power; that handling this retreat from greatness would necessarily mean making the best of many a bad and botched job; and that, in getting such things done, presentation and performance were of the essence. If people could be made to *feel* that something was well accomplished then, however much some of the evidence might contradict this, and however different things might seem in retrospect, at the time that was in practice more than half the battle won. So, throughout his mature professional life, Mountbatten played the losing hand of British decline with such finesse, assurance and aplomb that it often seemed as though it was not happening: reversal became advance, failure was really success, defeat was presented as triumph, and each setback appeared as a new initiative. And it worked. For in many cases, the performance was so persuasive, the illusion so complete, that it became, in a sense, its own reality, The *Kelly* may have been sunk rather ignominiously, but it made a morale-boosting legend of heroism and fortitude. Mountbatten may have been a posturing prima donna in South-East Asia, but that was exactly what the situation required. Indian independence may not have been the transcendent triumph that Mountbatten liked to make out, but compared with such bloody disasters as the Congo and Vietnam it was, indeed, a remarkable accomplishment.

To Mountbatten's critics, all this was but further evidence that he was a self-serving opportunist with his eye to the main chance: by helping Britain decline, he helped himself advance. But to his admirers, it merely showed that his judgment of events was wise and farsighted, that he was prepared to take on difficult, messy and unglorious jobs in the line of duty, and that he carried them out with a brilliance and success that no one else could have rivalled. For in the difficult circumstances of national decline, the very things for which Mountbatten was so often criticized were positive assets: the vanity, the charisma, the royal connections, the desire for publicity, the determination to take on almost any job and make a go of it. All this made it possible for Mountbatten to reconcile the British to their decline in a way that no one else ever managed: partly by presenting it in an honourable, flamboyant, exciting and even occasionally misleading form; and partly by ensuring that, even amid the traumas of independence and de-colonization, Britain never completely alienated third world or American opinion. Hence the many apparent paradoxes: the man of royal blood who was hated by the die-hard right; the prince charming of progressive instincts; the imperial undertaker who never wore black. As often happens, the IRA got the wrong victim: they thought they had murdered the last symbol of Greater Britain; in fact they had killed the foremost architect of little England.

That surely will be Mountbatten's place in British history: something which he himself would never have admitted, and which Ziegler does not adequately explore. And that, in turn, is the real explanation as to why he was so decorated and rewarded. Many people in Britain are honoured, not so much for what they have achieved, but to console themselves for their loss of *individual* power. Mountbatten was honoured, not because of who he was, but because he consoled the British people for their loss of *national* power. He was always in retreat, yet never in disarray; marching down the hill, but inevitably leading from the front. He played the part of the Duke of York with the panache of Prince Rupert.

(1985)

NOTE:
1. Philip Ziegler, *Mountbatten* (London, 1985).

# PART TWO

# CREATIVITY

# 7

# The City in History

Down the centuries and around the world, the cumulative massing in cities of humans and houses, of men and machines, of women and workshops, of children and churches, of people and pavements, has provoked a range of reactions at once varied and ambiguous, delighted and bewildered. Should cities be a source of pride or of shame, objects of wonder or of disparagement? Is mankind their victim or their beneficiary, their creature or their creator? Some have seen cities as repositories of hope, abundance, fulfilment and variety, which provide most of the things that make life worth living. Others regard them as cesspits of iniquity, squalor, disappointment and despair, as the negation, not the essence of life. In one guise, as Garden Cities or as Beautiful Cities, they bring about the New Jerusalem; but in another, as Coketown and Megalopolis, they merely realize the modern Babylon. To some, cities make civilization possible; to others, they are its greatest threat. Either way, they are conventionally associated with action, with movement, with things happening, rather than with inertia, with repose or with non-events. They are not quiet places for those who want to rest in peace.

Accordingly, the very idea that cities might be objects of veneration rather than celebration, of nostalgia instead of excitement, seems something of a contradiction in terms. Going to town, painting it red, setting it on fire, are urban activities unlikely to engender feelings of mellow and elegiac wistfulness. And the same is true, if in rather a different way, of suffocating on the London Underground, contemplating the black ghettos of Washington, or shuddering at the red light districts of Amsterdam. But in Britain, at least, there are real signs of profound changes in urban conditions, which may portend equally profound changes in urban attitudes. Our great provincial cities, which have for so long stood as the very emblem of urbanity and the embodiment of civic pride, are now economically desolate, politically threatened, and psychologically in retreat. And even London, once the great world city and the world's greatest city, is now rapidly becoming a frontier town cum banana-republic capital, its houses and heritage bought by the foreign rich, its inhabitants increasingly engaged in dishing up Ruritanian rubbish for today's jet-propelled Christopher Robins.

In the most literal sense of the word, Britain is ceasing to be a civilization: its cities, once so robust, so secure and so autonomous, are becoming one with Nineveh and Tyre. As our economy deindustrializes, our towns disintegrate: buildings fall down, businesses go bankrupt, unemployment soars, football crowds riot. Nor does the urban future look much brighter: North Sea oil may have flowed, but it has not created a British Denver or Dubai; the micro chips may be down, but no Silicon Valley has so far come out of them; economically as well as meteorologically, there is no English Sun Belt. When our great cities flourished, we regarded them at best equivocally; now they are almost moribund, it can only be a matter of time before we begin to view them nostalgically. And who better to usher in this new world we are in the process of losing than Mark Girouard? In this, his most ambitious book to date, he takes us on a grand tour of cities round the world, from medieval times to the present.[1] In four hundred sumptuous pages, he provides a celebration of the city so panoramic and so picturesque, so engaging and so enjoyable, that it is bound to be – and deserves to be – another best seller. With the council house as with the country house, his Midas touch is sure.

As with one of his previous books, *Cities and People* is subtitled *A Social and Architectural History*, his aim being to see why towns were built as they were by tracing the links between their appearance and design, and the needs of the men and women who lived in them. He divides his story into three parts, beginning with 'The

THE CITY IN HISTORY

City Reborn', which opens with a tremendous flourish, as he evokes the jewelled wealth, the arcades and bazaars, the churches, domes and turrets, of early medieval Constantinople, the biggest, richest and most sophisticated city of its time, floating like a vision above the waters of the Bosporus, the cross-roads of east and west. This leads into a discussion of the international trade in oriental spices and European wool, and to an account of the sluggish growth of western cities as marketing, manufacturing and banking centres: Florence, Sienna, Pisa, Genoa and Ghent. He describes the houses, the shops and the markets created by these early entrepreneurs; he looks at the places of worship and of education provided by the church and the town halls; he considers the bridges and fortifications constructed by the local secular power; he evokes the temporal and physical pattern of this early urban life; and he illustrates all this with vivid set-pieces devoted to Bruges and Venice.

But it is only in the second section, appropriately entitled 'The City Triumphant', that Girouard establishes his major theme: towns as places of leisure, recreation, variety and enjoyment, and the buildings which were put up so as to make this possible. Once again, he begins with another arresting evocation, this time of seventeenth-century Rome, with its fountains and triumphal ways, its churches and its palaces, its tourists and its touts: cosmopolitan, grand, complex, full of variety and extremes, it was the prototypical modern metropolis. But the major urban developments of this early modern period lay elsewhere, as the Baltic and the North Sea superseded the Mediterranean as the main avenue of trade and foci of urban growth. Accordingly, Amsterdam and Paris are explored in detail: the one as a city devoted to the making of money, the other as the town more interested in spending it. This in turn brings Girouard to fashionable urban society, with its spas and seaside resorts, its parks and promenades, its coffee houses and assembly rooms, all most brilliantly exemplified in Bath. He leaves this sophisticated vista with evident regret, to investigate the growth of government cities, with their parliament houses and royal palaces, their hospitals and dockyards; and then ventures even further afield to trace the export of such western cities abroad, especially to the Americas and the East Indies.

His last section, on 'The Exploding City', contends with the almost exponential growth and proliferation of western towns during the last two hundred years, and vividly conveys the pace, the scale and the excitement of this development. He begins with a depiction of Engels' Manchester, the 'shocker' of the early Victorian period, the first great modern industrial metropolis, with its factories and its chimneys, its mills and its canals, its steam engines and its warehouses, which slowly evolved into something more civilized. From there, he moves on to London, the first great suburban city, and explores the making of Regent's Park and St John's Wood, the rise of the villa and the semi-detached house, and their gradual spread to the provinces. After a brief pause in Paris to witness the birth of the boulevard, he rushes us across the Atlantic in time to see the rise of the skyscraper in Manhattan and Chicago, and then takes us round the world, stopping off at Vienna, Buenos Aires and Tokyo. Finally, he looks at Garden Cities and the Town Planning and City Beautiful Movements, those early essays in urban escape and reform which reached their fullest, most extensive and most self-destructive fruition in Los Angeles: where downtown is nowhere and suburbia is everywhere – a failed Jerusalem, a low-density Babylon.

So succinct a summary can hardly convey the range and the riches, the diversions and the delights, of this fascinating and audacious book. The prose is always vigorous and attractive, and the text is full of wise and witty aphorisms. The illustrations are an endless source of pleasure: culled from an astonishingly wide range of sources, beautifully reproduced, and a constant reminder that cities are as much things of the eye (as well as the nose and the ear) as they are of the brain. The set-piece evocations, of medieval Constantinople, Renaissance Rome, industrial Manchester and contemporary LA, are admirably done, with effectiveness and economy, affection and detachment. The range of the coverage – from medieval Pisa to twentieth-century Dallas, from the Spanish in Mexico City to the British in Calcutta – is quite extraordinarily wide. From beginning to end, *Cities and People* reads with all the vigour and immediacy which one might expect of the book of the television series – something which it is not, but definitely should have been.

But to describe it thus is also to highlight the weaknesses inseparable from such an approach. In its words as well as in its pictures, *Cities and People* is fundamentally a succession of snapshots, a series of scenes, rather like Kenneth Clark's *Civilisation*, but with the culture taken out and the cities put in. Girouard, like Clark, is a tourist in time, and like all such explorers, is bound to engender criticism – for the places he chooses to visit, for the way he treats them, and for the point of view he puts across. For some, this book will seem – despite its undeniable breadth – a classic piece of western parochialism: there is nothing on the ancient civilizations of China, the Americas or the Near East; the great urban societies of Greece and Rome are ignored; and the contemporary third world gets very short shrift. And for others, the cities that he *does* include will sometimes seem too briefly and breathlessly treated: Canberra and New Delhi get scarcely a paragraph between them; Spain and Scandinavia are barely touched upon; London as the world metropolis is hardly discussed; and the industrial city is written off in fourteen pages, half of them photographs. It may, indeed, be salutary to see how transient and parochial our own great cities look in this broader perspective; but on occasions, this grand-tour approach verges on the superficial.

And even when Girouard does pause long enough to examine some cities in detail, the treatment is not always satisfactory. The aim of this book is to do for the city what he has already done so successfully for the English country house: namely to explain the evolution of the built form, not in terms of architectural history narrowly conceived, but rather as a response to broader human developments. To explain the history of the English country house over five hundred years in terms of changes in the structure and function of the English landed élite was a difficult enough enterprise. But to try to do the same thing for western cities during one and a half millennia within the compass of one book is a scarcely realistic undertaking. The buildings, the lay out, the morphology, of any *single* city in any one place at any particular time, can only be explained in this way with reference to an astonishingly complex amalgam of geographical, political, social, cultural, technological and ideological forces. To try to understand the whole urbanization process in this way necessarily leads to generalizations which lack bite and to explanations which seem rather banal: there were churches in medieval towns because religion was important, factories in industrial towns because manufacturing was important, and so on.

It cannot really be said that this gets us very far: Girouard takes city buildings and city people essentially at their face and their pictorial value; he does not probe behind or beneath to reach the inwardness or the underside of the city; he conveys no deeper sense of the urbanizing process and phenomenon. As he himself readily admits, the viewpoint which unifies this book is personal rather than methodological, idiosyncratic rather than intellectual. He writes, unabashedly, as a member of the upper middle class ('the suburbs are still a strange land to me'), surveying the city from his second floor living room in Notting Hill, and writing essentially about the places and the people he likes and knows. But while this makes the book vivid, it also makes it partial. He is much better on nobles, bankers and merchants than on businessmen, the lower middle classes and the proletariat. He is more interested in town halls, theatres and assembly rooms than in factories or suburbs or slums. He prefers the fashionable recreations of the early modern towns to the rather arid life of its medieval precursor or the more popular pastimes of its industrial successor. He likes his cities hierarchical and paternalistic, serene and civilized; there is little sign in his account of conflict or coercion, of exploitation or inequality. Just occasionally, the lower classes become troublesome, but on the whole, they know and keep their place.

To the extent that most of the beautiful and enduring city buildings are the product of the higher classes and culture, rather than the lower, this approach is entirely legitimate. Many urban activities, especially those of the poor and the weak, do not require purpose-built settings, and so do not impinge directly on the city's appearance. But in all societies, the majority of town dwellers have come from towards the lower end of the social scale, and since they have made at least as big an impact on cities as their betters, any book on the subject which treats them as a silent, passive and largely absent majority is not confronting the city head on – either as a collection of people or as a collection of buildings. There are, in this book, very few criminals, deviants or derelicts; there are no Pooterish suburbanites or servants; there is no treatment of the world of Mayhew or of Booth. Yet, collectively if not individually, these people did things to buildings, *and buildings did things to them*: made them work, made them ill, made them think, made them die. Cities and people, buildings and occupants, interact in more ways than one, and at more levels than just the top. Viewed in this broader perspective, Girouard's vision and version of the city seems too establishment, too élitist, too escapist: a *Country Life* view of the town, which can hardly fail to captivate in 1985.

So it is not surprising that when he reaches the twentieth century, he has very little to say, and most of that is not exactly cheerful. Today's cities don't seem as much fun as they once were; they are probably less beautiful than at any previous time in their history; in the third world they are threatened with numbers and problems beyond control and almost beyond comprehension; and throughout the west, many are going the same way as Britain's blighted towns, albeit more slowly. Much that was done to them in the 'sixties appears in retrospect to have been both unnecessary and disastrous: the planners got their plans wrong, the urban renewers tore down a great deal that should have been conserved, and many of the new towns are so insecurely established that they may never grow old. Today, Girouard suggests, there seem to be only two urban options remaining in the west: the vertical city, like Houston, dominated by its downtown skyscrapers; and the horizontal city, like LA, with its endless freeways and low density housing. Neither of these appeals to him much: the skyscraper city because it is boring, inhuman, and dies at night; the spreading city because its low-density dispersal denies the very essence of human life: face-to-face contact, interaction, excitement, variety.

Cities, he resolutely concludes, will continue: but he has hardly convinced himself enough to convince anyone else.

According to Girouard's tripartite division, cities have been reborn, have triumphed and have exploded: and on such a ballistic trajectory, that only seems to leave dispersal, disintegration and fall-out to follow. Perhaps the metaphor has got out of control. But contemporary experience rather suggests otherwise. The view from Notting Hill may still be acceptable, but from Brixton and Toxteth, to say nothing of Cairo and Calcutta, it most definitely is not. And if Girouard himself seems to find cities of the past preferable to those of the present, then what must be the feelings of those in the slums and the council estates, the ghettos and the shanty towns? Whether deliberately or just plain unavoidably, this book is at once a celebration of cities and a requiem for them: and together, these two moods are very much the handmaids of nostalgia. Over twenty years ago, Lewis Mumford wrote an apocalyptic book about our urban condition, and called it *The City in History*. Increasingly, in the 1980s, that seems to be just where our cities are going, and where they belong. But whether they can or should rest in peace is rather a different matter.

(1985)

NOTE:

1. Mark Girouard, *Cities and People: A Social and Architectural History* (London, 1985).

# London's Urban Fabric

It is almost impossible to say something completely correct about London; and it is equally difficult to say anything entirely erroneous. Whatever is written about a town so vast and varied, whether by city residents, provincial visitors or foreign observers, is likely to be at least and at best partially valid, which may explain why the literature on London is so lush. By the late eighteenth century, it was the largest city in the world, unique not only in the number of its inhabitants, but also in the range of its functions. *Pace* Dr Johnson, there was not in London all that life could afford; but it provided more opportunities for living and buying than all provincial English towns combined. Unfailingly attractive, and inexorably centripetal, London dominated England to an extent not rivalled by any other capital in any other country, drawing to itself the crown, parliament, government, the law, commerce, finance, fashion and culture, thereby concentrating in one swollen metropolis all those diverse urban functions which, in the United States, were divided up between Boston, New York, Philadelphia and Washington, and in France were shared by Paris, Versailles, Lyons, Marseilles and Bordeaux. So, as Henry James explained, 'one has not the alternative of speaking of London as a whole, for the simple reason that there is no whole of it . . . Rather, it is a collection of many wholes, and of which of them is one to speak?'

Which, indeed? One matter which preoccupied many mid-eighteenth and mid-nineteenth century observers was the extreme contrast between the wealth which was generated and garnered in London, and the poverty-stricken nature of its appearance. 'The capital of the richest nation in the world' was also 'the least beautiful city in the world'. Unrivalled in 'opulence, splendour and luxury', it was nevertheless 'inconvenient, inelegant, and without the least pretensions to magnificence or grandeur'. Affluence and effluence dwelt side by side; its streets were more likely to be paved with gold or garbage than with slabs; and its buildings were non-monuments to non-monumentality. The comparison between Trafalgar Square and the Place de la Concorde, Buckingham Palace and the Louvre, the Mall and the Champs-Elysées, and Regent Street and the Rue de Rivoli, merely underlined the fact that the British were amateurs in the grand manner. The city whose 'towers, domes, theatres and temples' Wordsworth celebrated in a rare moment of urban empathy, was more candidly described in *The Prelude* as a 'monstrous ant-hill', 'gloomy' and 'unsightly'. Like the making and losing of the British Empire, London was both burnt and built in a fit of absence of mind. The strands of its fabric (like the fabric of its Strand) were distinctly unimpressive.

The first twentieth-century writer to confront this conundrum historically was Steen Eiler Rasmussen, a Danish architect, town planner and Anglophile, whose book, *London: The Unique City*, was published in 1934, and is now deservedly, if tardily, reprinted.[1] As a lifelong observer of the great metropolis, he came to share Henry James's view that it could only be written about satisfactorily from a partial and particular perspective. 'A description', he noted, 'of a town of ten millions is utter nonsense, unless one considers the subject from a special angle, and can thus reduce to a chosen few the endless number of facts.' Accordingly, he devoted his book to explaining what it was that made London the uniquely delightful city he believed it to be, by investigating 'that part' of its history 'which can help us to understand the city of the present day'. And the novelty and importance of his findings are well borne out in three other books which, although written several decades later and from a variety of standpoints, are all in great measure following the trail which he blazed. Whether by describing what was built, or by resurrecting what was not, they are all concerned, like him, with London's conspicuous lack of monumentality.

For Rasmussen, London was unique because, unlike the 'concentrated' cities of the Continent, it was spatially 'scattered', characterized by unrestricted growth and organic development, by private enterprise and private property, by leasehold estates and one-family houses. In turn, this was explained by the conflict between Westminster (the bastion of the Crown) and the City (the stronghold of commerce) which, uniquely among European capitals, was emphatically resolved in favour of the latter. As a result, London was dominated by private wealth, individual freedom, political independence, commercial values and domestic virtues, rather than by absolutist power, tyrannical rulers, state interference, centralized bureaucracy and despotic grandeur. The defeat of Wren's grandiose plan for reconstruction in 1666 symbolized the triumph of the citizen over the sovereign and was, for Rasmussen, a 'good thing'. For him, the abiding English virtues were (in alphabetical order) balance, decency, fair play, refinement, reserve, reticence, simplicity, tolerance and understatement, all of which were exactly and fittingly reflected in the homely squares, the welcoming parks and the tidy Underground of London. At a time when the English seemed increasingly attracted by such alien and Continental notions as high rise housing, Rasmussen sought to awaken them to the merits of their own capital, and to urge them to stay loyal to their national characteristics. 'He who learns to know the English way', he concluded, 'cannot but admire it.'

Half a century on, this safe and cosy picture seems less convincing. Much of the city of which Rasmussen wrote so affectionately has been levelled by the bomb and the bulldozer. Problems of race, crime and violence make London today seem both more sombre and less unique than in the 1930s. It is no longer 'a pleasure to go down into the stations of the Underground'. His self-confessed Whiggism now seems more distorting than illuminating. Selectivity may be necessary in writing about London, but what conviction can a general argument about the city carry which is made by ignoring slums, suburbs and poverty, as well as churches, markets and great buildings, and also the docks, the railways and the government? And, in this revised edition, his attempt to prove that Milton Keynes is the direct descendant of Bloomsbury seems about as plausible as trying to show that Michael Foot speaks with the authentic voice of the Levellers. More fundamentally, the central argument of this book, that London's homely architecture is the product and expression of Londoners' homely virtues, is chronologically unsound. Most of the buildings whose praises Rasmussen sings were completed by 1800; but most of the characteristics whose merits he acclaims were, on his own admission, products of the Arnoldian public school, which did not come into its prime for another half century or so.

Any book fifty years old is likely to seem wrong headed in some ways, and Rasmussen is no exception. But his interest in the relationship between political structure, social attitudes and architectural form, and his more specific concerns with leasehold estates and one-family houses, have been profoundly influential. One eloquent and stylish illustration of this is Donald Olsen's book (another gratifying reprint), which begins where Rasmussen left off, by trying to assess the role of the great urban, aristocratic, leasehold estates in the making of the urban fabric.[2] Combining the power to plan with the inclination to do so, more interested in long-term appreciation than short-term profit, and preferring coherent planning to piecemeal development, these great estates exercised formidable power over the building, preservation and remaking of the urban environment, thereby influencing profoundly the social, economic and architectural character of certain parts of London. The way in which they did so is illustrated with reference to two such estates: the Bedfords, whose involvement in urban development ran from Inigo Jones's highly innovative Covent Garden piazza in the 1630s, via the creation of Bloomsbury's Georgian delights, to the development of Figs Mead, a model lower-class suburb, in the 1830s; and the Foundling Hospital estate, to the east of Bloomsbury, developed from the 1780s to the 1820s, and reaching its social and architectural summit in Brunswick Square, so beloved of Isabella Knightley.

By giving equal weight to the limitations on such landowners' powers, and by stressing that for them town planning was very much the art of the possible, Olsen shows that the influence of the great urban estates on the making of London's fabric was rather less than Rasmussen may have thought. Covent Garden, for instance, was conceived and begun as the Belgravia of its time. But the upper classes did not stay long; the lower classes followed them; and the establishment of the market there was but a recognition that this trend could not be reversed. Likewise, in Bloomsbury, the high hopes initially entertained were proved vain. The upper classes preferred Mayfair; it took half a century to build and let the houses in Gordon Square; the building of Euston Station close by did untold damage as heavy traffic invaded the hitherto sequestered streets; and 'creeping decline' proved irresistible, as houses were converted into tenements or just left vacant and decaying. Despite the very real power which urban landlords such as the Bedfords possessed, they could not force builders to build, tenants to come, or occupants to stay. Contemporary radical polemicists may have depicted such great ground landlords of London as 'Mogul monarchs' and 'Persian satraps'; but in many ways they were as frustrated and restricted in their building schemes as were the monarchs themselves.

As Olsen explains in an admirably detached introduction to this second edition, this was a highly subversive message to preach in the 1960s, when the book was first published. At a time when the white-hot technological revolution was in full (if retrospectively feeble) blast, and when British, French and Americans were replanning and rebuilding their cities with the limitless funds and buoyant optimism of big spending liberal governments, Olsen's argument was one to which official ears were largely deaf. For if his history of the well-run and powerful Bedford estate had any contemporary lesson, it was this: however carefully thought out and vigorously executed any town planning scheme might be, there were very real limits to what it might realistically accomplish. Today, however, the market is once more in the ascendant; government is in retreat; council houses are for sale; and planning is undermined from within and discredited from without. And, ironically, this makes Olsen's second conclusion as subversive now as was his first a generation ago: planning may not achieve miracles, but it can, in the right circumstances and at the right time, achieve *something*. His great landowners may have been forced into 'strategic retreats'; but there were also 'partial victories' and 'minor triumphs'. Much of Bloomsbury, which Rasmussen evoked so beguilingly in chapter nine of *The Unique City*, is no more. But anyone walking round Bedford Square today – 'the most complete and best preserved of all Georgian squares in London' – will instantly recognize the force of Olsen's argument.

The fact that this description derives from Muthesius's book indicates his indebtedness to Olsen and, in turn, to Rasmussen.[3] Again, he is interested in private not public wealth, in leasehold estates and control, and in the British preference for one-family houses rather than multi-storey living. And, although Muthesius rightly warns that architectural history has concentrated too much on London, he devotes much of his book to the great metropolis, arguing as he does that fashion in housing, like taste in clothes, diffused downwards and outwards from there. So his starting place is familiar: Covent Garden and Bloomsbury, 'the model for all later developments of terraces, squares and regularity in general'. More than Olsen, however, his book is a tract *for* the times, rather than against them. In the 'thirties, Rasmussen urged the English not to be beguiled by flats. But, for a generation after the Second World War, his warnings went unheeded: terraced houses were demolished as insults, eyesores, abominations, while tower blocks were constructed as progress, improvements, the future. But the belated discovery that flats were often merely slums in the sky, combined with the revived appeal of smaller, warmer, safer houses in our bleaker, straitened world, means that the terrace is once again sought after as a past that does work, while flats are avoided as a future that does not. A decade ago, Muthesius's well-disposed, elegantly-written and exquisitely illustrated evocation of the terrace would have been inconceivable; but now it will be found adorning the bookshelves or coffee tables of many a gentrified dwelling.

As a pioneer in this subject, Muthesius rightly sets his own terms of reference. The terraced house originated in upper-class London, reaching its apogee in those early nineteenth-century extravaganzas in Belgravia, Regent's Park and Carlton House Terrace. It was also adopted by the highly emulative middle classes, who produced their own provincial versions in spas like Bath, Clifton, Cheltenham and Leamington, and in resorts like Brighton, Folkestone, Eastbourne and St Leonards. By the mid-nineteenth century, aristocratic demand had tailed off, and the middle classes had abandoned the terrace for suburban villadom. But for the working classes, the terraced house remained the principal form of residential accommodation until the end of the nineteenth century. Within this loosely woven narrative structure, Muthesius explores the ways in which landownership, development and the increased organization of the building trade influenced the form and appearance of the terraced house; he investigates its stylistic evolution, from late eighteenth-century Classicism to mid-Victorian gothic revival to *fin-de-siècle* eclecticism; and he describes the great array of building materials: stone in the south-west, stucco on the south coast, and brick almost everywhere – silver grey in Reading, purple in Luton and white in Cambridge.

As these diverse and varied examples imply, the difficulty with the subject is that there is no such thing as the ideal type of terraced house, which makes it almost impossible to relate social change to architectural evolution. There was so much local variation – from one-storey miners' cottages in Sunderland to back to backs in Leeds to terraced flats in Tyneside – that it is hard to generalize even about working-class homes. And while it may be true that a twenty-roomed town house in Belgravia and a four-roomed dwelling in the Black Country were merely variations on the same basic theme, the buildings, locales, amenities and occupants had no more in common, for serious analytical purposes, than *Upstairs Downstairs* has with *Coronation Street*. The extensive discussion of bathrooms, kitchens, water closets, gas cookers and the like is very interesting; but it is not at all clear what it has to do with the majority of terraced houses which, even in the early twentieth century, were still lacking in many of these basic amenities. Why, otherwise, was so much slum clearance necessary after the Second World War?

As Muthesius rightly notes, many extravagant schemes for terraces collapsed, as builders went bankrupt or supply exceeded demand. 'We shall never learn', he notes, 'of all those grandiose projects which remained entirely on paper.' One such was for a terrace at Norwood in the 1850s, which is included in Barker and Hyde's attractive anthology of freaks, follies and fantasies from the seventeenth century to the present day.[4] Of the many discarded designs and rejected plans, everyone will have their favourite. For grandeur, there is Wren's abortive 'Great Model' for St Paul's; Telford's magnificent 600 foot single span London Bridge; Waterhouse's 'skyscraper' design for the Law Courts on the Embankment; and Seddon and Lamb's 550 foot gothic tower at Westminster commemorating imperial worthies. For megalomania, there is Inigo Jones's Whitehall Palace for Charles I (a combination of the Escorial and the Baths of Caracalla); John Martin's three-storey Thames-side quay (which looks like something bizarre out of *Cleopatra*); and a scheme for standing the Crystal Palace on its end as a 1,000 foot high memorial to Albert (the *Towering Inferno* before its time). For foolishness, there is a monument to Nelson in the form of an 89 foot high trident (described by one contemporary as 'a gigantic toasting fork'); an Eiffel Tower at Wembley (one version of which was to provide accommodation for a colony of 'aerial vegetarians'); and a Tower Bridge encased in glass (so as to keep out the rain). And for long-running farce, there are the many abortive attempts to re-plan Piccadilly Circus, from Norman Shaw in 1904 to Holford in 1968.

Like Muthesius, this book is very much a product of our times. As the authors admit, in words reminiscent of Olsen's, there has been a 'lull' in grand government schemes of city planning and improvement, so it seems an appropriate time to consider whether these unrealized dreams represent capital gains or losses. Clearly, if these palaces, squares, bridges, thoroughfares, memorials and churches had been constructed, London would be much more monumental than it actually is. The fact that it has not celebrated genius, grandeur and greatness to the extent of Paris, Rome or Vienna is not owing to a lack of ideas or effort. Nevertheless, on the ground, if not on the drawing board, the terraced house has usually triumphed over the triumphal arch. In part, this is because of climate. Open squares and arcaded buildings need the sunshine of the Mediterranean rather than the grey, soggy skies of London to be set off to best advantage: umbrellas and monuments do not go well together. Moreover, many of the proposers of such schemes were frauds or fanatics, crooks or crackpots, inflexibly infatuated with their own inflexible projects, men like Colonel Trench, the hero (or, rather, joker) of the book, whose schemes for a royal residence in Hyde Park, for a pyramid in Trafalgar Square the height of St Paul's, and for a Thames-side elevated railway, earn him the prize of folly-maker in chief.

But, as Muthesius, Olsen and Rasmussen have all implied, there is more to it than that. Quite simply, the English have never been very good at monumental architecture. One only has to look at the pompous, preposterous ponderosity of Sir John Soane's numerous and unrealized designs for a Triumphal Bridge, a Royal Palace, a Temple of Victory, and a National Entry into the capital, most of which look like working drawings for the set of *Ben Hur*, to see the force of this. As Rasmussen himself put it half a century ago, 'in almost all periods, English monumental architecture has been ordinary and conventional in character.' And it has been thus because the opportunity for it has always been limited. Londoners may not exemplify all of those characteristics listed in Rasmussen's A to Z guide to their virtues, but they are sufficiently cautious, conservative and sentimental to resent and oppose much large-scale tampering with their city's fabric. As Barker and Hyde put it: 'London is an architectural mess, but London likes it that way.' So, perhaps, Rasmussen was right all along, as this survey of what was not built merely corroborates his explanation of what was. We are back where we began, with the triumph of individual initiative over government intervention.

But are we? Is this really how it is and how it was? The timing of the publication and reissue of these four books suggests, on the contrary, that the values which they describe and celebrate are not the only ones which have influenced the making of urban London. They may have prevailed in the mid-eighteenth and mid-nineteenth centuries, and they may be in the ascendant again now. Hence, in part, the revival of Rasmussen and Olsen and the appearance of Muthesius and Barker and Hyde. But this has not always been so, as the earlier reception accorded to Rasmussen and Olsen makes clear. When the one wrote initially in the 'thirties, it was in vain, ineffectual protest against the impending trend towards high-rise monumentality; and when the other wrote in the 'sixties, it was an equally unsuccessful attempt to question the dominant belief in the power of government to re-plan our cities. From the 1940s to the 1970s, in building as in everything else, laissez-faire was out, and government intervention was in. And, in terms of the making of London's fabric, this meant a period of state assertiveness directly descended from such earlier episodes as Charles I and Inigo Jones in the 1630s, Charles II and Wren in the 1660s, George IV and John Nash in the 1810s and 1820s, Lord Esher and Aston Webb in the 1890s and 1900s. Viewed in this light, the paternity suit concerning Milton Keynes should be resolved in favour, not of Bloomsbury, but of Wren.

*Pace* Rasmussen, there has always been, throughout London's building history, a constant tension between state intervention (whether royal or democratic) and private initiative (whether aristocratic or individual). Sometimes the pendulum has swung from the one to the other; sometimes they have both flourished simultaneously. In other words, the conflict between state absolutism and individual initiative, which Rasmussen thought was so emphatically and constantly resolved in favour of the latter, was actually much more indecisive in its outcome. Sometimes the state won; sometimes the private sector. But the victories were rarely complete enough to justify writing the history of London's buildings on the assumption that either one had prevailed for most of the time. And, just as private initiative experienced those 'strategic retreats' and 'partial victories' which Donald Olsen outlined, the same was true of state-sponsored schemes as well. Both achieved something; neither achieved everything. Many schemes for terraces failed, just as some schemes for monuments did not succeed. The Bedfords got a modified, partially successful Bloomsbury, and George IV got a modified, partially successful Regent Street. The private sector accomplished less than Rasmussen thought; the public sector accomplished more.

For all its powerful and seminal insights, the approach pioneered by Rasmussen, and embodied to a lesser or greater extent in all these books, has had the effect of presenting an interpretation of London's past as if it were the only interpretation, by giving undue stress to private initiative while all but ignoring government activity. What is really now needed is a study of London's fabric which does not embrace either of these views to the exclusion of the other, but does full and overdue justice to the interaction between them. Like almost everything else written about London, this would still be only a partial vision, neither totally true nor fundamentally false. But some partial visions are more impartial than others.

(1983)

NOTES:
1. Steen Eiler Rasmussen, *London: The Unique City* (reissue, London, 1983).
2. Donald Olsen, *Town Planning in London: The Eighteenth and Nineteenth Centuries* (reissue, London, 1982).
3. Stefan Muthesius, *The English Terraced House* (London, 1982).
4. Felix Barker and Ralph Hyde, *London As It Might Have Been* (London, 1982).

# Mayfair

When, in *The Importance of Being Earnest*, Lady Bracknell imagined the terrible spectre of social revolution, she spoke feelingly of 'acts of violence in Grosvenor Square'. In this, as in her later strictures against 'the Brighton line', she demonstrated a sound understanding of the social geography of late nineteenth-century London. For while Berkeley Square might boast its nightingale, and Belgrave Square was saluted in *Iolanthe*, neither quite rivalled the *cachet* of Grosvenor Square, the most glamorous address in London, the social centre and status summit of Mayfair, where the rich, the well-born and the powerful lived lives of exclusive, glamorous opulence and privileged, aristocratic grandeur. Some indication of Mayfair's stately, splendid and sumptuous past may be gleaned from the acknowledgements page in this appropriately stately, splendid and sumptuous volume, where names like Abercorn, Derby, Mountbatten, Scarbrough and Weymess surge before the reader's eye, in a veritable cascade of coronets.[1]

Since Lady Bracknell's time, there have, indeed, been 'acts of violence' in Grosvenor Square – both social and architectural. The *landed* élite has largely ceased to be the *governing* élite; many much-reduced magnates have quit London altogether for the embittered seclusion of the shires; and others have adopted a lower residential profile among the chic apartments and smaller houses of Chelsea and Knightsbridge. 'Aristocracy', Nancy Mitford noted over twenty years ago, 'no longer keeps up any state in London', and their once-great Mayfair houses, with their splendid decor, lavish furnishings, spectacular works of art, and retinues of servants, have also vanished, or been given over to less blue-blooded uses. Today, they are one with the dodo and the

Dreadnought, surviving only in the elephantine memories of elderly dowagers, and in the escapist, nostalgic fantasies recreated in high-class soap operas like *Brideshead Revisited*. In Grosvenor Square today, the Uncle Sam who lords it over the west side is not some latter-day Courtauld relative, but a very different creature altogether. Lady Bracknell might be mollified to learn that Mayfair retains its high status and exclusive reputation: but the riches and power to which it now plays host are institutional and governmental rather than patrician or titled.

The Mayfair Estate came into the Grosvenor family through an advantageous marriage in 1677 between Sir Thomas Grosvenor and the heiress Mary Davies, who also brought with her other London lands which later became Pimlico and Belgravia. Enjoying enormous natural advantages of location, from which indifferent early management could not detract, Mayfair was developed from the 1720s, and by the end of the eighteenth century was established as the home of the *beau monde*, a position which it retained as long as the *beau monde* lasted. It was the ground rents thus created, subsequently augmented by revenue from Belgravia and Pimlico, which inflated the Grosvenors from insignificant Cheshire squires into glittering ducal millionaires. By the mid-nineteenth century, they were described as 'the wealthiest uncrowned family on earth', and fifty years later their income was being measured in hundres of thousands of pounds – figures which almost defy the calculation of contemporary real equivalents.

Combining stupendous wealth with an upright character, the first Duke of Westminster was 'the *beau idéal* of a Victorian gentleman' – a high-minded, evangelical philanthropist, owner of one of the finest private art collections in the world, and an outstandingly versatile sportsman. On his death in 1899, it was noted that 'he could pass from the race course to a missionary meeting without incurring the censure of the strictest'. But this could not be said of Bend' Or, his grandson and successor as second duke, who was as much a public figure as his immediate forebear – but in rather a different way. In 1919, he was obliged to resign from the Lord Lieutenancy of Cheshire because of the circumstances of his first divorce – and there were still three more wives to come. 'Whose yacht is that?' Amanda asks Elyot in *Private Lives*, as they stand on their hotel balcony looking out into the moonlit Mediterranean. 'The Duke of Westminster's, I expect,' he replies. 'It always is.'

When Bend' Or died in 1953, Henry Channon (who was himself 'riveted by lust, furniture, glamour, society, and jewels') described him as 'a mixture of Henry VIII and Lorenzo Il Magnifico', and believed that his wealth was 'incalculable' – a view which, predictably, Her Majesty's Government did not share. They valued his estate at more than £10 million, and it was rumoured that a special government department was set up to undertake the collection of death duties. Today, in addition to Belgravia and Mayfair, the family trustees own estates in Cheshire and Scotland, and have other holdings scattered around the world, especially in the old white Dominions. Contemporary estimates of their total wealth start in the region of one hundred million pounds, and work steadily – if speculatively – upwards from there. By comparison with many of their landed cousins, who slum it in safari parks, the Westminsters have been extraordinarily successful in keeping their estates and augmenting their riches across the generations.

During the late nineteenth century, large parts of Mayfair were redeveloped, and this phase in the estate's history coincided with a broader pattern of destruction and rebuilding throughout much of London. Indeed, it was in this immediate context that the *Survey of London* was born. In 1894, C. R. Ashbee, a young East End architect, with a passionate interest in the Arts and Crafts Movement, was so outraged by the demolition of the Old Palace at Bromley-le-Bow that he set up a Committee for the Survey of London Monuments, which planned to publish lists of all important buildings within twenty miles of Aldgate. Two years later, the recently-formed London County Council began to take an interest in Ashbee's Committee, and agreed to pay its publishing costs, provided that the area was extended to the whole metropolis. The first instalment, on Bromley-le-Bow, appeared in 1900, price 10s 6d, and during the next fifty years, a further twenty-five volumes appeared.

As this early history makes plain, the *Survey of London* began life as one of those ventures in historical preservation and national self-regard which burgeoned in the 1890s and 1900s, including the National Trust, *Country Life*, the *Burlington Magazine*, the *Victoria County History*, the *Dictionary of National Biography*, and the Historical Monuments Commission. All were concerned with England's past, and many were born out of the fear that the most cherished and varied of the nation's traditions – the parish and the county, the rural craftsman and the village smithy, the country house and the cathedral close – were under new and powerful threat from agents of destruction as diverse as the county council and the property developer, the internal combustion engine and suburban blight. Publications such as *Country Life* and the *VCH* were suffused with a dreamy, wistful, elegiac nostalgia for a vanishing rural England: they were expressions of rustic lament rather than manifestos of vigorous conservationists.

But the *Survey of London*, although much inspired by this feeling, was also more aggressive, more didactic and more forward-looking in its interests. For in seeking to compile a list of all buildings of architectural merit or historical significance within the metropolis, it aimed, as Ashbee explained in his introduction to the first volume, 'not only at giving a record, but also at suggesting a policy'. By watching and registering 'what still remains of beautiful or historic work in Greater London', it was hoped 'to bring such influence to bear from time to time as shall save it from destruction'. In safeguarding the best of London's fabric for the future, it sought to stimulate 'that historic and social conscience which to all great communities is their most sacred possession'.

It was this powerful preservationist instinct which explained both the appearance – and the weaknesses – of the large, expensive and well-produced volumes of the *Survey* which appeared during the ensuing half century. For, despite their academic appearance, they were more the manifestos of committed preservationists than the work of professional scholars. With a few conspicuous exceptions, such as the trilogy on Whitehall, the majority of volumes were myopic in interest, amateurish in research, and antiquarian in tone. The archival material on which they depended was at best thin, and the dating and attribution of buildings was often based on very flimsy evidence. Buildings constructed after 1800, which by this time constituted the majority of London's fabric, were ignored. And parish boundaries were slavishly adhered to even when they resulted in some bizarre and even meaningless units of investigation. No attempt was made to relate the buildings thus described to the social, political, economic or cultural milieu of which they were both product and expression, and matters such as change, causality and explanation were not addressed, even indirectly. There was, in short, no real *historical* engagement with London's past at all.

By the early 1950s this approach was becoming ever more difficult to justify, especially when compared with such important, pioneer works as S. E. Rasmussen's astonishingly innovative *London: The Unique City* (1934) and John Summerson's now classic *Georgian London* (1945). So influential have these books become that, in retrospect, their novelty and audacity is hard to appreciate. But at the time of publication, they were milestones in the history of architecture, showing how the details of individual buildings could – and *should* – be related to broader historical questions, concerning the structure of landownership, the nature of speculative building, and the dynamics of urban life. Compared with these powerful, innovative, historical studies, the *Survey* volumes seemed about as up to date as St Patrick's Cathedral on Fifth Avenue. Moreover, after half a century's painstaking endeavour, only fifteen of the two hundred-odd parishes of the City and County of London had been investigated, which gave an ominous relevance to the rather breezy prediction of the editor of the first volume, who had freely admitted that the *Survey* was 'a work that may, perhaps, never be finished'.

Accordingly, in the early 1950s, the LCC drastically reformed the whole series. They appointed a professional historian, Dr F. H. W. Sheppard, as full-time general editor, and provided him with a research staff whose massive, unflagging archival researches have been so vital to the *Survey*'s rejuvenation. Unlike its closest cousin, the *VCH*, which has remained – despite valiant efforts – imprisoned in the iron web of its own antiquity (and antiquarianism), the *Survey* has been successfully liberated from its preservationist past, and transformed into a work admirably professional in execution, and impressively historical in content. Although topography and architecture remain the paramount concern, each volume published since 1957 has begun with a general commentary on the social and economic aspects of the area dealt with. In addition, all buildings are now documented and described (where possible) down to the present day. And on occasions even the parish boundaries have been disregarded in favour of more realistic units of study. From the outside, the fifteen-odd volumes which have appeared under Dr Sheppard's auspices look very similar to those which went before. But in terms of content, they have little more in common with them than a co-residential Oxbridge college of today has with its medieval and monastic predecessor.

The result has been a series of studies which have increasingly exhausted the superlatives of their critics. Volume XXXVI, for instance, investigated the Parish of St Paul, Covent Garden, and not only provided a magisterial history of Inigo Jones' piazza, but also, in its account of the Bedford Estate, made a major contribution to the study of patrician urban landownership. And three years later, in the next volume, the *Survey* boldly cast off its central London straitjacket, and bravely entered the suburbs, in a study of Northern Kensington which combined quantitative skill, meticulous scholarship and evocative flair so powerfully as to beat most urban historians at their own game. Quite rightly, one reviewer acclaimed the volume, and the *Survey*, as 'the noblest yet most indulgent work of urban iconography ever conducted'.

In addressing itself to the Grosvenor Estate in Mayfair, therefore, the *Survey of London* has taken on a subject fully worthy of its own grandeur. With its carefully designed, tastefully planned, beautifully produced and meticulously proof-read volumes, which now throw as much light on broad questions as they do on specific buildings, the *Survey* is both a Mayfair among monographs and a Grosvenor Square of general surveys. Indeed, in its splendid appearance, its coherent yet flexible planning, and its long-term conception and perspective, it rather resembles those master plans drawn up in the eighteenth and nineteenth centuries for the patrician owners of metropolitan acres. All too regrettably, however, this aristocratic analogy may be further extended: for in the case of this particular volume, one also needs a ducal income of almost Westminster dimensions to be able to afford it.

Because the Grosvenors' Mayfair archives are so extensive and important, it was wisely decided to publish an extended general survey of the social, administrative and architectural history of the estate as a separate volume which, by a happy and contrived coincidence, appeared in 1977 to celebrate the tercentenary of the Grosvenors' acquisition of their London acres. This companion volume investigates the estate in exhaustive detail, street by street and house by house, piling on evidence concerning the architects, builders and occupants with an almost suffocating intensity. Here is a veritable prosopography of bricks and mortar, which does for Mayfair's buildings what the *History of Parliament* does for Westminster's MPs. Had Sir Lewis Namier been endowed with the interests of Sir Nikolaus Pevsner, he might have written just this sort of book.

As a result, it is more a work to be dipped into than to be read at a sitting, a manual of reference and information rather than of narrative and interpretation. Utilizing every possible visual aid – a large and detailed map, ninety-six pages of plates, and many quite superb plans and line drawings, – the reader is taken on an exhaustive conducted tour of the estate. As we are led along the pavement, the general history of each street is outlined, in terms of its fabric, its occupational usage, and its social tone. At each front door – whether it is to a house, a church, a block of flats or Claridge's – we pause and enter. Room by room, we are taken round; changes and alterations made over the years are described; where there have been previous buildings on the site, we are given their history; and we leave with a list of the principal occupants as a parting gift. From the workmen's dwellings of Gilbert Street via the coachmen, grooms, victuallers and farriers of Bourdon Street, to the surviving Georgian splendours of North and South Audley Street, the varied texture of Mayfair life, and the corresponding diversity of its buildings, are beautifully displayed. Predictably and appropriately, the high spots in this grand tour are the detailed history of the houses in Grosvenor Square, the story of the life and death of old Grosvenor House and its subsequent rebirth, and the account of the nineteenth-century grandeur, and twentieth-century transformation of Park Lane.

The delicious effect of all this is to make the reader an eavesdropper on architects at work and aristocrats at play. We meet Robert Adam giving 26 Grosvenor Square its magnificent eighteenth-century interiors; J. T. Wimperis concocting his splendid *fin-de-siècle* Queen Anne extravaganzas for the rebuilding of Mount Street; and Edwin Lutyens having fun and games over the designs for the new Grosvenor House. At 75 South Audley Street, we encounter Lord Bute (was he really 'the theoretician of absolutism'?), uneasily enjoying his ephemeral triumph as George III's first minister. Nearby, in South Street, we come across Catherine Walters, the last Victorian courtesan, on one side, and Lord Melbourne, whose house boasted sixteen servants 'all thieving and drunk', on the other. Further west, in Park Lane, we notice one house where Disraeli resided before he had climbed to the top of the greasy pole, and another where the widowed Lady Palmerston lived, after her husband had fallen off it. Finally, and perhaps appropriately, a brace of divorced duchesses: Violet, one of Bend' Or's temporary wives, at 71 South Audley Street, and Margaret, Duchess of Argyll at 48 Upper Grosvenor Street, which she kept as a private residence until as recently as 1978.

More generally, this wealth of detail provides ample support for the generalizations developed in the earlier companion volume. In particular, it shows both the scope and the limits to the power of aristocratic landowners to mould the urbanization process according to their own preferences. The first Duke, for instance, was often successful in his late nineteenth-century rebuilding programmes, improving the tone of some of the meaner streets, and ridding the estate of its surfeit of eighteenth-century hostelries. But when, in the twentieth century, the great grandees began to abandon their town houses for smaller dwellings and apartments, there was little that the Westminsters could do but to accept this trend and re-plan their estate accordingly. Like many other Londoners, they did not wish to see Park Lane become Park Avenue: but they had little real choice in the matter. All they could do – and *did* do – was to ensure that, if such redevelopment had to come, then it must be to the highest possible standards. Accordingly, Park Lane and Mayfair rightly remain the two most expensive sites on the 'Monopoly' board, and this magnificent book goes far in helping us understand why.

(1981)

NOTE:
1. F. H. W. Sheppard (editor), *The Survey of London*, volume 40, *The Grosvenor Estate in Mayfair*, part II, *The Buildings* (London, 1980).

# The Stately Homes of England

No artifact in modern England has been the object of such fanciful, romanticized and well-articulated veneration as the country house. Yet it is important to remember that this is, in fact, a relatively recent development. The main reason why so many great mansions were demolished from the Tudor to the Victorian period was so that their owners might move with the times, and thus put up new and improved versions instead. Nineteenth-century novelists, like Surtees or Trollope, tended to give minutely detailed accounts of country-house life, but they were more prosaic and precise than rapturous and rhapsodic. But during the first half of this century, there was a significant change in attitudes, with the result that one of the most common set pieces in popular fiction became that magical, glamorous, enchanted moment when the central character first set eyes upon the mansion which frequently dominated the novel. So, when Harriet Wimsey (*née* Vane) visits Denver Ducis for the first time, Lord Peter assures her that the drive is indeed one mile long, that there are deer roaming in the park, and that peacocks do in fact strut upon the terrace. As he rightly observed, 'all the story-book things are there'.

Such scenes, evocative rather than detailed, more fanciful than factual, abound in the works of Buchan and Brett Young, in Waugh and in Wodehouse: their country-house world was, in Mark Girouard's apt phrase, 'mellow, dignified, creeper-clad, and bathed in perpetual sunshine'. Nor is it coincidence that this became the conventional wisdom at the time when, for the first long period in four centuries, few new country houses were being built by the old territorial élite, and many old ones were being vacated by their original owners. Although far from extinct, country house life during the first forty years of the twentieth century was not lived with quite the same sense of effortless, exuberant ease which had characterized it a hundred years before. And, since the Second World War, even this Indian summer has turned to autumn: the creeper has withered and the sunshine faded. The death toll recorded by Roy Strong, Marcus Binney and John Harris in *The Destruction of the English Country House* tops nine hundred, and few writers today set contemporary novels in country houses, as they did even a generation ago.

Yet, as James Lees-Milne correctly notes in his attractive if angry anthology *in piam memoriam* Bladesover, 'One of the many contradictory qualities of the British is to revere, and even lament, the things they are in the process of destroying.'[1] This is not, of course, a universally valid dictum. Many lost causes in this country pass unnoticed, unmourned and unlamented. But there can be no doubt of its applicability to the stately homes of England in the 1980s. Contemporary novelists may no longer gush or enthuse, but throughout the nation as a whole, the plague of country-house nostalgia rages with ferocious, uncritical and seemingly incurable vigour. By some mysterious process of non-reasoning, the stately-home world that most of us never knew has become the world we ourselves have lost, and thus the world we desperately want to find once more: the only paradise we seek to regain is the one which was never ours to lose in the first place.

James Lees-Milne's pocket anthology provides fascinating fodder for such elegiacally-conditioned digestions, even though it also contains an unexpected (and, perhaps, unintended) antidote to the current cult of the country house. Drawing widely on the printed memoirs, diaries and correspondence of natives and foreign visitors, he compiles a memorable picture of life in the English stately home, as described by some of its more outspoken and opinionated habitués, the cumulative effect of which is to leave an overriding impression of eccentricity and bad temper. We meet Sarah, Duchess of Marlborough, lamenting her 'misfortunes to suffer very great mischiefs from the assistance of architects'; Sir

John Cope of Bramshill, whose 'apartments are so vastly spacious that one generally sees Sir John toward the winter put on his hat to go from one room to another'; John Mytton of Halston Hall, who consumed between four and six bottles of port a day, and once set fire to his night shirt to frighten away the hiccoughs; Benjamin Disraeli, gazing into the fire at Hughenden, murmuring 'dreams, dreams, dreams', and being refused in marriage by the Countess of Cardigan because his breath smelt of 'the ill odur of politics'. And there is also – as one might expect – the by-now-obligatory quota of quotes from *Brideshead*.

Funnily enough, it is not only the people, but also the houses, which emerge rather less saccharine-sodden than one might have expected. In the first place, as Lees-Milne points out, many contemporaries (especially eighteenth-century) were highly critical of the mansions of their own day: Westcombe House 'must have been built by somebody that is mad'; Blenheim was 'execrable within, without and almost all round'; Kedleston 'would do excellently for a town hall'; Hardwick had 'vast rooms, no taste, much indifferent tapestry'; Powderham was 'not worth a halfpenny'; and Hagley was 'deficient in water and gravel, two great charms'. To judge from such opinions, contemporaries like Horace Walpole and Arthur Young would have regarded the present cult of the country house with amazement and incredulity. Moreover, the life which was actually lived within their walls emerges as far from beguiling. Most mansions were cold, gloomy, eerie, filthy, smelly and insanitary; they were too grand or too small, too plain or too ornate, too shabby or too vulgar; the food was bad, the company often boring, and there was little to do except hunt; and the servants were frequently dishonest or incompetent, while the nannies were sometimes wicked and tyrannical.

In the light of all this, it is not entirely clear why the editor waxes so eloquently angry at the demise of a way of life which, even as described in his own anthology, seems relatively unappealing. Whatever may be said in favour of the country house as a mode of government, way of life, shrine of culture or architectural artifact, there is clearly much to be said against it too, in part because so many country-house owners seem to have been so peculiarly insensitive to, and unappreciative of, their privileged surroundings and position. From the 1880s, however, such devil-may-care indifference could no longer be successfully sustained, as the landed establishment was increasingly forced on the defensive. Such, at least, is the argument of Heather Clemenson's admirable study of 500 English landed estates during the last 100 years.[2] The late nineteenth century, she suggests, was an especially trying time for landowners, as their political power, landed wealth and social status were undermined by the agricultural depression, the reform of local government, the extension of the franchise, the imposition of death duties, the introduction of industrialists into the peerage, the Liberal attack on the House of Lords, and the disproportionately heavy losses suffered by the landed élite in the First World War. The result was that most landowners stopped building houses or buying land; there were massive sales of acres and mansions immediately before and after the First World War; and in the 1930s the actual demolition of country houses became a noticeable trend for the first time.

So, although Lees-Milne is quite correct in asserting that country-house life survived until 1939 virtually intact, it is clear – at least in retrospect – that the writing was on the wall from the 1880s. It is against this background – which might usefully have been filled in more thoroughly – that Clive Aslet sets his tastefully-written and beautifully-produced account of country houses built in England between 1890 and 1939: the final flowering of this ostensibly and intermittently arcadian way of life before the Second World War, the demise of living-in servants and the rise of taxation brought it to an end.[3] Here is nostalgia at the end of the road (sorry, lane), the last fling of the private patron as country-house client and the architect as country-house designer. By this time, of course, the patrons were an unprecedentedly mixed bag, as very few of them were authentic landowners. Reduced rents, diminished acres and eroded confidence meant that only the super-rich, such as the Portmans, Norfolks, Cadogans and Butes, with incomes massively augmented from mineral royalties and urban rents, could still afford to build. But, in the main, the patrons tended to be the new late Victorian and Edwardian millionaires: brewers, contractors, newspaper tycoons, financiers and Americans, with enormous (but not always respectable) riches, who found an admirer in Edward VII and an outspoken critic in H. G. Wells.

Faced with such varied material, Aslet sorts his houses into two basic types: the social and the romantic. The social house was built on the grandest of scales for the richest of the rich: some patricians, most parvenus. Smart, glossy, luxurious and up-to-date, such mansions boasted telephones, automated laundries, lifts, sewing-machines, marble bathrooms and central heating. They were all of a piece with bridge, women and champagne; with gargantuan meals, extended waistlines and dispeptic digestions; with pheasant shoots, the baccarat table and big game hunting. One such house was the staggering, swaggering baroque of Bryanston for Lord Portman; another was the castellated, constipated confection of Skibo for Andrew Carnegie; and a third was the ebullient, flamboyant Renaissance of Sennowe Park for Thomas Cook's grandson. These houses were for social advancement, self-indulgence and conspicuous consumption, where display meant more than beauty, opulence was preferred to taste, and wealth mattered more than lineage. As Harold Nicolson explained:

> Edwardians were vulgar to a degree. They lacked style. They possessed only the hard glitter of their own electric light: a light which beat down pitilessly upon courtier, ptarmigan, bridge scores, little enamel boxes and plates of food. They lacked simplicity.

It was in conscious reaction against such bloated, boorish excesses, and in deliberate pursuit of reticence, enchantment and 'simplicity', that other country-house patrons – still affluent enough to afford expensive, handmade products, but less gorged with wealth than the super-rich – opted for the romantic house instead. Two extracts from Lees-Milne express the lyrical, idyllic ideal they sought to re-create: one is Henry James's evocation of Compton Wynyates's 'ivy-smothered brickwork and weather-beaten gables, conscious old windows and clustered mossy roofs'; the other is Waugh's celebration of Brideshead as a house 'that grew silently with the centuries'. The results were such warm, mellow, glowing, welcoming houses as Deanery Garden and Plumpton Place (by Lutyens, for Edward Hudson, proprietor of *Country Life*), Rodmorton Manor (by Ernest Barnsley, for the banker Claud Biddulph), and Hilles (by Detmar Blow, for himself). Here was the setting for a simpler way of life, less artificial and self-indulgent, more artistic and literary, a world lit up by devotion to dying rural crafts, romantically identifying with the land and the countryside, and characterized by traditional values, anonymous craftsmanship and oak furniture. While the social house had an affinity with Harrods (or Selfridges), the romantic house was closer to Liberty's (or Laura Ashley).

Whatever their differences in style and purpose, both types of house were exercises not only in escape but also in self-deception. Owners of social houses aspired to make them powerhouses, to entertain the King and members of the Cabinet. But insofar as high politics remained a country-house pursuit, it was still carried on in the homes of the Derbys, Devonshires and Salisburys, who despised 'middle-class monsters' – be they buildings or businessmen. The social houses were power-houses only in the sense that they were wired for electricity. They also sought to give the semblance of landed life, the illusion of a great mansion in the midst of a broad-acred estate. But none of these houses was the centre of a self-contained, self-sufficient economic unit; nor were they rooted securely and socially in their locality. The estates were rarely of more than a thousand acres and were more likely to be used for sport than farming; the houses were sustained by revenue from the Stock Exchange or South Africa; and instead of spending half the year in the country, renewing local contacts, the owners now motored down from London for the weekend. These were country houses only to the extent that they were houses in the country, symbols of self-made triumph rather than expressions of hereditary grandeur. Their affinity with such stately homes as Chatsworth or Blenheim was architectural but not functional: they were the playthings of plutocrats not the GHQs of grandees.

As for the romantic house, it, too, was a sham from start to finish. These houses expressed a love of land and hatred of industry: but the money which made possible this arcadian self-indulgence in most cases derived from this much-despised source. Although these houses appeared to have grown silently with the centuries, in fact they exploded noisily with the days, as their owners, too impatient to let time take its course, demanded the illusion of instant antiquity. By definition, such Arts and Crafts houses should not be *machines* to live in. But most owners wanted the quaintness of the past with the technology of the present: a Garden of Eden with the serpent removed but the servants retained. As Waldorf Astor explained before embarking on his millionaire's Tudor fantasy of Hever Castle, he wished to live 'in comfort in his medieval stronghold, having no desire to call up from the past the phantoms of the plague'. And at its worst, such naive and selective romanticism turned into plunder, pillage and rape, as crazed, obsessive, megalomaniac fanatics like William Randolph Hearst ransacked Europe for furniture, pictures, staircases, fireplaces and roofs that might be fitted into their Xanadu-like dream homes.

Not surprisingly, the inhabitants of these fantasy houses seem at least as bizarre as those who flit across Lees-Milne's pages. There was Andrew Carnegie, welcoming his sovereign to Skibo with the catastrophically accurate salutation 'Hail fat Edward.' 'That's you,' Carnegie added, pointing, just in case the King had misunderstood. There was William Randolph Hearst, described by Teddy Roosevelt as 'an unspeakable blackguard', who told his wife that St Donat's Castle, his recent Welsh purchase, was Norman. 'Norman who?' she replied, wondering. There was William Waldorf Astor, who was so anxious to hear his praises sung in the press that he instructed his office to release the false news of his death so he might enjoy his obituaries, and who kept the public out of Hever grounds so effectively that it was supposed his middle name was Walled-Off. There was Sir Philip Sassoon, the homosexual politician who added a bachelors' wing to Port Lympne around a Moorish courtyard which Honor Channon likened to a Moorish brothel. And there was Lord Charles Beresford, on a country-house weekend, bursting into a darkened bedroom he thought was occupied by his lover. 'Cock-a-doodle-do,' he cried lustily as he leaped on the bed – only to find himself between the Bishop of Chester and his wife. One of the houses in Aslet's catalogue is described as 'now a mental institution'. To judge by the antics described here, some of them always were.

As these stories imply, Aslet is better at anecdote and illustration than at argument and analysis, largely because his material is too refractory to be put into neat conceptual categories. The houses were so diverse, and their owners were so varied, that it is impossible to link social change and architectural development as Mark Girouard did in *Life in the English Country House*. And the mansions were not of sufficient complexity or decorative interest to justify the extended individual treatment that their nineteenth-century predecessors received in *The Victorian Country House*. Even the distinction between the social and the romantic house seems too crude for comfort: what were Hever or Skibo or Bailiffscourt – romantic in form but social in intent? It is also not at all clear that the inter-war world (when the country-house practices of Lutyens, Kinross and Blomfield all but collapsed) can be treated in the same way as the years of high Edwardian opulence. Nor is the analysis of 'the servant question' entirely satisfactory. There may have been anxieties about domestic help in the early years of the twentieth century: but there were still well over one million of them employed in 1939. And the chapter entitled 'The Road to Good Taste' seems an unconvincing (and unexplained) amalgam of Arts and Crafts oak dressers, Louis Seize gilt sofas and Modern Movement glass tables.

At the most general level, however, Aslet is surely correct in asserting that the Second World War had a much greater impact on life in the English country house than the First – on both the social and romantic houses of which he writes, and also on Clemenson's more authentic stately homes. In some ways, of which as yet we know very little, the Second World War was the country house's finest hour. Demolitions were temporarily halted, and many mansions were put to use in the service of the state, as military hospitals, convalescent homes, POW camps, training centres and command headquarters. The Battle of Waterloo may have been won on the playing-fields of Eton, but the D-day landing was planned in Inigo Jones's double-cube room at Wilton. Yet in other ways, these were terrible times, as owners watched helplessly the inevitable destruction and abuse which requisitioning brought with it, made worse by the loss of servants, the limited supplies of fuel, and further increases in taxes. The best pictures of this twilight world are the prologue and epilogue to *Brideshead* and the splendid, poignant volumes of Lees-Milne's own diaries: *Ancestral Voices*, *Prophesying Peace*, and *Caves of Ice*. But, as Clemenson correctly remarks, a complete history of the country house in wartime has yet to be written.

The same is true for the period since then. The decade after the Second World War witnessed renewed sales of land on a large scale, the greatest demolition ever of country houses, and the sale of many which survived to local authorities or educational foundations. And, although government intervention has effectively curtailed further destruction since the mid-1960s, the combination of rising capital taxation, spectacularly increased fuel costs, and spiralling land values, has led to a further disposal of houses and estates, of which the sale of Mentmore to Indian transcendentalists, and Warwick Castle to Madame Tussauds, have been the most famous. By 1980, one quarter of the mansions in Clemenson's original survey were demolished or ruined, and one half of the families who had owned land in 1880 had parted completely with their estates and their home. And, with the levying of CTT and the prospect of even higher taxation from any future radical government, it may be that the remaining mansions and estates will not survive another generation. 'Perhaps,' Clemenson concludes, 'this time the private sector has cried wolf with some justification.'

Yet in other ways, as Clemenson quite correctly admits, the wolf has been kept from the door so successfully and so resourcefully that Lees-Milne's lament that landowners have been 'liquidated by the state with constant thoroughness' seems much over-stated. The late 1950s and early 1960s saw a great revival of country-house life: in his preface to the second edition of *Brideshead*, Waugh admitted that the book had become a panegyric preached over an empty coffin; and in the days of Macmillan's cousinhood government, Chatsworth and Hatfield seemed still to be the power houses they had always been. And the opening of stately homes to the public on a commercial basis – pioneered by the Marquess of Bath at Longleat in 1949 – has enabled their owners to tap new sources of revenue, both public and private. In the eighteenth century, Arthur Young regretted 'the vile custom of not being able to view a house, without paying for the sight, as if it were exhibited by a showman'. But nowadays, showmanship is the key to survival. And survival there certainly has been. After all, nearly eighty per cent of Clemenson's houses are still standing; half remain in private ownership; and one third of the families who owned mansions and estates in 1880 continue in possession. Although the stately homes of England may no longer prove that the upper classes still have the upper hand, they have certainly survived dissolution in the twentieth century more successfully than did the monasteries of the sixteenth.

In a sense, then, the most fascinating and equivocal phase in the history of the country house is in our own time, since 1940, for which Clemenson provides the statistical skeleton to which someone else might add the flesh. As is always the case in writing of landowners and country houses, the most difficult task will be to strike the correct balance between change and continuity, decline and survival, nostalgia and realism, saccharine and scholarship. That point is well illustrated by considering Gladstone's prediction, made in the 1890s, that one hundred years hence, England would still be a country in which the great landed estates would remain intact. To the extent that they are much less intact than they were in Gladstone's day, we need to know why. But as the 1990s come closer, with every likelihood of that prediction being at least partially borne out, we need to know why this is, too. It all depends on your point of view and precision of vision. The great

danger in weeping over what has been lost is that you cannot see
the truth for the tears. And the trouble with too much nostalgia is
that it makes you go blind.

(1981 and 1983)

NOTES:
1. James Lees-Milne (editor), *The Country House* (Oxford, 1982).
2. Heather A. Clemenson, *English Country Houses and Landed Estates*
   (London, 1982).
3. Clive Aslet, *The Last Country Houses* (London, 1982).

# Sir Edwin Lutyens

Lutyens lives! After three decades in which his reputation has been in ashes, the most esteemed English architect of his time, whose death on New Year's Day 1944 was mourned as if an emperor had passed, now returns in triumph to his phoenixed pedestal. That is the message of this torrent of books which have recently gushed from the architectural presses, pouring abundant and enthusiastic praise on Lutyens and his works.[1] Written primarily by a young generation of architects and architectural historians, they emphatically reinstate the interpretation eloquently enshrined in the great Lutyens Memorial published in 1950, where Christopher Hussey, in his 600-page biography, and A. S. G. Butler, in his three volumes of plans, plates and commentary, acclaimed Ned as 'the greatest artist in building whom Britain has produced'.

Even as this monument was being constructed, Lutyen's star was already in eclipse. In 1931, he had criticized modern architecture for its 'unfriendly and crude pretensions' and its 'haphazardness, lack of grammar and inconsequence', comments unlikely to endear him to the angry young men of the time. So, with the modernists in the ascendant after his death, they took their revenge. In no sense a Pioneer of Modern Design, Lutyens was pointedly ignored in Pevsner's teleological tale, *An Outline of European Architecture*. 'Our greatest architect since Wren' was caricatured as 'the greatest folly builder England has ever seen', a 'twentieth-century architect of prodigious gifts, who contributed nothing whatsoever to the main streams of development in twentieth-century architecture'. 'Perhaps one day,' Pevsner once observed, with a crushing lack of conviction, 'Lutyens' wisdom will be recognized as effortlessly as I recognize his folly.' Now, as disillusionment with modernism blossoms, that day of recognition has definitely and defiantly dawned.

It is, however, far from effortless. Taken together, these books run to over a thousand pages: not since the Lutyens memorial volumes has a British architect received such concentrated and weighty attention. Of necessity, such two-dimensional tributes convey only a limited impression of a supreme practitioner of this quintessentially three-dimensional art form. To get a sense of Lutyens in the round, it is best to begin with the exhibition in his honour which is running at the Hayward Gallery.[2] The imaginative use of furniture and other Lutyensiana, set in an appropriately surprising succession of rooms and spaces, decorated with some of his best-known stylistic motifs, and concluded with spectacular scale models of the Thiepval Memorial Arch and Liverpool Metropolitan Cathedral, give a vivid and enveloping sense of Lutyens and his world. Here is an accomplished display in the Grand Manner, a gourmet guide to Lutyens, proclaiming, according to the catalogue, 'the joy of architecture'.

Like the exhibition, the catalogue explores Lutyens' works chronologically and his styles thematically, from Vernacular to 'Wrennaisance' to neo-Georgian to Elemental Classicism, as displayed in two hundred country houses, monuments and memorials by the score, offices, castles, cathedrals and embassies in bubbling profusion, all topped off by one house for the Viceroy in India, and another for Queen Mary's dolls in London.[3] For fifty years, from the 1890s to the 1940s, Lutyens' imagination teemed with plans and projects: the creative flair, sustained inventiveness and unfailing exuberance overwhelm, intimidate and demand admiration. Not surprisingly, the catalogue commentary requires the combined efforts of Colin Amery, Mary Lutyens, Jane Brown, John Cornforth, Gavin Stamp and John Summerson to do justice to an architect whose career, in its range, dimensions and accomplishments, outshines Wren, Vanbrugh and the Adam brothers. Cloud capp'd towers, gorgeous palaces, solemn temples: Lutyens made them all.

As Prospero's words appropriately imply, Lutyens' preference for bricks and timber, stone and slate, rather than for steel and concrete, plate glass and box girders, betokened a greater affinity with the world and values of Renaissance humanism than with the utilitarian impersonality of the Welfare State. *When Democracy Builds* was the title of an ardent and prophetic lecture by Frank Lloyd Wright, Ned's near contemporary. But for Lutyens, democratic government could 'only work through compromise, leaving its conscience in the hands of accountants'. Hospitals, schools, factories, cinemas and underground railway stations had no place in his eternal realm. To the extent that he thought about it at all, Lutyens took the established order as he found it, and built for those who could afford it. Unlike Sherlock Holmes, his clients were almost invariably illustrious: patricians and parvenus, politicians and plutocrats, prelates and proconsuls.

The singlemindedness with which Lutyens sought his élite commissions, and the certainty with which he told his clients what he would give them, explain much of his success in the first phase of his career, in the 1890s and 1900s. Marrying the daughter of Lord Lytton, Disraeli's Viceroy, was a good start, putting Lutyens on that country-house circuit where he preferred fishing for work to fishing for trout. And one successful commission almost invariably led to another. Through a relative of Gertrude Jekyll's, he met Reginald McKenna, which brought him two country-house projects and, in the inter-war years, extensive work and consultancy for the Midland Bank. Having designed Goddards for Sir Frederick Mirrieless, he followed that up with Overstrand Hall for Lord Hillingdon, his business associate. Such clients were unfailingly won over by Lutyens' boyish charm and irresistible innocence. 'He could not spend his money – until he met me,' Lutyens boasted proudly of the Yorkshire businessman (implausibly named Ernest Hemmingway) for whom he designed Heathcote, complete with black marble stairs, when his client had requested oak. 'His buildings,' Christopher Hussey conceded, 'were often very expensive, and sometimes not wholly convenient' – one facet of his work which places Lutyens closer to the modern movement than his detractors might allow.

But the most important contact, which again came through

Gertrude Jekyll, was with Edward Hudson, who launched *Country Life* in 1897. Once more, there was a string of important commissions; Deanery Garden, Lindisfarne Castle, Plumpton Place, and the *Country Life* building in Covent Garden, Lutyens' first big city venture. More importantly, it gave Lutyens access to a journal which, from the time of Gertrude Jekyll's article on Munstead in 1900, became his foremost champion and publicist, as John Cornforth explains in his fascinating essay on the *Country Life* connection in the Lutyens exhibition catalogue. From 1907, many of the articles on Lutyens' houses were written by Lawrence Weaver, and combined carefully-composed illustrations with an uncritical and sympathetic text that displayed Lutyens' work before a wide and interested audience. 'The influence of Mr Lutyens is good, strong and increasing', Weaver concluded, 'his art gives me a large personal pleasure.' The benefits to Lutyens of such generous publicity must have been immense.

Most of Lutyens' early mansions were not so much country houses as houses in the country – rustic retreats for the urban rich rather than sumptuous palaces for landowning magnates, the visual by-product of that concern for cherished yet vanishing rural past which took less concrete form at this time in such ventures as the National Trust, the *Victoria County Histories* and, of course, *Country Life* itself. Lutyens' houses brilliantly caught this elegiac mood, with their muted texture and friendly asymmetry, mellow gables and homely chimneys. Ingeniously adjusted to the contours of the site, and sensitively constructed in local, 'traditional' materials, they created a comforting picture of instant antiquity. The shapes were gentle but exciting, the designs were gratifyingly inventive yet reassuringly traditional, and the gardens of Gertrude Jekyll softened the outlines, so that the houses seemed to emerge naturally from the landscape, rather than to have been fitted on to it. Thus conceived, these beautiful, dreamy variations on traditional themes touched the same wistful, nostalgic chords as Elgar's early compositions.

For Elgar, the shift from the Severnside sylvan of 'Enigma' to the expansive, '*nobilmente*' themes of Pomp and Circumstance and the

First Symphony was a relatively ordered and organic progression. But for Lutyens, the transition from the Home Counties vernacular of Munstead to the imperial splendour of New Delhi, was less easily accomplished. Classicism may have been the 'High Game'; but the altitude took some getting used to, and he needed time to learn the rules. Some of the early designs, such as the abortive plan for London County Hall in 1907, were borrowed from Wren and Inigo Jones, without paying any interest. Others, like the Rand Regiments' Memorial in Johannesburg of 1911, dished up Edwardian Baroque at its most pompous and flatulent. Moreover, in this premier league, the referee could be stern and the spectators unbending. Unlike Herbert Baker, who was at his best on committees, Lutyens dismissed them as 'horrible, ignorant and unsympathetic', and was too intent on being a great man to learn the arts of compromise and conciliation. But while charm and insistence worked wonders with rich and indulgent private clients, they cut no ice with economy-minded administrators, as shown in a small way by the failure of the Dublin Art Gallery and the Edward VII Memorial, and on an appropriately enlarged and epic scale at New Delhi.

Fortunately for Lutyens, this 'big work', the most glittering commission given to any English architect since Wren, came along at exactly the moment when he had fully mastered the 'High Game'. But, as Robert Grant Irving's fascinating study in the architecture of politics and the politics of architecture makes abundantly clear, there was far more to the making of New Delhi than the design of the buildings. Quite appropriately, his narrative is dominated by political events rather than artistic endeavour: the initial decision to transfer the capital was greeted with disapproval by the India lobby in England and dismay by the European community in Calcutta, who feared that their town was to be reduced, Titipu-like, to the rank of a village; the assassination attempt on the Viceroy, Lord Hardinge, held up planning and decision-making at a vital stage; the First World War brought building almost to a standstill; and the subsequent commissions of inquiry imposed further and drastic economies. As a result, the city took nineteen years to build, and was occupied by the British for only another sixteen: by the time it was completed, the Raj to whose power and permanence it was supposed to be a monument was about to join the previous Delhi dynasties in the dust.

Under these circumstances, the most remarkable fact about New Delhi is that it was built at all. The political background was less than propitious; there were interminable wrangles over the choice of site, style and architect; and the cost soared to three times the original estimate. Especially during the years 1916–22, imperial administrators like Crewe, Hardinge, Chelmsford and Montagu were preoccupied with waging war against Germany and peace against Gandhi, and were trying to steer India, with what initiative they could still command, towards dominion status. In this grown up world of men and affairs, Lutyens was out of his depth, a bird of paradise in a chicken run, an irritating prima donna whose petulant complaints offended and exasperated those in power, and profited him nothing. 'Absorption in my profession', he explained rather coyly to one Viceroy, 'has prevented me realizing the rules that control bureaucratic methods.' For Baker, architecture was the art of the possible; for Lutyens, it was the art of perfection. Lutyens got his buildings; but Baker got his gradient.

Not surprisingly, this committee city did not give entire satisfaction. It set bureaucrats in surroundings which deceived by their grandeur and endangered by their isolation. Baker's two Secretariats were over-blown, windy, ponderous Edwardian Baroque, salted and spiced with Indian motifs which were decorative but not integrated. Nor was Lutyens' record unsullied: he was not at his best as a town planner; the Viceroy's House (especially the dome) suffered from being twice replanned to conform to new and reduced estimates; and he was inexcusably negligent in not spotting that Baker's adjusted gradient would spoil his splendid vista along King's Way to Viceroy's House. But there were many redeeming features, too: the authentic and unrivalled synthesis of east and west; the brilliant fusion of public grandeur and private domesticity; and the astonishing vision of the massive, horizontal house floating effortlessly on the garden like a magic carpet. 'Poor old Christopher Wren', Edward

Hudson exclaimed, 'could never have done this.' When Lutyens left Viceroy House for the last time as its supervising architect, he kissed its walls.

By the time he reached the last phase of his career, the Delhi commission, combined with his war-memorial work, had turned Lutyens into a major public figure. As Irving's book shows, Lutyens handled his masters in India with little finesse; but he seems to have fared rather better when joining with the Imperial War Graves Commission. This work also enabled him to develop his elemental Classicism to new levels of abstraction, which made it a superb vehicle for expressing the tragedy of war. Baker, who preferred homely, vernacular, sentimental crosses, found Lutyens' war memorials too tight-lipped, lacking in patriotic or Christian feeling. But therein lay their mysteriously vital force: gaunt, bleak and desolate, searingly and poignantly proportioned, stripped of consoling frippery and sculptural pomp, such masterpieces as the Thiepval Arch and the Cenotaph caught the prevailing mood of baffled and bewildered bereavement as appositely as Elgar's cello concerto.

Unlike Elgar, however, Lutyens kept going, driven on by the need to earn as much as by the compulsion to create. The flow of country houses dwindled in the later years, but never dried up completely, and included the fairytale Castle Drogo, the farewell vernacular of Plumpton, and the final Classical flourish of Middleton Park. His consultancy work for the Midland Bank and for the Westminster Estate resulted in some audacious flights of fancy in the Poultry Head Office and in the new Grosvenor House. And his wartime Presidency of the Royal Academy enabled him to plan a new, post-war London, Wren-like in its grandeur and its abortiveness. But the consuming passion of his final years was the Liverpool Metropolitan Cathedral, whose astonishing scale and complexity is fully revealed in John Summerson's outstanding contribution to the Lutyens exhibition catalogue. Had it been completed, it would have surpassed St Paul's in style, size and subtlety. But the patrons chickened out: *Si monumentum requiris, noli circumspice.*

★

Perhaps because they are written by architects and historians rather than psychoanalysts, none of these books gives an entirely satisfactory picture of Lutyens as a man. Nor do they relate his personality to his architecture with complete conviction. Inadequately educated, temperamentally insecure, financially anxious and sexually maladroit, his 'Olympian attitude, careless of mankind' signified an unshakeable belief in his own powers. Conversationally inarticulate, given to excruciating puns or ill-judged bawdiness, he could be the most zestful and life-enhancing companion. 'Duff and I', Lady Diana Cooper recalls, 'would give up anything if Ned Lutyens was free for lunch – he was such fun.' Flippant, irreverent and facetious in his public manner, he was driven all his life to create, to succeed and to greatness. Now a king, now a jester, part Puck, part Palladio, sometimes Peter Pan, sometimes Napoleon, the public and private Lutyens were uneasily juxtaposed: the architect who could synthesize discrepant styles and harmonize spatial dissonances with such unfailing assurance and panache never really got his act together as an individual.

For it was in his buildings, rather than in his life, that he resolved these contradictions in a creative synthesis of unique force and originality. The last of the great romantic architects, who was also beguiled by the geometrical allure of the Classical mode, he devised with the intellect means to reach ends that were conceived in passion. In an endless succession of buildings, mass and sprightliness, repose and power, solidity and wit, order and playfulness, protean silhouettes and adamantine strength, anchored movement and balanced rhythms, were brought together so as to give his work what he once described as 'the power within itself'. At one level, it was all a huge joke, with disappearing pilasters, staircases which vanished into arches, straight lines that were really curved, flags which were made of stone: nothing was quite what it seemed to be. But at another, the Olympian deities of style and space, line and logic, meant that everything was too serious for speech. 'Architecture', he once observed, 'should begin where words leave off.' In one guise, it was the 'High Game', to be played with zest and gusto; in another, it was an omnipotent, demanding, jealous god, who had to be served and appeased. 'There is that in art', he noted, 'which transcends all rules – it is divine.'

That, for Lutyens, was ultimately what mattered. For despite the many Establishment commissions, he was no 'architect laureate'. 'Talking of sentiment and politics frightens me,' he once remarked. Wit, jauntiness, insouciance, characteristics in Lutyens which so dismayed and baffled Baker, were not the attributes of a tame imperial builder. Temporal power, regal splendour and imperial pomp held no allure for him, making him at once an infuriatingly inflexible colleague and a transcendently gifted architect. Baker's architecture was politically serious but stylistically suspect; with Lutyens, it was the other way round. Baker's heroes were Rhodes and Milner, and his heart was given to the Kindergarten and the Round Table. But Lutyens' masters were Newton and Wren, and his deities were more abstract and absolute: geometry and proportion, the ruthless pursuit of divinity in his art and immortality for himself. 'The architect', he proclaimed, in a statement of towering and intimidating certainty, 'should work according to his aesthetic ideals, not cater to the sentiments and prejudices of the populace.'

If the interpretation embodied in these new books establishes itself once more as the prevailing Lutyensian orthodoxy, then the architect will have been justified in his belief that his creations would outlast the world which commissioned them and the critics who misunderstood them. Even as he worked on New Delhi, he read Gibbon's *Decline and Fall*. 'The Viceroy', he noted, 'thinks only of what the place will look like in three years' time. Three hundred is what I think of.' Like Prospero's insubstantial pageant, the life to which Lutyens' building gave shelter and substance has largely melted into thin air. The viceroys have vanished and their raj is rubble; his country houses are increasingly being converted into hotels and schools; even Remembrance Day is hardly a day to remember. But because Lutyens' loyalty was to eternal verities and transcendent truths rather than to transient empires and ephemeral politics, his work is as playful and powerful today as it was when first conceived. Unlike the modernists who succeeded and reviled him, Lutyens' vision was no baseless fabric. The cloud capp'd skyscrapers, the solemn supermarkets and the gorgeous car parks may all dissolve. But Lutyens lives!

(1982)

NOTES:
1. Daniel O'Neill, *Lutyens: Country Houses* (London, 1980); Roderick Gradidge, *Edwin Lutyens: Architect Laureate* (London, 1981); Robert Grant Irving, *Indian Summer: Lutyens, Baker and Imperial Delhi* (London, 1981).
2. Hayward Gallery, 'Lutyens: The Work of the English Architect Sir Edwin Lutyens (1869–1944)', 18 November 1981 to 31 January 1982.
3. Hayward Gallery Exhibition Catalogue, *Lutyens: The Work of the English Architect Sir Edwin Lutyens (1869–1944)* (London, 1981).

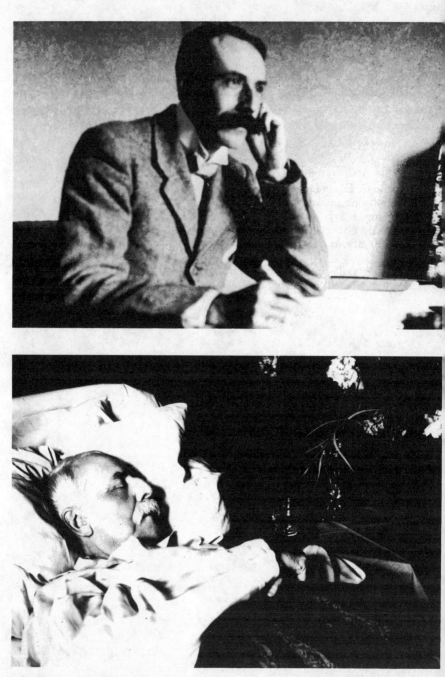

Elgar having just completed *The Dream of Gerontius* (top), and "Elgar on his deathbed." Reproduced by kind permission of The Elgar Foundation, Broadheath, Worcester.

# 12

# Sir Edward Elgar

There is a famous photograph of Elgar taken at the moment he had completed the orchestral scoring of *The Dream of Gerontius*. He wears a buttoned-up jacket and a wing collar, and sports a walrus moustache of formidable proportions. In dress and demeanour, he looks stiff, starched and stuffed: Colonel Blimp before his time. And yet the eyes suggest a very different personality: dreamy, passionate, visionary, a man of poetic imagination with his sights set surely on the sublime. Which of these is the real Elgar? Both? Either? Neither? It is difficult to be sure. For the picture is not only contradictory, it is also deceptive: a carefully contrived self-image masquerading as a spontaneous and unselfconscious record. The pensive pose, with the left hand on the cheek, and the gaze wistfully directed towards some distant horizon, was deliberately struck by Elgar while a lunchtime visitor went out to get his camera so as to record the moment for posterity. The resulting photograph was Elgar as he wanted to be seen, yet giving away more than he knew: the tradesman's son trying too hard to conceal the fact that he was.

Throughout his life, and even more so since his death, Elgar has presented a bewildering variety of images to his photographers and his public, his friends and his biographers. His temperament was quite extraordinarily complex, cross-grained and contradictory; his delight in what Ernest Newman called 'public mysterification' was as revealing as it was perverse; and his creative output has meant very different things to different people of different generations. The result is a personality easily evoked in part, but rarely encapsulated in full. From his friendship with

Ivor Atkins, Elgar frequently emerges as a cheerful, chuckling countryman; but in his letters to A. J. Jaeger, he often appears as an agonized and anguished artist. To Dora Penny, he was a happy-go-lucky and affectionate family man; yet to Rosa Burley he seemed extremely difficult and often profoundly unhappy. In his heyday, before 1914, he was widely acclaimed as Britain's unofficial musical laureate, the nation's greatest composer since Purcell; between the wars, he was derided as the pompous quintessence of self-satisfied Edwardian circumstance; and now, in our post-imperial, nostalgia-crazed times, he has re-emerged triumphantly, to provide the backing to all sorts of soap operas, from royal weddings to *The Jewel in the Crown*.

Not surprisingly, each of Elgar's major biographers has chosen to stress a different aspect of this varied enigma. Diana McVeagh kept the life and the works rigidly separate, argued that the man was less important than the music, gave a reticent and discreet account of his private life, and admitted that much of his output probably *was* as vulgar as his inter-war critics had claimed. Percy Young believed that the man and his music were inseparable, and presented Elgar as a 'two-worldly character', torn between the private poet of Worcestershire (who wrote great music), and the public poseur of London (who did not). In what remains the best and most moving book on Elgar yet written, Michael Kennedy provided the first psychologically-plausible portrait, of an anguished and lonely man, who yet became a music maker, a seer of visions and a dreamer of dreams. And even more recently, Michael De-la-Noy has depicted Elgar in yet darker colours, as a neurotic, depressed, contorted, desperately unhappy man, who conquered the world but never learned to love it, and who found happiness only in the ephemeral euphoria of composition.

So, although Elgar has sometimes been out of fashion, he has never been out of print. Even when his reputation was in the doldrums, the Elgar industry was rarely working short time; since the centenary of his birth in 1957, output has progressively increased; and now, in the year of the fiftieth anniversary of his death, it is positively booming. Of all the many Elgars by whom we have been inundated this year, the most monumental and much-discussed has been that of Jerrold Northrop Moore. For over a quarter of a century, and ever since he left America, Moore has been working singlemindedly at this subject; he has given innumerable lectures and broadcasts; he is a joint editor of the *Elgar Complete Edition* and a Trustee of the Elgar Birthplace at Broadheath; and he has already published books about Elgar on record and Elgar in pictures. Now he has produced his *magnum opus*, *A Creative Life*, together with a shorter study, *Spirit of England*.[1] Although he pays handsome tribute to Elgar's previous biographers, these two books are emphatically the fruits of his own immense labours. He has read everything that has been published on the subject; he has talked to everyone remotely connected with Elgar, including his daughter Carice, who did not die until 1970; and he has made unprecedentedly full use of the rich Elgar archives at Broadheath and in the Worcester and Hereford Record Office. In weight and work, these books together dwarf all previous Elgariana.

The twice-told tale unfolded here is by now very familiar in its outlines. For the first forty years of Elgar's life, there was little to suggest that genius, greatness and *Gerontius* were to come. He was born poor, provincial and Catholic; he was a self-educated musician; and he eked out a meagre living by teaching the violin and by conducting a band at the local lunatic asylum. He married an older woman who was above his station, but it proved to be the making of him, for Alice Elgar never doubted her husband's genius. But it took a long time to flower. Their first direct assault on London in 1889–91 was a humiliating failure, and most of Elgar's compositions in the 1890s were indifferent cantatas and oratorios commissioned by local choral societies, tenth-rate words set to second-rate music. As Moore perceptively observes, if Elgar had died in his early thirties, like Schubert, he would be completely forgotten today. If he had died at thirty-five, like Mozart, he would be recalled in specialist books on English music as a minor figure. Of all the great composers, he was among the latest to develop, and he never ceased to resent this.

Then, in 1898, at the age of forty-one, he wrote the *Enigma Variations*, a heartfelt tribute to those friends who formed a cross-section of the local society, in which he had lived and struggled, yet also, paradoxically, the vehicle by which he was able to escape from such provincial obscurity. Their success and popularity was immediate and abiding, and ushered in a period of golden creativity, as the late developer became a middle-aged prodigy. Nothing could stop him, not even the catastrophic first performance of *Gerontius*. Two overtures, two concertos, two symphonies, three oratorios and four *Pomp and Circumstance* Marches triumphantly vindicated Alice's belief that she had married a genius. Considering how unmusical the English prided themselves on being, Elgar was loaded with honours and degrees; he was given a knighthood and the OM; he was swept up into the arms of the Establishment; and even Edward VII recognized a good tune when he heard one. By 1911, Elgar was one of the most famous men in the land: the hoped-for glory had come.

But in 1920, Alice died, and Elgar the composer died with her. As the last verse of *The Music Makers* had predicted, with inadvertent clairvoyance, he now became 'a dreamer who slumbers and a singer who sings no more'. For the rest of his life, there was intermittent talk of a third oratorio, of a grand opera, of a piano concerto, and of a third symphony: but nothing significant emerged. Honours continued to cascade: the Mastership of the King's Musick, two more knighthoods and a baronetcy (although not the sought-after peerage). But now they were consolation for the loss of creative power, rather than recognition of its continued potency. In London, Elgar shambled from club to club, but he resigned from the Athenaeum when Ramsay MacDonald was elected; and in the country, he shuffled from house to house, accompanied by his devoted dogs and dogged devotees. He recorded his works for the gramophone, but at the concert halls, the public stayed away in droves. They wanted *Façade*, not *Falstaff*, the *Sea Symphony* not *Sea Pictures*. For the last decade and a half of his life, Elgar was living in an alien world: the 'massive hope in the future' which had inspired the first symphony had gone; he became convinced that his music was as worthless as his life; and he ended it, as he began it, in the provinces.

Although the contours of Elgar's life have long been established, Moore's meticulous research necessarily embroiders these familiar themes. There is the young Elgar, back from a successful performance of *King Olaf*, putting his head on his mother's lap, and confiding that he was frightened at the prospect of fame. There is the truly extraordinary extent of Lady Elgar's devotion, fervently thanking God whenever Edward wrote beautiful, wonderful, sublime, magnificent music – which in her eyes he invariably did. There is the dreadful deprivation inflicted on their daughter, Carice, constantly and firmly kept both down and out, so that she should not disturb The Genius at work. There is the contemptible treatment meted out by Novellos, his publishers, which reached its nadir when Elgar produced only two-thirds of his oratorio *The Apostles*, whereupon they initially proposed to pay him only two-thirds of the previously agreed sum. And there is the astonishing episode of the abortive third symphony, on which Elgar was working when fatally struck down by abdominal cancer. The BBC, who had commissioned the work, and were anxious to get results, wondered whether Elgar's fading thoughts might be shifted from his stomach to his symphony by cutting his spinal cord, so as to alleviate his pains.

Some of the insights into the music are equally arresting. How, at the age of ten, Elgar scribbled down a tune at Broadheath in 12/8 time, which prefigured a number of mature themes, as in the second symphony. How *Gerontius* was written as a wager against his own insecure faith, and how, by allowing such a terrible first performance, the Almighty let him down. 'I always said God was against art,' he concluded, despairingly. How Jaeger pushed Elgar into accomplishing more and better music than he dared to believe he could, by insisting that he rewrite parts of *Enigma* and *Gerontius*. How Elgar shaped the mass of thematic material into the coherent and structured form of the symphonies and the concertos. And how difficult life was for him, simultaneously working on two or three new compositions, conducting his music up and down the country, correcting proofs of new pieces, and arranging rehearsals and performances well in advance. It cannot always have been easy to be the dreamer of dreams when the world was so full of nightmare practicalities.

Yet, for all these occasional and illuminating touches, for all the well-intended labour that has gone into the making of these two books, Moore's Elgar project is massively flawed, both in conception and execution. *A Creative Life* is grotesquely gargantuan, a scissors-and-paste monstrosity, suffocatingly obese yet structurally invertebrate. The treatment is inexorably chronological and inadequately analytical; there is far too much quotation from words and music; the proportioning of the chapters is wholly unsatisfactory; the prose rarely rises above the commonplace, and is often woolly and pretentious. The author has become so obsessed with his subject that he has lost all sense of proportion or audience. As he rightly points out in the preface to *Spirit of England*, 'it is not necessary to recall every small detail'. Yet in *A Creative Life*, that is precisely what he does, describing Elgar's life week by week, day by day, hour by hour. In biography, as in everything else, nothing exceeds like excess: here we need less of Moore, more of less.

The author's conception of Elgar's creative life is as flawed as his exposition. To be fair, it is difficult for anyone, however accomplished, to write of the creative process without occasionally sounding pompous or ponderous, precious or pretentious. The ways of God-given genius necessarily remain ultimately unfathomable and inexplicable. And it is quite notoriously hard to relate an artist's creative endeavours to his life and times, especially in the case of music, the most abstract art of all. But even so, Moore's effort to fuse Elgar's life and work into a single whole is less successful than previous distinguished attempts. All his life, Moore argues, Elgar's creative mind fed on his past experience, in such a way that 'each new adventure in theme and form could be understood as the spiritual biography of the whole man'. And it was also in his compositions that Elgar reconciled the contradictions presented by his father's humdrum musicality, as a tuner of

pianos, and his mother's poetic yearnings, as an unfulfilled visionary. So, for all these reasons, Elgar was always reaching back to his
Broadheath boyhood. 'I am still', he recalled in later life, 'at heart
the dreamy child who used to be found in the reeds by Severnside,
with a sheet of paper, trying to fix the sounds and longing for
something very great.'

Undeniably, this stress on remembrance and reconciliation
helps to explain *some* of Elgar and *some* of his music. Indeed, the
notion that his work expresses nostalgia recollected in creativity is
something of a commonplace, while the powerful influence of the
dominant, romantic mother/wife figure has long been recognized. But these insights do not explain everything and, in
flogging them to a thousand-page death, Moore tells us rather less
about Elgar than he might, and rather more about himself than he
knows. At the end of *Spirit of England*, the author emerges as a man
deeply into nostalgia, disillusioned by the darkening experience of
contemporary living, disenchanted by present-day cults of speed
and success, preferring England to America, and Worcestershire
to London. And, at the beginning of *A Creative Life*, he further
tells us how his mother has constantly 'shown me ways of
drawing on the past to enrich the present'. Good for her. And
good for him. But it is not at all clear that Moore can project
his own personality on to that of Elgar quite so easily or so
crudely as he does in these books. There is, presumably, more to
Moore than mummy and memory, and there certainly was to
Elgar.

By so limiting his approach, Moore gets into many difficulties
which a less narrow-minded treatment might have avoided. He
eschews obvious explanations, when they don't fit his
framework, as when he stresses that Elgar's frequent recourse to
youthful sketchbooks was evidence of his nostalgia. But many
unnostalgic composers have done likewise, and in Elgar's case, the
usual reason was that he had to meet deadlines for new compositions, and so had no choice but to draw on old material. It also
leads to some far-fetched speculations, as when Moore argues that
Elgar never wrote a piano concerto because that instrument was
the symbol of his father's trade, and of his own lower middle-class

origins which he was trying to throw off. Above all, Moore is far too uncritically reverential in his use of Elgar's own recollections. For Elgar was not only a music maker, but a myth-maker as well, whose words about himself were often as deceptive as his photographs. And one of the myths which he cultivated most assiduously was that of always being at heart the dreamy little boy on Severnside. Moore elevates this imaginative reminiscence into the fundamental impulse of Elgar's creative life. Yet De-la-Noy devastatingly disposed of it as a 'trite and scarcely believable fairy tale'.

The purpose of any serious biography should be to get behind the myths of, by and about its subject, not to perpetuate them: and this Moore never attempts to do. As a result, he leaves whole areas of Elgar's character, about which we now know a great deal, either unexamined or undiscussed. His obsession with being photographed, his occasional outbursts of bad temper, and the innumerable chips on his shoulder (of which there were sufficient to supply all the fried fish shops in Worcester and Malvern combined), go largely unexplored. The perennial anxiety over money, the interminable wanderings from one rented house to another, and the need for constant reassurance, are described, but not discussed. The astonishing contrast between the music, so often tender, passionate, decisive and exuberant, and Elgar himself, who was rarely if ever any of these things, is not looked into. Above all, for a book which is so obsessed with the idea of creativity, it is quite extraordinarily evasive about sex. The account of Elgar's abortive engagement in 1883, and the analysis of his relationship with his wife, is distinctly thin, even prudish. And the platonic flirtations between Elgar and Dora Penny, Rosa Burley, Alice Wortley and Vera Hockman, get very short and stuffy shrift. Moore rather grandly dismissed such matters as 'idle speculation', reflecting 'only the wishes of the speculator'. Perhaps so. But what is sauce for the goose is sauce for the gander: quite why Moore, mother and nostalgia should have a monopoly of Elgarian speculation is not at all clear.

So, even as psycho-biography, this approach to Elgar is too

limited, too obsessively obsequious. But what is also missing is a broader vision, a capacity to stand back from Elgar's tortured and self-indulgent psyche, so as to see his life and work in that wider historical and musical perspective from which so much of its significance derives, and without which no real picture or understanding is possible. For example, Moore suggests, quite correctly, that in some ways Elgar was an ordinary lower middle-class provincial boy, with commonplace aspirations to upward social mobility, but with very uncommonplace means of fulfilling them: as he made music, so music made him. True. But the implications of this go largely unexplored. By conquering the oratorio, the symphony and the concerto, Elgar also conquered the court, the country and the establishment. Music was the means to fame and fortune, royalty and royalties, and having got them, the creative impulse all but dried up. On receiving the OM in 1911, he admitted that 'there is now nothing left for me to achieve'. And there was also precious little left for him to compose. In any analysis of Elgar's career, it is important to remember that, in large part, fame was the name of the game.

Of course, like all social climbers, Elgar also suffered from vertigo and, being Elgar, there was enough in his case for several Hitchcock films. As with his Broadheath background, the gong-grabber is part of the explanation, but not the whole. And the same applies to the notion that he was the 'spirit of England'. Undeniably, he appeared in one guise as the Tory party at its trumpets and triangles. But he was also a composer of cosmopolitan background and European reputation, and Moore makes no real attempt to see or understand him as such. Elgar's music owed much (but what, exactly?), to Mendelssohn, Schumann, Brahms, Berlioz, Dvorak and Wagner; many of his first and foremost English admirers had names like Jaeger, Richter, Schuster and Speyer; his work was widely performed in Italy, Russia and the United States; in Germany, *Gerontius* and the first symphony received ecstatic receptions, and Richard Strauss was fulsome in his praise. It is cosy, comforting and partly correct to stress Elgar's Englishness, to present him as a Cockaigne-like compound of Malvern water and Worcestershire sauce; but before 1914, in inspiration as much as in impact, he was also one of the giants of the international musical scene.

As such, Elgar was one of the last great figures of the Romantic movement, and that consideration, too, needs greater attention than Moore gives it, not only in understanding Elgar's creative phase, but also in explaining the onset of his musical menopause. For him, as for Dukas, Sibelius, Ives and Rachmaninov, the First World War crushed their capacity to compose. In each case, there were plausible personal reasons: but such a widespread phenomenon suggests that deeper movements were at work. For Elgar, 1914 ushered in twenty baffling, bitter and bewildering years. The end came in 1934, a bad year for English composers' lives, but a bumper year for their deaths. Holst and Delius both sang their swan songs and Elgar, his spinal cord still intact, his third symphony still in fragments, did the same. In his last illness, he lay in bed with a gramophone by his side, playing his own music, which serenaded him into the next world at 78 rpm. As with the *Gerontius* picture, this final photocall was carefully arranged. Once again, Elgar took no chances: the pose was struck, the camera clicked, and the image was preserved. But which? Was it Colonel Blimp in sight of some celestial Eastbourne? Or the visionary and dreamer on the edge of eternity? Or the tradesman's son on the brink of Pooterish Paradise? It is still difficult to be sure. The real enigma is not the *Variations*: it remains Elgar himself.

(1985)

NOTE:
1. Jerrold Northrop Moore, *Spirit of England: Edward Elgar in his World* (London, 1984); idem, *Edward Elgar: A Creative Life* (Oxford, 1984).

A view of Manchester (overleaf). Engraving by Thomas Higham after a drawing by George Pickering, first published in E. Baines's history of the *County Palatine and Duchy of Lancaster* (1836).

"Manchester, 10th October 1851" by W. Wyld (following pages). *The Royal Library, Windsor Castle.*

# PART THREE

# HISTORY

# 13

# Urban History

Earlier this year, I was travelling by train along the East Coast Corridor from Washington to New Haven. Visually, the most spectacular part of the journey is when, after leaving Penn Station and burrowing under the East River, the train picks its confused and faltering way through the Bronx, and allows the passenger an extended backward glimpse of the Big Apple. In the distance cluster the concrete stalagmites of the Manhattan skyscrapers, glittering and glinting in the sunlit smog, and waiting patiently for the Monet who never comes; while on each side of the tracks spread the inchoate jumble of turnpikes, railways, bridges, docks, factories, warehouses and homes which make up the suburban sprawl of Greater New York. Here, embodied in its most spectacular physical form, is the city in its Janus-faced guise as the redeemer and the betrayer of mankind, simultaneously holding out the prospect of the more abundant life, and the threat of the more untimely death. From the heights of a Park Avenue apartment block, New York stands for wealth, opportunity, enjoyment. But from the slums of Queens, it spells poverty, deprivation, misery. My travelling companion contemplated this vast and varied urban vista for a moment, and asked: 'How does it all work?'

It was to the answering of this superficially simple but substantively complex question that the late H. J. Dyos devoted his academic life. During the 'sixties and 'seventies, his energetic activity as teacher, writer and propagandist established urban history as a new sub-discipline, which exploded with the speed and suddenness of an American frontier town. In 1966, he arranged a conference at Leicester University, the proceedings of which were published as *The Study of Urban History*, and which put the subject on the map. Three years earlier, he had founded the Urban History Group, for whom he edited the *Urban History Newsletter*, later extended into the *Urban History Yearbook*. He wrote stylishly and extensively on urban transport and suburban life, and constantly exhorted his colleagues to address the city directly and in its totality, rather than merely incidentally, as passers by. He edited *The Victorian City: Images and Realities*, a book as bulging and burgeoning as its subject. He planned conferences, founded journals, edited series and commissioned books with the bustle and gusto of a Hollywood mogul. At Leicester University, where he became the first Professor of Urban History in Britain, his office looked more like the headquarters of a shipping line than the study of an academic. When he died too young in 1978, he had established an international reputation as an 'academic phenomenon', as 'Olympian Dyos', a soubriquet which happily acknowledged both his Greek ancestry and his tycooning talents.

For an outsider, who had left school at fifteen and come late to academe through the army scholarship scheme, it was a remarkable achievement of almost Smilesian dimensions, as a cottage industry was transformed into a multinational empire through single-handed entrepreneurial skill and inspirational zeal. But as Dyos himself always admitted, he was as much catalyst as creator, for there were deeper reasons why, at this time, history should have gone to town in so emphatic, energetic and exuberant a manner. In the 1960s and early 1970s, urban life became the focus of public debate and political attention to an extent which had not been known in Britain since the 1840s and 1880s. Throughout the western world, problems of race, poverty and housing attracted social workers, sociologists, planners and politicians, who sought to mobilize the burgeoning resources of welfare-state capitalism to remake the Victorian city in the image of the twentieth century. As the railway viaducts, slum terraces, hospitals, factories and schools were levelled to the ground, and as the high-rise blocks, council houses, urban motorways, shopping malls and multi-storey car parks were put up in their place, it did indeed seem as though the city as destroyer was being destroyed, and that the city as deliverer was being delivered.

Urban history as defined and developed by Dyos was very much the product of this contemporary milieu: conservationist, interdisciplinary and policy oriented. He believed strongly that the Victorian city was the prototypical modern metropolis; that the way they lived then was the best guide to understanding both the way we live now and the way we yet might live. So he campaigned vigorously to preserve the most important archives and artifacts of the nineteenth-century city, and constantly sought to build bridges between historians of the city's past, students of the urban present, and planners of the metropolitan future. For he recognized that the city was so extraordinary a phenomenon that urban history could not afford to be an exclusive preserve, but must provide a forum where scholars from many subjects might converge and converse. At Leicester in 1966, he gathered together geographers, planners, architects and sociologists, as well as transport, local, municipal, political, social and economic historians. And their collective interests encompassed the city from the early modern period to the present and well beyond. Between them, they established the identity of urban history in Britain for the next decade: catholic in approach, latitudinarian in ideology, lacking in theoretical rigour, preferring stylish evocation to quantitative analysis, and relying on individual scholarship rather than group research. All that really mattered was the commitment to the city in history. How was it made? What was it like to live in? What was its function as an autonomous, independent variable in the historical process? How – in short – did the city actually work?

One of Dyos's major concerns was that the amount of published material which might legitimately be labelled urban history was not commensurate with the claims he made and the ambitions he entertained for the subject. In particular, he believed that a great deal of significant and important research was undertaken by graduate students, and lay inaccessibly buried in their unpublished dissertations. One of the many schemes with which he was toying during the last years of his life was to devise a way of making such work more readily available, and the series *Themes in Urban History* is the posthumous result.[1] The first four volumes, each with several lengthy sections derived from dissertations written during the late 'sixties or early 'seventies, have now appeared: county towns before the industrial revolution (Warwick, Ipswich, Winchester and Bath); British urban planning from the 1880s to the 1920s (who the planners were, and what they did); the genesis and growth of suburbia (Acton, Chiswick and Ealing, Bromley, Bexley and Headingley); and the municipal politics of great industrial cities (Leeds, Manchester and Bradford). Together, these books greatly extend our knowledge of established subjects in urban history, and they are prefaced by elegant, stimulating, well-judged introductions from editors who are experts in each field, and who were all friends or protégés of Dyos himself.

Predictably, these volumes well illustrate many of the strengths and weaknesses of doing and viewing urban history the Dyos way. The book on suburbia is written mainly by urban geographers, and that on town planning by town planners. That disciples of these disciplines are prepared to write for such a series speaks well of Dyos's interdisciplinary endeavours; but there are worrying signs that the authors have not fully escaped from the straitjackets of their own particular specialisms, nor heeded Dyos's exhortation to address the city directly, and as a whole. The planning contributions are very much the history of the planners, by the planners, for the planners, which tell a relatively narrow, self-enclosed and Whiggish tale of how the profession came to be the way it is, and leave out such broader historical considerations as ideology, popular pressure, the political milieu, and comparisons with Europe and North America. In the same way, the studies of suburbia are written essentially from the geographer's standpoint. They are not so much concerned, as Dyos was in his history of Camberwell, to relate the general process of urbanization to its particular manifestation in one place, nor to evoke the sight and sound and smell of the suburban community. Rather, their main preoccupation is to test and illustrate morphological theories, which inevitably leads to over-schematic accounts pitched at rather an arid and abstract level. In more senses than one, the result is no more than semi-detached urban history.

The contributions to the other two *Themes* volumes are more conventionally historical, and so are far more sensitive to, and concerned with, the city as the substantive historical variable. Here the problems are more those of the thesis than of the discipline. In both cases, there is much meticulous research and detailed description, but rather less argument, explanation, hypothesis and generalization. And, as with the planners and the geographers, the prose rarely attains the lucid level of the editors' introductions or of Dyos's own writing. With the conspicuous exception of Gatrell's essay on the middle classes and incorporation in Manchester, the volume on municipal reform looks at local government in Leeds and Bradford well within the familiar perspective established by Hennock and Briggs. And the second-ranking towns which form the subject of Peter Clark's volume are so diverse in their history, and have left behind such limited data concerning population, poverty and occupation, that it is very difficult to gain any overall impression of what it all adds up to. Taken together, these volumes are useful and informative rather than seminal or exciting, adding to our knowledge but not transforming our understanding of the urban past. To the extent that this is what Dyos had in mind, the objective is admirably achieved; but it is not entirely clear where any of these subjects goes from here.

In the normal course of events, this would not matter, for historical research is necessarily a slow, accretive and evolutionary process. But the decade which has elapsed since most of the original work on which these volumes rest was completed has witnessed major changes – both in the urban milieu and in urban history. Like their Victorian predecessors, the remodelled cities of the 'sixties and 'seventies have only partially lived up to their promise of abundance, equality and modernity: we have seen the future of concrete jungles, vandalized shopping malls, blighted council house estates and slums in the sky, and we have decided that in many ways it just doesn't work. And this urban disillusionment, combined with the tighter official purse strings of Thatcherism and Reaganomics, means that the government and the planners possess neither the will nor the wealth to rebuild our cities again. Even the sociologists have rather lost interest: they no longer see the city as an autonomous object, *sui generis*, to be addressed directly, but rather as the dependent variable, the outcome of larger forces which should be studied instead. Moreover, from a global perspective, the urbanization process seems to be slowing down, and in Britain, the economic base of many of our once-great cities seems eroded beyond repair. In one way and another, we increasingly live in a de-industrializing, post-urban world, beyond the factory and beyond metropolis, and the implications for urban history are mildly disquieting. For while economic history can survive without industry, it is rather more difficult for urban history to survive without the city.

To make matters worse, Dyos was not only the first, but also the last tycoon. When he died, Leicester University did not establish his personal chair, a decision which it would be polite to label small-minded, and more accurate to call a disgrace. In the last year of his life, Dyos had become increasingly concerned that the urban history boom was about to burst; that the subject was losing its coherence, confidence, identity and direction; and that the contraction in the numbers of graduate students was draining away its future life blood. Accordingly, he determined to launch another super-conference, to chart the progress made since the seminal Leicester meeting, and to give the subject a shot in the arm for the next decade. The conference duly took place in August 1980 and, suitably rewritten, reorganized and augmented, the proceedings now appear as *The Pursuit of Urban History*, a work which may turn out to be as much a milestone in the subject's progress as was *The Study of Urban History* a decade and a half before.[2] In terms of personnel, there has been a major change: only two of those who wrote for the earlier volume appear in its successor; a new generation of urban historians can be glimpsed emerging; and the coverage is much more international in scope. In terms of subjects, too, there has been a significant shift of emphasis: away from the old Dyos staples towards more fashionable contemporary interests. While the *Themes* series is an attractive retrospective of urban history done the Dyos way, the *Pursuit* volume is a stimulating foretaste of the shape of things to come.

Whether by accident or by design, there is an ambiguity about the title of this volume which well reflects urban history's current condition: self-questioning, still in mourning, and awkwardly if excitingly caught between two different generations of practitioners. Is urban history the object or the agent of pursuit? Is this book about the search for a subject, or the study of the subject? Two-thirds of it (too much) is largely devoted to these methodological questions. Are all towns generically alike, regardless of their location in time and space? Is any town fundamentally the same, one hundred years on, or two centuries before? Is a town a town whatever it is, something so self-evidently commonsensical that the question is mere pedantry? Today it seems less easy to answer these questions with positive conviction than was possible in Dyos's time. And clearly, if it is difficult to make the case for anything being exclusively or generically urban, then it becomes even harder to argue for the autonomous subject of urban history. Indeed, some critics have argued that urban history is no more than a fashionable bandwagon, a spurious exercise in interdisciplinarianism, falsely claiming credit for work that would have been done in any case under more traditional labels. And others have urged that, in a western world where the vast majority of the population has been urbanized for well over a century, urban history is merely an empty shorthand term for the history of everything and of everyday life.

The chest baring and navel gazing to which such questions and criticisms give rise is not without its uses. But it does seem to be taken to excess here, if only because many of urban history's present doubts and difficulties are by no means exclusive to itself, but are in large part the result more of external circumstances than of internal weaknesses. Most subjects in the humanities and the social sciences are in crisis at present, with diminished government funding, reductions in the number of PhD students, and drops in undergraduate enrolments. Many of Clio's offspring are at least as self-questioning and divided as urban history: economic history is riven with methodological disagreement; social history is as sharply split ideologically; women's history still searches for intellectual coherence; third world history has fragmented almost to the point of disintegration; and much political and constitutional history is unreadably tedious. In short, urban history seems neither more nor less healthy than most historical subspecialisms at the present time. The only real difference is that, compared with these other subjects, it lacks those professors, journals and courses which ensure that it will go on whether people believe in it or not. If urban history were more securely entrenched and established within the structure of university history teaching, much of this angst and anxiety would evaporate.

In any case, when it comes to doing the subject rather than searching for it, urban historians produce excellent and fascinating work, which convinces by its merits if not necessarily by its label. This is well shown in the central section of this book, which contains eight substantial essays, impressively indebted to the cumulative labours of urban historians over the last decade, and drawing with confident and comforting alertness on the most influential academic disciplines of the moment: semiotics, structuralism and anthropology. Studies of the urban fabric and municipal government have been superseded by investigations of civic ceremonial and antiquarian boosters; the heroes of *The Study* were Robert Park and Asa Briggs, but now it is Clifford Geertz and Michel Foucault who hold the stage; and the single city to which scholars turn most often for inspiration is no longer early twentieth-century Chicago but late twentieth-century Calcutta. Accordingly, the current concerns are with the management of public and private space, with kinship, the family and gender divisions, with total institutions and urban culture, with subjective perceptions and structures of meaning, and with urban ideology, images and ideas. Here are subjects and questions every bit as lively and as topical as those addressed over a decade ago, offering (as Dyos had hoped) emphatic evidence that, in the anxiety-ridden early 'eighties, it is easier to renew urban history than it is to reverse urban decay.

From very different standpoints, two essays address themselves to the past, present and future of urban history and urban life, from the sort of broad perspective which Dyos himself most favoured. Eric Lampard offers convincing evidence that, in global terms, the urbanization process is virtually at an end, and that in western Europe, the impact of high technology is breaking that link between cities and industry and numbers of people which has been taken for granted since the early years of the industrial revolution. And the result, as Donald Olsen argues, is that cities may now be reverting to their pre-industrial functions as works of art, symbols of prestige, centres of conspicuous consumption, and domes of pleasure. Juvenal's Rome, rather than Dickens's 'Coke-town', may well be the more appropriate urban paradigm for the future, already foreshadowed in the Denver of *Dynasty* and the Dallas of *Dallas*. But the end of the urbanization process as it has occurred during the last two hundred years does not thereby mean the end of urban history. For if the city is once again to be remade and refashioned, this time in the image of the micro chip rather than of the planner, then we shall need more urban history, not less.

But this is both to anticipate and to simplify. For between the nineteenth-century age of great cities, so beloved of urban historians, and the late twentieth-century prospect of urban dispersal, so essential to up-market soap opera, came the intermediate era of megalopolis. Predictably, perhaps, urban history done the Dyos way never really got to grips with this most explosive manifestation of the city – for it was too global a phase of urban development to be of much relevance to a subject which remained deliberately and self-consciously rooted in English metropolitan experience. Yet it cannot be denied that in the twentieth century, national clusters of towns have been dwarfed by international networks of much larger urban agglomerations, and that the provincial pessimism of Dickens's 'Coketown' has been super-seded by the global gloom of Mumford's 'Necropolis'. As Anthony Sutcliffe rightly puts it in his introduction to a second volume of edited essays, 'the rhythm of the giant cities dominates our globe'.[3] And, since this has been true for most of the twentieth century, it is high time that urban history in England caught up with it.

Accordingly, this book is much to be welcomed as a pioneering foray into the recent, international urban past, and sheds much-needed (if sometimes ill-focused) light on the world cities of yesterday – if not always of today or tomorrow. As befits its subjects, *Metropolis 1890–1940* is international in coverage, inter-disciplinary in approach, and cosmopolitan in authorship. In one of its two substantive sections, the subject is explored thematically and intuitively, in a group of essays which investigate the response to the great metropolis of the intellectuals who tried to understand it and the artists who aspired to evoke it. And this is balanced by a cluster of complementary papers which describe in detail the making and management of seven super-cities. Here, in 450 tightly-packed and well-illustrated pages, a distinguished team of historians, planners, geographers and scholars in the creative arts confront both the images and the realities of the modern metropolis in a work which, in its strengths and weaknesses, stands as a fitting, if perhaps unintended, sequel to Dyos's earlier blockbuster on *The Victorian City*.

So far, so good. But – as Dyos himself recognized – there are real difficulties in pinning down a subject so protean and so amorphous as the great city. If, as it now seems commonplace to admit, it is difficult to define the urban element in urban history, then how much more problematic is it to isolate the specifically big-city element in the history of the metropolis? Even the cities included here seem in some ways an odd assortment. Where is Chicago, whose architecture was, for much of the period, synonymous with the very idea of metropolis, and whose school of sociology was crucial in putting the big city on the agenda of twentieth-century thought? And where is Los Angeles, whose freeways and clover-leaf junctions were as important a pointer to the metropolitan future as the skyscrapers of Manhattan? Why, on the other hand, is the Rhur included, when it was never more than an uneasy agglomeration of urban villages, which never achieved metropolitan status or identity? And where does Moscow fit in? It may have been the metropolis of Communism, but as a city it was smaller that Vienna or Chicago. And in any case, this book is about castles on the ground, not in the air.

As these questions suggest, the real difficulty is that these cities seem to have very little in common during this period except that they were all big, or very big. London and New York suburbanized very rapidly; Paris and Berlin more slowly; Moscow hardly at all. Some were capital cities; others not. Some were ports; others not. Some were in democracies; others in dictatorships. For New York, 1890 to 1940 was a golden age; for Paris it was a lull between two storms; and for Moscow, the dates are almost meaningless. By 1940, these great cities do not seem to have been very much more alike than they had been half a century before. The skyscrapers of New York had not yet been built anywhere else, and London could still be portrayed, not entirely implausibly, as a unique city. As Peter Hall puts it in his rather subversive general chapter, 'by 1940, the great metropolitan cities were still at very different stages of evolution'.

If the common realities of the metropolis seem elusive, it is hardly surprising that the contemporary images of it were correspondingly blurred and diffuse. In a post-Freudian era, most creative figures were more interested in exploring the inner life of the mind than in representing the outer life of the world, and those who addressed the city did so indirectly, and largely unaware that there was anything special about it. The many commentators and pundits of the time looked at all large towns, and gave no special treatment to the few super-cities. Among visual artists, the French Impressionists were as interested in water lilies as in the Thames at Westminster, and the German Expressionists rarely depicted the city at all. Among contemporary novels, it was Joyce's *Ulysses* which caught most powerfully the sense of contemporary bewilderment which the metropolis allegedly engendered: but his subject was Dublin, not Gotham City. Only a tiny minority of movies took the great metropolis seriously at all; it was technically almost impossible to shoot films in city streets; and in any case, the majority of inter-war cinema goers were more interested in Fred Astaire and Ginger Rogers. In music, the response was so varied, from the representational to the atonal, as to make generalization quite impossible. And in architecture, much of the best design work was undertaken in relatively small cities like Stockholm, Copenhagen and Amsterdam.

It is not at all clear where this leaves the images and the realities of the very big city during the first half of the twentieth century. Like any book which opens up a subject, *Metropolis 1890–1940* is more exploratory than definitive, and this is just as it should be. But it does not automatically follow that the flag under which this particular pioneering expedition has been mounted is in fact the correct one. The conference at which many of these chapters originated as papers was sponsored by the Planning History Group, and the book arising out of its appears in a series called *Studies in History, Planning and the Environment.* In short, as Anthony Sutcliffe concedes in his introduction, this book is not so much the product of urban history pushing forwards, as of planning history pushing backwards. Planning, we are told, is now in a mess. And to give it renewed confidence and sense of purpose, what better than to look at how it all began, during the first age of the great metropolis? How far did the image makers put across a picture of the giant city which influenced what the planners were thinking about it? How far, in turn, did the planners actually influence the metropolis? And how far can this dialogue between the city and the planners before the Second World War shed some light on what has happened since?

The planning historians are to be congratulated, not only for putting the big city on the agenda of research and discussion, but also for devising an approach to it so ingenious as to bring it within the ambience of their own applied and essentially anachronistic field of historical vision. But it is an uphill struggle trying to answer any of these elaborately-posed questions in anything but the negative. It cannot be shown if (or how) the planners were influenced in the inter-war years by the creative image makers. Nor did the planners themselves achieve very much: they lacked the power and the money, and they never could decide, even among themselves, whether they should abolish or tame or improve the great city. So it is not at all apparent what any of this has to do with the golden age of skyscrapers and freeways which characterized the thirty years after 1945, still less with the era of disenchantment which has set in since. The editor, who is far too accomplished an urban historian to be persuaded by the special pleading of his own introduction, coyly admits that 'the theme, the periodization and the choice of cities' are all open to doubt and to question. How right he is! As self-conscious planning history, this book is, inevitably, an unsuccessful treatment of a non-subject. But as an inadvertent piece of urban history, pushing the subject forwards into the twentieth century, it is very promising indeed.

These six books between them embody the work of over fifty scholars from three continents, and add up to nearly two thousand pages. A subject which can generate so much interest and so much output can hardly be said to be dying. On the contrary, urban history as exemplified in these books has more in common with the burgeoning cities of the American sun belt than with the decaying dinosaurs of the north-east seaboard. Indeed, as this wealth of material makes abundantly clear, the subject bears a striking resemblance to that very process of urban growth which it is one of its prime purposes to describe, evoke and explain. In some ways, it is sprawling, congested, uneven, over-crowded, with too much speculation, some jerry-building, and occasional blind alleys. But in others, it is imaginatively conceived, soundly constructed and vigorously executed, full of life and promise. If God made the countryside, then agricultural history is merely another branch of theology, best left to country parsons. But since it is incontrovertible that mankind made the town, there must always be urban historians prepared to answer the city-dweller's simple yet central question: 'How does it all work?'

(1983 and 1984)

NOTES:
1. Peter Clark (editor), *Country Towns in Pre-Industrial England* (Leicester, 1981); Anthony Sutcliffe (editor), *British Town Planning:*

*The Formative Years* (Leicester, 1981); Derek Fraser (editor), *Municipal Reform and the Industrial City* (Leicester, 1982); F. M. L. Thompson (editor), *The Rise of Suburbia* (Leicester, 1982).

2. Derek Fraser and Anthony Sutcliffe (editors), *The Pursuit of Urban History* (London, 1983).

3. Anthony Sutcliffe (editor), *Metropolis, 1890–1940* (London, 1984).

# Economic History

The covers of two of these books[1]* display very similar views of Manchester, the 'shock city' of early nineteenth-century England. One is for 1836 and the other for 1851, and both embody a familiar picture of the Industrial Revolution: of factories pouring out goods, and chimneys belching forth smoke; of burgeoning exports, spiralling output and rising productivity; and of improved land, unceasing labour, accumulating capital and inspired enterprise. Here is an epic drama: Coketown in the making, the workshop of the world in operation, and the factors of production in fertile fusion. Taken together, these two illustrations project an image of the Industrial Revolution as an heroic happening, characterized by vigour, energy, inventiveness and courage, or (depending on your point of view) by exploitation, cruelty, avarice and shame. Either way, to look at these pictures, to visualize the events which they capture for a moment, and to imagine what is required to render such changes historically comprehensible, is to see at once why Floud and McCloskey claim that 'economic history is an exciting subject'.

Or is it? Undeniably, in the years from the mid-1950s to the early 1970s, economic history *was* exciting, as an ever-expanding army of scholars, stirred by the theories of development economists, and buoyed up by the apparent successes of the post-war welfare state, turned with relish to Britain's industrial past, partly to test and refine the grand generalizations of Toynbee, the Hammonds, Clapham and Ashton, and partly to see what (if any) guidelines that past might yield for those who wished to transform that

*See illustrations between pages 130 and 131.

Sahara Desert of the present into the Sunset Boulevard of the future. As a result, the *Economic History Review* scintillated with provocative, seminal and wide-ranging articles, many of them nurtured and inspired by that most creatively entrepreneurial of editors, M. M. Postan. Major controversies, such as the storm over the gentry and the standard of living debate, were fought within its pages, as the protagonists assailed each other like Punch and Judy – with a great deal of punching, if rather less judiciousness. And a wide variety of substantive problems – the growth of population, capital accumulation, home and overseas demand, technological change and innovation – were identified, investigated and then synthesized in a new generation of late 'sixties textbooks which remained the last word for undergraduates until the appearance of Floud and McCloskey's volumes.

Since then, the wheel has turned again, as these second-generation generalizations have themselves been further tested and refined. But the scrutiny to which they have been subjected has been fundamentally altered by the emergence of the 'New Economic History', which rose to prominence in the United States in the late 1960s, and which has profoundly shifted the subject's status, from being a client of history to a vassal of economics. The two most famous works in this genre were both written by Robert Fogel, who was thus established as midwife and guru, entrepreneur and high priest, of this new cult. The first, *Railroads and American Economic Growth*, was an audaciously conceived study which cut the iron horse so emphatically down to size, by exploring a hypothetical late nineteenth-century American economy *without* railways, that some critics wondered whether Professor Fogel himself was any longer on the rails. The second, *Time on the Cross*, was a co-authored, revisionist investigation into the economics of the American slave experience, which made many people cross at the time by suggesting that slaves did not fare as badly on the Ante-Bellum plantations as had generally been supposed. Both these books were bold and brash, trumpeting their new methodology with such messianic zeal and impassioned conviction that it seemed only a matter of time before old-fashioned economic historians became the hand-loom weavers of their generation – cottage industrialists overtaken by the new technology, and doomed to sad decline and slow extinction.

From the beginning, this 'New Economic History' was characterized by a distrust of literary and impressionistic evidence, by a heavy reliance on quantitative data elaborately manipulated and computed, by the explicit and widespread employment of economic theory, by the careful specification and testing of hypotheses, and by the use of the counter-factual technique, which required imagining how an economy would have evolved if certain specified 'factors' had not actually been there – a sophisticated version of the 'If Napoleon had won the Battle of Waterloo' school of history. Old-fashioned economic history was condemned for its unsystematic and unscientific marshalling of unreliable data; the new discipline ardently aspired simultaneously to bring economic standards of logic to history and historical standards of fact to economics; and its practitioners spoke with relish of having 'captured' the *Journal of Economic History* and moulded it to their new creed. The military metaphor well reflected the embattled and belligerent status of the new economic historians, who soon found themselves waging war on two fronts: crusading against the infidel without, and quarrelling among themselves within. And the weapons with which these battles were fought were fashioned in the white-hot heat of the 'sixties technological revolution. The solitary scholar-gladiator of old, replete with lance and trident, was replaced by a new model army of research assistants, computer experts and applied economists who, under the guidance of a lab-coated field-marshal, launched massive bombardments with all the scholarly firepower (and some of the strategic futility) of a Somme offensive.

Not surprisingly, it took longer for this approach to catch on in England (where economic historians had always tended to be historians first and economists second, and where the vast sources required for such projects were initially harder to obtain) than it did in the United States (where the circumstances in both cases were rather the reverse). So although there have been some important individual studies, *The Economic History of Britain since*

*1700* is the first full-scale attempt to apply the 'New Economic History' systematically and comprehensively to this country's industrial past. The result – as befits its neo-classical presuppositions – is a book carefully tailored to the requirements of the market: the paperback version is moderately enough priced for undergraduates; there is a large and comprehensive bibliography of the latest research findings available; each of the short chapters is written by an expert on the subject; and the statistical methods and economic theory which are employed are fully explained. The editors and publishers are to be congratulated on producing two volumes which serve both as an up-to-date guide to the development of the modern British economy and as a monument to the methodological changes which have taken place within the discipline during the last decade and a half. This work is not merely the history of an economy in the past: it is also a progress report on economic history in the present.

But is the result, as the editors hope, *exciting*? Does it convey in words the drama which is so vividly caught in the picture on the cover of volume one? And does it suggest that British economic history has been revived and reinvigorated by the importation of this new trans-Atlantic methodology? The volumes are so well-intentioned that it would be agreeable to answer positively: but it is rather harder actually to do so. In the first place, much of the writing is arid and bleak: if the contributors *are* lit up by the substantive or methodological excitement of what they are doing, they certainly keep their ecstasy very much in check. Of course, it is difficult to write lively, high-coloured prose when the subject-matter requires graphs, tables and statistics in profusion, and when complex concepts and theoretical jargon must be deployed with precision and care. But even if, as the editors candidly admit, economic history is concerned with 'the dullest parts of human life', that is no justification for writing it in the dullest sort of human prose. Indeed, as the welcome and characteristically zestful contributions of Professor McCloskey himself eloquently demonstrate, there is really no need to write like this at all – although his predilection for literary allusion does lead him mistakenly to suppose that the Holmes-and-Watson story about the dog that didn't bark in the night comes from *The Hound of the Baskervilles*. High marks for coincidental correlation, low for causal attribution.

It is also rather unfortunate that, because of the time-lag in the diffusion of this innovation across the Atlantic, this book has come out at the very moment when, in the United States, there is a growing recognition that the 'New Economic History' has not lived up to the great expectations which were initially (if in retrospect rather naively) entertained of it. The climacteric of Cliometrics has come and gone: so the time is not exactly propitious for the appearance of these two volumes. Despite the massive assaults that have been launched on subjects such as the economics of slavery, very little sure ground seems to have been gained, and there are growing doubts as to whether this new methodology can be used authoritatively on any but the most trivial of projects. The statistical data available, even for the nineteenth century, seem so fragile as to belie the elaborate manipulations to which they are subjected, and the whole concept of the counterfactual – of inventing what did not happen in order to explain what did – seems altogether too clever by half (= 50 per cent). Above all, there is a real and growing anxiety about the ominously ahistorical nature of an enterprise which is so wedded to the application of neoclassical economic theory that it cannot accommodate more diverse modes of human behaviour; that it assumes a static, equilibrium economy when its real concern is with change over time; and which presupposes perfect competition, full utilization of resources, rational and profit-maximizing entrepreneurs, and non-interference by government, when it is clear that no past society has ever conformed to these fanciful assumptions.

Certainly, there is much in *The Economic History of Britain since 1700* which will lend support to doubts such as these. The first volume in particular seems conceived extremely narrowly: among the more conventional topics of economic history which might have been included but which go virtually unmentioned are entrepreneurship, the City, war, government, banking, taxation and the trade cycle. There is no sense of the regional nature of the

English economy; Ireland and Scotland are completely ignored; and Wales fares little better. Apart from one chapter which rushes bravely and breathlessly through social change, there is no awareness of religion, ideology, social attitudes or cultural values, still less any attempt to come to terms with contemporaries' experience of what was happening. And, on the positive side, even those subjects which *are* included are treated in a negative and curiously narrow-minded way. Canals, steam power, railways, cotton, capital, technological change, exports, free trade, home and overseas demand, are analysed in turn, and each is pronounced not to have been 'indispensable' to economic development. 'The phrase-turner in economic history,' we are grandly informed, 'yearning for romance in the counting house and the factory', who delights 'in verbal play with big events and big machines', is not merely disappointed: he is positively assailed. The idea of the Industrial Revolution as an heroic happening, as conventionally embodied in the picture on the dust-jacket, is seen as at best atypical and at worst a myth.

Of course, there is much in this which is of value. It is important to have established that old and crude notions about cotton or steam-engines or exports being leading sectors can no longer be sustained. And it is especially comforting in these days of rapid de-industrialization to be told that, even as late as 1860, the Industrial Revolution was 'the central event in modern Britain more in *memory* than in *happening*'. But if everything once thought to be big and indispensable is now presented as small and insignificant, it is not entirely clear, historically speaking, what such a reformulation accomplishes. After all, no one would say that Floud and McCloskey's book is indispensable: but, since they presumably wish us to read it because of its substantive contents, that is hardly the point. To limit discussion of what are still recognized as the major themes of the Industrial Revolution to proving that none was as important as was once thought seems a curiously myopic way to proceed. Railways may not have been 'indispensable': but they were still, apparently, more important than any other single 'factor' mentioned in this book. The heroic events may not have been typical: but, as the cover eloquently demonstrates, they did actually happen. To evaluate everything with reference to this rather bizarre criterion is to miss most of the really important historical questions. What happened? How did it happen? What is the dynamic interaction between the different factors of production? How did the machines work? How can this be evoked and explained in terms which were humanly comprehensible to contemporaries then and to their descendants now? 'Economic history,' the editors tell us in their introduction, 'is not a story.' Perhaps it would be better history if it were.

This view of the Industrial Revolution as being something of a non-event, to be appropriately commemorated in non-writing, is all the more ironic because the other book which sports a Mancunian dust-jacket, Wrigley and Schofield's *Population History of England*, is partly concerned to argue precisely the opposite case: that the economic and demographic changes in England at the end of the eighteenth century constituted 'a radical break with the past' of a 'decisive nature', 'one of the most fundamental of all changes in the history of society'. In the classical age of the Industrial Revolution, they argue, it first became possible for a nation to experience considerable population expansion while not merely avoiding the hitherto ubiquitous Malthusian poverty trap, but while actually *increasing* standards of living. Hitherto, they explain, any increase in population sooner or later outstripped the growth of productive resources, so that, in response, prices rose, real wages fell, and population growth was halted. But from the late eighteenth century, this relationship was decisively broken, as increased output and productivity made it possible to sustain growing population and expanding incomes simultaneously.

For the whole period with which they are concerned, Wrigley and Schofield argue that the major determinant of population growth has been the birth rate, itself primarily influenced by the age at which people married, which was in turn a leisurely response to economic circumstances, usually lagged by a generation or more. This conclusion is reached after an exhaustive collection and ingenious manipulation of the records for baptisms, marriages and deaths which are found in 404 sample parish registers. The result of their labours is a clear picture of the major trends in English population growth – of expansion for a century from 1540, of stagnation from the Civil War to the early 1700s, and then of a renewed upswing from the middle of the eighteenth century. Early Modern England, the authors note, was characterized by low mortality and also low fertility, unlike many underdeveloped countries of the post-war world. So, the key to growth was the rise in fertility which, especially in the later eighteenth century, is to be explained by the decline in the age and increase in the frequency of marriage. Significantly, they also show that it was only at the very end of the eighteenth century that the rates of English population growth surpassed the previous high levels of expansion reached in the late sixteenth century, and also began to outstrip the general level of population expansion in contemporary Europe. Most important for those who have watched the debate on the causes of English population growth as bemused spectators will be Wrigley and Schofield's substantial assertion that old beliefs in the importance of the falling death rate cannot now be convincingly sustained.

Of course, doubts are bound to persist and, to their credit, most of them are candidly ventilated by the authors themselves. Despite their heroic efforts, it is difficult to believe that they can satisfactorily have overcome all the inadequacies of the raw data, and it is particularly unfortunate that the two most important turning-points, in the mid-seventeenth and late eighteenth centuries, are those when parish registration was least comprehensive. There are bound to be reservations about the use of the venerable Phelps Brown and Hopkins index of real wages as a reliable guide to the standard of living which is such a central concept for their argument, and it is a source of regret, especially from the late eighteenth century onwards, when the experience of economic growth was so diverse and localized, that the figures are only given in aggregate form, which must conceal some major variations in different areas of the country. Even so, it is difficult to see how their basic findings could be undermined or improved upon, and the authors are surely right in defending their work from 'exaggerated scepticism'. Such a defence is, in fact, hardly necessary, since few would deny their remarkable achievement in linking complex biological, social and economic processes over four centuries and more. In the breadth of its conception, the scope of its coverage, the range of skills and techniques displayed, and the subtlety and strength of its argument, *The Population History of England* is a work of remarkable virtuosity, combining the panoptic vision of the parachutist with the meticulous scholarship of the truffle hunter.

For Wrigley and Schofield, as for Floud and McCloskey (in whose first volume an abridged summary of their population findings is printed), the great divide comes in the last quarter of the nineteenth century, when the classical age of what was (or is mistakenly supposed to be) the Industrial Revolution came to an end. For the 'New Economic Historians', one particular way in which this latter phase differs is that there is far more data available, and this is reflected in the greater size and density of Floud and McCloskey's second volume. For those already familiar with McCloskey's work the general argument of this later book will be instantly recognizable. Far from experiencing a Great Depression, largely caused by entrepreneurial failure, the British economy in this period, characterized by an adequate supply of labour and capital, was in fact more productive, resilient and successful than is often supposed, not least because entrepreneurs behaved in a way which was sensible and rational. 'From damnation to redemption' is the verdict passed on that much maligned figure, the late Victorian businessman – insofar as he mattered at all. But, as the arguments of the first volume have already made plain, nothing was really indispensable: entrepreneurship, empire, free trade, overseas investment, the lot. Once more, nothing is big, fundamental or revolutionary: mundane realities rule.

The advantage of this approach for the later period is that it does seem to impose some welcome conceptual rigour on the concept of economic failure. How, after all, does one define decline: by comparison with what has gone before, or with contemporary rivals, or with what might have been the expected performance of the economy? How much popular anxiety at the time was merely because of a realization that other nations were catching up, as they were bound to do, rather than because Britain was doing less well than she might have done? To pose these questions is to cut through much of the flabby thinking which has characterized earlier scholarly treatment of this period; to try to answer them, however, is to illustrate once more the limits and drawbacks of the 'New Economic History'. Is it realistic to suppose full employment prevailed in late nineteenth century England? Was capital really being utilized as efficiently and as rationally as possible? Did the market actually work? Is it possible to reach agreement on what the expected performance of the economy should have been? It is significant that Pat Thane (to whom another social history scamper is entrusted) is clearly somewhat sceptical of all this, and it is noteworthy that B. W. E. Alford bravely resurrects the thesis of entrepreneurial failing in his treatment of the inter-war economy. The biggest problem with this second volume is that there is no sense of when, if ever, Britain became an industrial nation: if not before 1860, and if not after 1914, when, if at all, did it happen?

The difficulties in writing about economic decline, or more generally about the economic history of Britain in the last century, are well illustrated in two books of rather old-fashioned economic history.[2] M. W. Kirby bases his tale of woe on the assumption that British economic decline began around 1870, which, bearing in mind McCloskey's argument that the economy was not yet mature in 1860, leaves a very short period in which the workshop of the world got its act together. His account of subsequent developments embodies judicious summaries of most secondary literature, although the balance of some of the chapters seems rather curious, as in his treatment of the 1940s, where he gives a great deal of space to the negotiations for US aid but says almost nothing on the nationalization of industry by the Labour government. His general theme is that 'Britain's economic decline has its origins in the past.' In a sense, of course, that is true: presumably all things in the present have their antecedents at an earlier date. But there are real difficulties with this superficially appealing notion. In part, this is because his somewhat routine explanations

– entrepreneurial failure, defective education, anachronistic social structure – need to take rather more extensive account of the wayward but important criticisms levelled at them by McCloskey than in fact they do. But it is also because it is not precisely clear how any of these issues can realistically be said to be continuous throughout Britain's recent history. Entrepreneurial failure is a very different thing in the 1980s than it was a century before, and the social structure, however defective it might be to its critics, is not the same as it was a hundred years ago. A theme retrospectively identified over time is not the same as a deep-seated cause.

In delicious contrast, Hamish Fraser's account of the rise of a consumer society (which took place at the very same time that Kirby and others see the British economy in decline) is good old-fashioned economic history at its best: it tells a story; it is well written; it is about real people; there is a sense of change and development; and there is a pleasing balance between the particular detail and the general argument. In essence, Fraser's picture illuminates the aggregates, tables and arguments assembled by Barry Supple in his essay on the same subject in the second volume of Floud and McCloskey. Here is the rise of a mass market, a revolution in retailing, and the transformation of light industry, with results which have lingered until our own day. For the last decades of the nineteenth century saw the appearance of such old faithfuls as fish and chips, New Zealand lamb, breakfast cereals and whisky; of Maypoles, Liptons, Sainsbury's, Lyons, Harrods and Selfridges; of the bicycle, the cinema and the yellow press; and of Hovis, Peak Freans and Huntley and Palmers. When Edward VII went to sea with Sir Thomas Lipton, it was noted with surprise that the King 'had gone yachting with his grocer'; when the first J. J. Sainsbury died, his last words were, reputedly, 'Keep the shops well lit.' 'To be conscious of our forefathers as they really were and, bit by bit, to reconstruct the mosaic of the long forgotten past' is an injunction of G. M. Trevelyan to his fellow historians which McCloskey cites with evident approval. Here, for once, is a work of economic history which does not lose sight of that paramount objective.

\*

Taken together, these books suggest that neither the new nor the old economic history has a monopoly of good or bad scholarship, plausible or wayward argument, bright or dull writing. Satisfying *either* of those jealous and demanding gods of historical method and economic theory is in itself a daunting and difficult task. Satisfying *both* is probably impossible, if only because the opportunity costs of venerating the one deity must of necessity be insufficient genuflection at the other's altar. Economists may lament that old-fashioned economic history may sometimes be insufficiently theoretical; historians are bound to be more concerned that the newer version is on occasions only incidentally historical. The problem with Cliometrics is that there is more to Clio than can be discovered merely by applying the tape-measure. 'A reviewer's job', McCloskey observes, 'is to raise plausible doubts.' In this case at least, the anxieties are real: I will show you fear in a handful of dust jackets.

(1982)

NOTES:
1. Roderick Floud and Donald McCloskey (editors), *The Economic History of Britain since 1700* (2 volumes, Cambridge, 1981); E. A. Wrigley and R. S. Schofield, *The Population History of England, 1541–1871: A Reconstruction* (London, 1981).
2. M. W. Kirby, *The Decline of British Economic Power since 1870* (London, 1981); Hamish Fraser, *The Coming of the Mass Market, 1850–1914* (London, 1982).

# London History

'Despite the recognized importance of the subject', Asa Briggs once remarked, 'there is no good general history of nineteenth-century London.' A generation on, that laconic lament lingers leadenly. It is not, of course, that there is any lack of material: on the contrary, books on Victorian London gush forth as profusely as water from a fractured main. The problem is that they are rarely good, not often general, and sometimes not even history. There are at once too many books on London, and too few – too many tourist guides, city biographies and suburban chronicles; too few studies of its politics, economy, society and government; and almost nothing which addresses the great metropolis directly, in its totality, as the world city. Significantly, the most comprehensive histories of nineteenth-century London were written at the close of the era they described, and little has been accomplished since. Historiographically speaking, yesterday's great wen has become today's black hole.

The difficulty is that nineteenth-century London was such a success story in some ways that historians cannot cope with it, and such a fable of failure in others that they do not want to. From one standpoint, London was the Cinderella of nineteenth-century cities, the inert, lifeless embodiment of economic backwardness, class fragmentation, political marginality, municipal stagnation and administrative chaos; while the provinces blazed the trail in economic growth, class formation, political radicalism, municipal reform and administrative progress. Compared to the Manchester 'shocker' of the 1840s, the Leeds *pas de seul* of the 1850s, and the Birmingham 'pantomime' of the 1870s, the London theatre of municipal life was dark, bleak and unappealing. And, just as the great provincial cities led the way in nineteenth-century provincial life, so they have pioneered the path in twentieth-century urban history. Although for H. J. Dyos urban history primarily meant London history, it has been much more provincially oriented for the majority of his disciples and devotees. Like most of Clio's clones, urban history is usually on the side of the big batallions, who have, accordingly, been billeted well to the north of Watford.

But although, in most ways, nineteenth-century London was an anachronistic, pre-industrial city of the past, in terms of numbers, it was the prototypical metropolis of the future. And therein lay its second difficulty. For its growth was so spectacular that contemporaries saw it simultaneously as too much of a city, and yet also as not really a city at all. Stretched too far, grown too big, London became merely an abstraction, a postmark, with no tangible centre, no one point of assembly, no clear geographical orientation, and no anthropomorphized sense of itself. The biggest urban agglomeration in the western world and the largest city in the land was merely a collection of villages with only the most blurred sense of civic identity. And if contemporaries then were at a loss to comprehend a community so large, diverse and multi-functional, how much harder is that task for scholars now? H. J. Dyos may have been correct in urging urban historians to address the city directly. But how is this possible when the metropolis in question housed one tenth of England's population in 1810, and one seventh in 1871; when it was simultaneously the seat of government, the home of the sovereign, the centre of the legal system and learned professions, the hub of the literary and scientific establishment, and the bastion of business and commerce; and when its name might be applied at one extreme to the single square mile of the City proper, or at the other to the financial capital of the entire world? Understandably, the most significant legacy which London's nineteenth-century inhabitants have bequeathed to its twentieth-century historians is fog.

The best work that has recently penetrated such Holmes-and-Watson gloom concerns the social massing of men and the physical massing of buildings in the nineteenth-century metropolis.

Several distinguished studies have investigated the relations between the workers, the petty bourgeoisie and the middle classes,
while another clutch of books has explored the making of the
urban fabric, both public and private, central and suburban. But,
as with all important research, the plugging of some gaps merely
emphasises the continued existence of others, and exposes some
new ones not even noticed before. What, for instance, were the
particular metropolitan links (if any) between these generations of
buildings rediscovered and generations of men revived? And what
was the substructure of London's economy, and the super-
structure of its municipal power, which profoundly influenced
both social relations in the city and the making of its urban fabric?
Studies centred on classes or on buildings must necessarily take
more for granted about the workings of the city economy and the
distribution of urban power than it is prudent to do. All too often,
London's economy is dismissed for its 'uneven development'
because the Industrial Revolution 'passed it by', while its government is supposed to be the embodiment of anti-absolutist political
values. But such easy assumptions have run far ahead of our actual
knowledge.

Although we still lack a full-scale economic history of nineteenth-century London, these four recent books greatly advance
our knowledge of London's recent political and administrative
history.[1] Yet even as they do so, they inadvertently illustrate
how daunting is the task which faces the historian of London's
recent past. Hone's study takes metropolitan radicalism in the
Napoleonic era, but finds it such an amorphous subject that the
sense of place, the awareness of the immanent urban location,
seems almost completely lost sight of. Goodway seeks to rescue
London Chartism from the endless condescension of provincial
posterity, yet at the end of it all, its 'failure' somehow seems as
inevitable as it always did. Owen's investigation into the workings of the mid-Victorian Metropolitan Board of Works, and his
more selective forays into local vestry government, depicts the
triviality and myopia of London's municipal affairs with such
verisimilitude that it is on occasions hard to sustain interest. And,
as Young and Garside show in their more extended treatment of

London's administration, the only way to cover such a subject over a long time span is to abandon the pretence that one scholar can do it all unaided. So, to differing degrees, they all serve to illustrate Young and Garside's observation that, in writing of London's recent past, the 'wealth of historical detail seems to impede the development of a more general understanding'.

Hone's book is the first attempt to investigate that dark age of London's radical history between Pitt's repressive measures of the 1790s and the assumed re-emergence of popular protest in the 1810s, in the aftermath of victory against France. Her aim is to 'throw light on the nature of radicalism by examining how and where change was sought, by identifying the radicals, and by describing their methods'. By taking London as a whole, and not just Westminster or the City, and by massive research into multifarious archives, parliamentary papers, newspapers and pamphlets, she is able to demonstrate with overwhelming evidential force the 'survival of radical activities and continuity of radical personnel throughout the war years'. Major leaders like Cartwright, Burdett, Tooke, Place, Hunt and Cobbett are reassessed, and several hundred hitherto unknown radicals are rescued from oblivion. We are taken into a twilight world of riots, processions and petitions, of radical societies and parliamentary collaboration, of programmes for reforming parliament, prisons, asylums and education, of the Despard Plot and the Cato Street Conspiracy. Never again will it be possible to dismiss London politics in the Napoleonic period as irrelevant or unimportant: for here, laid bare, is 'what the radicals did and how they did it'.

Nevertheless, despite its scholarship, its subject and its sub-title, the book cannot really be described as London history at all, as there is so little sense of place, economy or social structure. There is very little analysis, no map of London, no sense of the metropolitan environment, nor of how it influenced radical activity. Jim Dyos would have remarked that this book was only incidentally urban, and indeed only incidentally metropolitan. Much of the history recounted here concerns central government, the House of Commons, the Home Office, Irish insurrection, naval mutinies and provincial unrest. Of course, this formed an essential ingredient of London radicalism, but its particular metropolitan dimension goes largely unexplored. The economic and social underpinnings are rather breezily brushed aside on the grounds that 'so far as London is concerned, our knowledge of the metropolis as a geographical and socio-economic entity is probably adequate', and there is no satisfactory attempt to situate the multitude of radicals mentioned spatially, socially, economically or ideologically. The result is that, although we now know a great deal more about London's wartime radicalism, it still remains a curiously enigmatic episode in explicitly metropolitan terms.

Goodway's volume, which he rightly describes as 'the first full-length study to be devoted to Chartism in London', shows a much greater sensitivity to its urban setting. It gets off to a sure metropolitan start, not only with its dedication 'for Eric and Raphael, Londoners', but also with a map which helps to establish the significant locations of London Chartist activity. The first section offers a brief analysis of London's economy where, according to Goodway, fundamental changes in the mode of production from small masters to larger employers in the 1830s and 1840s led to a growth in proletarian consciousness which was the essential pre-condition for Chartist growth. There follows a Hone-like narrative of Chartism itself, which shows just how little happened in 1838–9, how the zenith of organization and agitation was reached in 1842, and how the high point of turbulence and revolutionary potential was arrived at in 1848. The third section investigates the role of the army and the constabulary, and argues that it was the success of the police in dealing with the crowds, and the Chartists' fear of military action against them, which goes far to explain the movement's relative failure. Finally (and thus rather oddly placed), Goodway returns to the opening theme of socio-economic change, and offers a necessarily sketchy 'economic history of the city in the Chartist decade', which shows more precisely the structure and circumstances of the trades which were politically the most involved.

On balance, his account is more successful as London history than as Chartist rehabilitation. Despite his wishes and words to the contrary, London Chartism remains 'minimal, ineffective, disorganised, passive'. There is insufficient evidence to support his assertion that 'the second quarter of the nineteenth century saw the making of a metropolitan proletariat', with a 'common consciousness', and the argument that activity was greater in the 1840s than in the preceding decade because the economy was more depressed is easier to state than to demonstrate. As has always been suspected, the Chartists did not organize very well, they quarrelled among themselves, and they only appealed to a limited section of the workers. London was too big, too fragmented, for easy mobilization, and there was no suitable, central location where a massed crowd might assemble and intimidate. The troops and police were efficient and the ruling class held firm. Even Goodway admits that a 'substantial proportion' of the special constables were workers, and the splendid daguerreotype which is reproduced of the 10th April 1848 gathering on Kennington Common is not a picture of a revolutionary mob or inspired leadership. Assuredly, some of the Chartists may have believed that they could overthrow the government, and may even have dreamed, plotted and organized to that end. But there was a large gap between their reality and their perception of it. Recovering their ardour does not enhance their credibility. London may have been 'a bastion of Chartism' with 'a powerful force', 'a mass party': but it still failed.

Both of these books are rather better at getting inside the minds and the mores of the movements they describe than at explaining why they actually accomplished so little. They both throw out ample hints and suggestions, but do not seem interested in following them up. Hone, for instance, mentions *en passant* the widespread popularity of Pitt's repression, and the fact that the war against Napoleon had a strong patriotic appeal. Likewise, Goodway writes of the skill of the police at crowd control (which seems well attested) and at social control (for which the evidence is rather less). But both writers, because they wish to stress the significance of their chosen episodes of London radicalism rather than place them in a wider historical framework, give less attention than they should to their own evidence that London was, quite simply, intrinsically inimical to such activity at that time. In 1816, for instance (as in Hone), Burdett admitted that there was 'an essential power in the people', but also conceded that there was an 'essential power at Hyde Park, at Knightsbridge, at the Tower, at Woolwich, at Hounslow, at Deptford and at Chatham. We are in fact, in this metropolis, in the midst of a circumvallation of forces'. And here, in Goodway, is Place to Cobden in 1840: 'London differs very widely from Manchester, and, indeed, from every other place on the face of the earth. It has no local or particular interest as a town, not even as to politics . . . London in my time, and that is half a century, has never moved.'

However visionary and ardent they might have been, these radical leaders knew that, whatever might be the position in the provincial cities, in London, the workers were poor and divided, and the authorities were powerful and rich. Moreover, as the seat of government, London was also the setting for major displays of consensual, conservative pageantry, which appealed very strongly to the 'flag-saluting, foreigner-hating, peer-respecting side of the plebian mind', but which receive scant attention here. To read these books, the only popular parading and processing by London working men in the first half of the nineteenth century was in pursuit of radical objectives. But what of the great patriotic displays and celebrations during the Napoleonic Wars, at the time of George III's Golden Jubilee, and even for the Coronation of George IV? And, during the Chartist era, what of the young Victoria's Coronation in 1838 and her wedding two years later? By definition, the London working man was more susceptible to this form of establishment propaganda than was his provincial comrade, simply because there was so much more of it in the capital city. In London, more than anywhere else, there was a strong dialectical relationship between radical and conservative crowd activity. To isolate the former is in some ways a great and often necessary aid to evocation and analysis. But, especially in the metropolitan context, it can sometimes distort as much as it illuminates, if only because the flowering and failure of London radicalism cannot be fully explained merely in terms of itself.

★

Although the other two books look at nineteenth-century London from rather a different standpoint – the working of government rather than the threats to authority – the metropolitan context is once again so overwhelming a force (and this time explicitly so) that the similarities are striking. The theme of 'failure' is once again pronounced. If London was too big for successful riot, it was also too big for successful government. Just as wartime radicalism and Chartism were 'failures', so, too, in their way, were the Metropolitan Board of Works and the London County Council. Indeed, as with these two studies of popular unrest, Owen and Young and Garside seek to reconsider the accusations of 'failure' levelled at the MBW and the LCC; but once more, the picture which emerges is really rather familiar. Moreover, the crowds on the streets and the governors in their vestries were further united in that, in both cases, their civic effectiveness was in part constrained by their necessarily limited perception of their urban environment. If London had been smaller, more uniform, more coherent, easier to grasp, then both radical leaders and zealous administrators might have accomplished more than they did. In this sense, London was (and is?) as inimical to the functioning of government as to its overthrow.

David Owen's authoritative study of the complexities of London's government in the days between Chadwick and the LCC was left regrettably incomplete and only in first draft when he died in 1965. But, thanks to the unobtrusive and tactful endeavours of some of his friends and admirers, the work has been revised and completed with great skill, so that the joins hardly show. The first section explores the workings of the MBW between 1855 and 1888, and treats the contemporary criticisms of incompetence, ineptitude, inefficiency and corruption with a certain wry, sceptical and ironic detachment. However much the Board may have mismanaged both its public affairs and its public image, especially in the 1880s, its achievements in the realms of drainage construction, embankment making and road building were certainly substantial and significant. And they were the more so because, as Owen shows in the second part of his book, the MBW was subjected, throughout its life, to constant criticism from the surviving City Corporation (whose affairs he unravels with masterly expository skill) and from the metropolitan vestries (four of which receive sample investigations). Here, on occasions in suffocating detail, are the politics and trivia of the parish pump par excellence: sewers and streets, parks and open spaces, gas and water companies, abbatoirs and cow sheds. As Owen himself coyly admits, many of his subjects are indeed 'small and excruciatingly complex'.

Fortunately, the reader is saved from sinking into the morass of metropolitan muddle by the endeavours of two of Owen's friends, who place his writings in a broader context. As Donald Olsen explains in his introduction, Owen's findings bear on three major questions about the government of nineteenth-century London. Was there to be one, centralized metropolitan administration, or many dispersed and fragmented bodies? Should local authorities, of whatever kind, be actively interventionist, or should they see their prime obligation as being to save the ratepayers' money? And should the government of London be undertaken by the elected few or by the participatory many? Throughout the nineteenth century, and well on into the twentieth, there has never been a clear answer to these questions. We still do not know. In an equally well-judged conclusion, David Reeder warns that, complex as Owen's account is, there was a great deal more to London's nineteenth-century government than Owen's book actually considers: the poor law, education and the working of metropolitan charities, to say nothing of the provisioning of transport and other amenities, were all separate, and in most cases private, enterprises. But perhaps the most challenging implication of Owen's work, which Reeder is quite correct in pointing out more explicitly, is the suggestion that, even if the MBW was more of a 'failure' than a 'success', it was probably no worse, given its powers, resources, tasks and responsibilities, than many provincial, municipal governments in the 1850s and 1860s. After all, such towns as Leicester after the Municipal Corporations Act and Birmingham before Chamberlain were not exactly in the vanguard of civic progress and municipal reform. Perhaps Londoners, and those who undertook the government of their city, suffered from an unnecessary inferiority complex, which historians have been too eager to accept and too loath to question.

Owen's detailed findings are also placed in the rather broader context of London's metropolitan history by Young and Garside, whose book not only tackles the biggest subject of the four over the longest time span, but also (and to some extent as a result) is the most cogently argued and conceptually sophisticated. At one level, it is an account of the development of London's government, which isolates three distinct evolutionary phases in the last century and a half. The first period, from 1837 to 1899, was the greatest age of reform, in which the competing multitudes of local interests were gradually subdued, and the newly-created LCC enjoyed a brief heyday of centralized power, only to be weakened by the subsequent creation of twenty-eight rival borough councils. From 1900 to 1939, the LCC was obliged to govern a metropolis where most suburban growth was taking place beyond its jurisdictional boundaries. This led, in the 'twenties, to attempts to grab distant, virgin land for housing redevelopment schemes, and as a result the LCC was likened to a wolf on the prowl among suburban chickens. But in the 'thirties, as Labour took over, attention shifted from the suburban periphery back to the inner city regions, and programmes of slum clearance and flat building became the preferred method of re-housing the working classes. Finally, since the Second World War, the continuing decentralization of the metropolis, and the accumulated demands for the reform of its government, ultimately led to the creation of the GLC in 1965. Where, if anywhere, we go next is not at all clear.

The narrative account thus baldly summarized is unfolded with great elegance and clarity. More ambitiously, it is the authors' professed aim to relate changes in the structure and politics of London's government to changes in contemporary perception of the city's spatial and economic circumstances. But, as they discover, there is a great lag in this process, as the London perceived by reformers to need reforming tends (in the manner of soldiers always fighting the last war not the current one) to be that of the previous, not the present generation. So, the setting up of the LCC in 1888 was in many ways a response to the diagnoses made and prescriptions offered back in the 1850s and before. And, as a result, by the time it was established, it was already out of date, as the extensive process of suburbanization had already given rise to a greater London well beyond the bounds of the LCC's jurisdiction. Only in the 1950s, however, as the Conservative Government took up the cause of a Greater London Council, was there any serious prospect of this problem being dealt with. And, once again, it was too late. For by the time the GLC was born in 1965, it was already a 'splendidly archaic monument' to Edwardian progressivism, rather than a timely solution to the problems of the late twentieth-century metropolis. For by then, and like all the great cities of the western world, London was already entering a post-metropolitan age, characterized by urban decay and inner city blight, the collapse of the industrial base which had hitherto underpinned such massive urban concentrations, and the rise of a new, high-technology, low density, non-urban economy. And the appropriateness of the GLC to such circumstances was, and is, somewhat tenuous.

As the authors themselves modestly admit, their book is 'as selective a reading of London's history as any other'. But they do themselves less than justice. Of course it is selective; but compared with the three other books reviewed here, it is more ambitious in the problem it tackles, and more rigorous in the posing of its questions. There should, perhaps, be more on the financial aspect of local government, on the interplay between ratepayers and councillors, expansionists and economizers, the city's own resources and its reliance on government funding, and the problems posed for London's finance by the shift of industry from the centre to the periphery. Surely, these considerations, too, must have influenced the timing and nature of local government reform. But in all conscience, the authors' field is already amply large enough. It is especially sensitive to the interplay, in a party political sense, between Whitehall and County Hall, and demonstrates with great authority how, in the 1880s and again in the 1960s, the Conservatives sought to remodel London's government in the belief that they themselves would capture the new civic Frankenstein. Ironically, they were no more successful at this under Macmillan and

Home than they had been earlier under Salisbury. For reasons that remain largely unexplained, constituency politics in London are one thing, but local government politics are quite another.

When reviewing the extant historical literature on modern London, Young and Garside note that 'even the best work is fragmented temporally, spatially or thematically'. Of necessity, given the state of the art, this is bound to be so. With a mass of detailed work still to be done, on subjects of fundamental importance, dissertations, monographs and learned articles are bound to predominate at the expense of synoptic, synthetic surveys. But as more books such as these appear, it will become increasingly possible to undertake a comprehensive history of power and government, party and politics, reform and administration, in nineteenth-century London. But the price paid is that, until such a stage is reached, we shall have to be contented with more books of meticulous scholarship and precise focus, which will convey a great deal of important information about their chosen subject, but lack a sense of London as a place on the map or as a drama in time, which can only come from taking a broader perspective. Meanwhile these books bring with them the hope that, in London's political history, such a broader perspective will one day be possible.

As far as the economic history of nineteenth-century London is concerned, the picture looks much less optimistic. As economic historians increasingly divide their energies between the worship of the computer and the writing of business histories, their interest in tasks of fundamental intellectual significance seems to have atrophied. And, since the city's economy must, in varied ways, underpin almost everything else, the lack of work on this subject must delay even further the prospects of a full-scale history of nineteenth-century London being written before the twentieth century is out. But if ever such a work (and it would, by definition, have to be a co-operative, externally funded venture) was undertaken, it should not only seek to recover the awe and bewilderment with which nineteenth-century contemporaries regarded the capital; but it should also impose on it, in retrospect, a coherence, unity and identity which only the passage of time can provide. It is the fate of contemporaries not to understand their metropolitan present; it is the duty of historians to do better at understanding their metropolitan past. In the meantime, we shall have to settle for Dyos's dirge, significantly reminiscent of Briggs's elegy: 'It is lamentably true that no comprehensive history of London has yet been written.'

(1983)

NOTE:
1. J. Anne Hone, *For the Cause of Truth: Radicalism in London, 1796–1821* (Oxford, 1982); David Goodway, *London Chartism, 1838–1848* (Cambridge, 1982); David Owen et al, *The Government of Victorian London, 1855–1899: The Metropolitan Board of Works, the Vestries and The City Corporation* (London, 1982); Ken Young and Patricia L. Garside, *Metropolitan London: Politics and Urban Change, 1837–1901* (London, 1982).

# Welfare State History

Asa Briggs has just produced three new books.[1] This piece of information is made even more remarkable by the fact that he has published twenty-six already. Admittedly, there are some, like *How they lived, 1700–1815* and *They saw it happen, 1897–1940*, which are largely collections of contemporary documents, and which have merely been awarded Briggs's benediction. And others, like *The Nineteenth Century*, and *Essays in Labour History*, are edited volumes, to which he has contributed only a chapter and an introduction. But the majority are authentic works by his own hand: textbooks, like *The Age of Improvement*; scholarly books, like *Victorian People* and *Victorian Cities*; picture books, like *The Power of Steam* and *Ironbridge to Crystal Palace*; bestsellers, like *A Social History of England*; and multi-volume blockbusters, like *The History of Broadcasting in the United Kingdom*. While lesser historians fiddle over footnotes, Briggs dashes off reviews; while they ruminate over reviews, he completes articles; while they agonize over articles, he manufactures books; and while they bother over books, he produces multi-volume works. As befits his position as the pre-eminent authority on Victorian England, Briggs has often been described as a steam-engine scholar, pounding along the tracks of historical endeavour like an express train at full throttle.

Yet this prodigious and unrivalled output has not been the product of limitless research time, nor of leisured and scholarly detachment. On the contrary, as well as being one of the best and the brightest, Briggs has enjoyed a parallel – and unparalleled – career as one of the great and the good. He has shouldered heavy burdens of academic administration, as Professor of Modern History at Leeds, as a founding father and Vice-Chancellor of

Sussex University, and as Provost of Worcester College, Oxford. He has walked the corridors of power, as a member of the UGC, as British representative to the United Nations University, and as chairman of a government committee on nursing. He has held a clutch of decorous and dignified offices, as Chancellor of the Open University, and as President of the WEA, the Social History Society, the Society for the Study of Labour History, and the Society for the Social History of Medicine. And he appears regularly on television, is an incorrigible conference-goer, and spends so much time jetting round the world on business that when he received his peerage, it was suggested by some that he might take the title Lord Briggs of Heathrow. If in one guise he is a supersonic G. M. Trevelyan, then in another he is the thinking man's Lord Mountbatten.

No one can travel so much, do so much or write so much without attracting his detractors: the greater the achievement, the larger the target. Compared with his immediate contemporaries, Briggs's writing lacks the combative forcefulness of G. R. Elton, the olympian grandeur of Owen Chadwick, the stylish verve of J. H. Plumb, the cosmopolitan allusiveness of E. J. Hobsbawm, and the impassioned radicalism of Christopher Hill. Some have criticized his work for being too bland, for lacking analytical bite, for being more concerned with experience than with explanation, for relying too much on frequently-recycled quotations, and for the way in which one book is so often and so obviously cloned from another. Others have noticed that his coverage of the nineteenth century is distinctly uneven: he is happier in the town than in the country, stronger on the middle classes than the aristocracy, has more feel for nonconformity than for established religion, and is more interested in public than in private lives. And even his most ardent admirers must sometimes regret that he has lavished so much time and energy on his vast history of the BBC (happily now abridged into one book), of which yet *another* instalment is promised in the near future. Appropriately enough, one of the volumes is called *The War of Words*. In this case, at least, it is a battle Briggs has not always won.

Yet the shortcomings are far outweighed by the strengths, chief among which is the simple but essential truth that Briggs has been almost as much the maker of Victorian England in our own time as the Victorians themselves were the creators of it in theirs. When he began to write, at the close of the Second World War, Victorian history barely existed as a serious scholarly subject. The outline of events was known, but it was not clear what the problems were, nor what attitudes to adopt. The influence of an earlier generation of ill-disposed critics, like H. G. Wells and Lytton Strachey, remained much stronger than it should have done. There were reminiscences and three-decker hagiographies, but the archives were either unavailable or unexplored. There was Elie Halévy's massive *History of the English People in the Nineteenth Century*, but it did not cover the crucial middle decades. There was G. M. Trevelyan's textbook, and his admiring biographies of Lord Grey of the Reform Bill, Sir Edward Grey and John Bright. And there was G. M. Young's masterly if elusive *Portrait of an Age*. As Briggs gratefully and graciously acknowledges in two of the essays reprinted here, both of these patriarchs influenced him profoundly: Trevelyan by urging the links between economy, society and politics; and Young by his stress on the uniqueness of each generation's historical experience.

Since 1945, there has been a boom in Victorian studies, and Briggs himself has done more to mould and create it than any other historian. He seems to have read everything the Victorians wrote for or about themselves; he has a remarkable feeling for people and places, buildings and artifacts, institutions and organizations; and he draws illuminating contemporary comparisons with the United States, France, Germany and Australia. He has tackled mainstream political and economic history, and tried his hand at biography; he is highly sensitive to art and architecture, poetry and literature, culture and ideology; and he has been a much-emulated pioneer in social, labour, urban, company and medical history. Yet unlike many sub-disciplinary chauvinists and proselytisers, he has never become imprisoned in these new frameworks, nor lost sight of the broader historical landscape. On the contrary, it is his capacity for making connections which is his most impressive gift: between social structure and political activity, between contemporary issues and contemporary writers, between Manchester and Birmingham, Melbourne and London. By such illuminating comparisons and aptly-chosen examples, Briggs has built up an unrivalled panorama of the range and riches of Victorian life.

But what has given Briggs's work its real immediacy and appeal is that, regardless of the particular subject about which he may be writing, the present and the past have always come together in his work in such a way that he has been above all else a contemporary historian. To some extent, this is because the Victorian period, which is at the centre of his historical universe, remains a world more lived in than lost: for many people, its town halls and churches, railway stations and grand hotels, suburbs and slums, still provide (if diminishingly) the setting for their existence; and for Briggs himself, life must often have seemed like a latterday parable of Smilesian endeavour triumphantly rewarded, as the Keighley Grammar School boy has taken his seat in the House of Lords. But Briggs's history has also ranged more broadly over the two centuries which separate the 1780s from the 1980s, and he has written extensively on the period since 1945, the very time when he himself has been so busy as an academic statesman. So it is not surprising that the slightly left-of-centre ethos of Welfare State consensus politics, which so dominated English life from Attlee to Wilson, has not only been at the forefront of some of his writing, but has also provided the unifying background and underlying value structure to all of it. For nearly forty years, Briggs has been the most 'relevant' of historians – of his time and for his time.

As he himself rightly and readily admits, 'historians cannot avoid reading into the past the preoccupations of the present'. And in his case, this means he has spent his prolific professional life as the Whig historian of the Welfare State – not in the crude, teleological sense of seeing everything in the last two hundred years as leading inevitably and inexorably in that direction, but more subtly, in that the aspects of the past which he has most frequently studied, evoked and celebrated bear a remarkably close affinity to the distinguishing characteristics of the Welfare State in its heyday. *The Age of Improvement*, for instance, is dominated by a rising and increasingly meritocratic middle class, by their sense of never having had it so good, and by their high-minded reforming ardour, which gradually created a more decent and wholesome world for everybody. Likewise, *Victorian Cities* explores how, in the age of the railway and the tram, and of the unprecedented massing of millions of people, urban society gradually came to recognize its problems, set about solving them, and so progressed towards a greater degree of control over itself. And *Victorian People* is unified by the themes of prosperity, national security, trust in institutions, belief in a common moral code based on duty and restraint, and in the virtues of free discussion, inquiry and investigation. The Welfare State in its prime could hardly be better described.

Throughout his writings, Briggs is primarily concerned with thought and work, inquiry and investigation, debate and discussion, progress and improvement. He knows that there is conflict and exploitation, squalor and misery, unhappiness and discontent, but these are not so much lamented for themselves as seen as the mainsprings to positive action. As a labour historian, he is less concerned to evoke dreadful working conditions than to show how these led to trade-union organization and a better deal for the employees. As an urban historian, he is interested not so much in the blighted environment as in the opportunities which big cities provided for middle- and working-class people to make a better world. And as the historian of the BBC, his main aim has been to show how a group of conflicting interests was gradually moulded into a great national institution, for the edification and improvement of the mass of the people. Accordingly, the heroes of Briggs's books are men like Joseph Chamberlain and Sir John Reith, who got things done and made things work, and institutional agencies of improvement, like voluntary societies, local government, royal commissions and civil service departments. Throughout Briggs's historical universe, the Welfare State mentality is there, even when the Welfare State is not: private lives are explored only with reference to the public stage; problems are

solved and objectives achieved, agreement is reached and consensus emerges; individual enterprise and sectional interests are
gradually fused into some shared sense of purpose for the common
good.

All this emerges vividly in the first two volumes of his collected
papers. Between them, the essays brought together here span
thirty-five years of indefatigable scholarship: some ante-date and
anticipate later books; others are retrospective ruminations on
subjects explored in greater detail; all can be read with pleasure and
profit. The opening section of the first volume reprints several
pieces in which Briggs considers how contemporaries tried to
make sense of the Industrial Revolution, how they tried to describe it and explain it to themselves. There is his famous essay on
the language of class, which explores the rise of collective vocabu-
laries and collective perceptions; the parallel study of the language
of the masses, which treats the same problem from lower down
the social scale; an account of those more quantitatively-inclined
Victorians, who deployed statistical modes of inquiry to measure
more precisely just what was going on; and a more impressionistic
piece which shows how, at the other extreme, writers and artists
tried to evoke the city, not as a statistical aggregate, but as a
particular place. Here are assembled a classic cast of Briggsian
historical personages: looking carefully, thinking hard, anticipating the future. As Briggs himself puts it, 'studies which begin with
the Victorian city end with the twentieth-century state'.

The second section draws together some of his earliest, most
substantial and most important work on nineteenth-century
towns, where he first developed the idea that political activity
might be explained with reference to economic structure and
social life. This, too, is a typically Briggsian approach, not dwelling on depression and distress, but seeing them as a spur to
endeavour, improvement and reform. And he was to use it again,
as a central theme of his masterly *History of Birmingham*, and as the
unifying thread in his virtuoso cavalcade, *Victorian Cities*. The
famous contrast which was developed in that book, but first
worked out in these early articles, was between Manchester, a city

of deep economic divisions and social cleavages, and Birmingham, a city of economic co-operation and social cohesion. So while in the one, political activity took the form of the middle-class Anti-Corn Law League, in the other it expressed itself as the Birmingham Political Union, with its agitation for Parliamentary and currency reform. Thirty years on, these pioneer pieces still impress: for the audacity with which they broke down traditional historical sub-disciplines; for their sensitivity – *pace* Mumford – to what were in fact very *un*alike industrial towns; and for their concern with 'the tangled nexus of private and public conflicts, compromises and decisions' which fashioned these particular communities.

While most of the essays in the first volume relate in some way to *Victorian Cities*, many of those in the second are more closely linked to the companion book, *Victorian People*. This is especially so in the first section, where Briggs tries to 'trace patterns of value through the experience of individuals' – not, in this case, politicians or administrators or investigators, but creative artists and intuitive commentators. There is a general essay on writers and cities in the nineteenth century, which shows how novelists came to terms with the newness, noise and numbers of the urbanizing world, in America, Britain, France and Germany. There is a well-crafted piece on Ebenezer Elliott, a middle-class Sheffield radical, who wrote poems about the steam engine and Free Trade for a working-class audience. And there are two rather slighter essays on Trollope as a traveller and William Morris as a Victorian. But the two best pieces are on George Eliot and Charlotte Brontë. In a study of *Middlemarch*, Briggs shows how Lydgate's success as a doctor and failure as a medical reformer can only be understood with reference to the contemporary debates on public health, both at the time when Eliot wrote and of the time in which *Middlemarch* is set. And his analysis of *Shirley* not only rehabilitates it as a commentary on Yorkshire Luddites but also notes, characteristically, that one sentence from it – 'misery generates hate' – provided the motto of Beveridge's *Full Employment in a Free Society*.

The remainder of the volume makes a less coherent collection. There are sundry essays on Victorian historians and the Norman

Yoke, on how nineteenth-century commentators looked to the future, and on how some historians play the same prediction game. And there are short and appreciative pieces on G. M. Trevelyan, G. M. Young and Gilberto Freyre, which tell us almost as much about Briggs as about the subject of scrutiny. But the most substantial essays deal with another quintessentially Briggsian topic: the interaction between health, medicine, politics and reform in the modern world. One study considers public health and public opinion in the age of Edwin Chadwick, and sees the fight for reform as a war on two fronts: experts battling against misunderstanding and ignorance and politicians and administrators crusading against prejudice, inertia and vested interests. A second piece explores the impact of cholera on nineteenth-century urban society, and shows Briggs in unusually polemical vein, largely at the expense of Professor Louis Chevalier, who saw cholera as a menace to be endured rather than as a problem to be solved. 'The forces of resistance to chaos and panic,' Briggs notes with stern and determined optimism, 'deserve as much attention as the chaos and panic themselves.' And there is a more general essay on the Welfare State in historical perspective, where Briggs deliberately tries to avoid Whiggish excess, but still feels moved to comment that 'shapes of the future flit through the changing past'.

Taken together, these essays are a remarkable testament to the range and vigour of Briggs's work (and there are two more volumes still to come). Of necessity, some are more substantial than others, and the passing of time has not treated all of them with equal respect. Briggs's picture of Birmingham as a unique city of collaboration and cohesion would not, now, command universal assent nor would his more general argument that urban politics can be so closely related to economic structure and social relationships. His constant preoccupation with public rather than private lives means that the recent shifts of interest among social historians are barely reflected here: sex and gender, childhood and marriage, bedrooms and bathrooms, shop-floors and households, seem rather more conspicuous by their absence than they would have done a decade ago. It is also noteworthy that, while Briggs emerges as a brilliant pioneer of social, urban, medical and labour history, he has been much less emulated in his attempts to bring together history and literature, background and text. As literary criticism becomes less historical and more introverted, and as historical scholarship becomes more quantitative and less impressionistic, the dialogue between these two disciplines, never loud, has become virtually inaudible.

More broadly, the real interest of this collection is that the overall view of the recent past which it articulates so powerfully is much less fashionable now than it was ten years ago. Briggs has never been in any doubt that the Industrial Revolution was a great leap forward, a time when the whole texture of society was totally transformed. But it has recently become more commonplace to argue that it was but a little local levitation rather than a national take-off into sustained growth. For Briggs, the power of steam, the impact of technology, the new processes of production, were crucial. But many historians now believe that their importance has been much overrated, and that very little change had really taken place by 1851, when Britain was the workshop – but not the factory – of the world. For Briggs, the rise of class-consciousness, the growth of big industrial cities, and the massing of millions of men and women in such new environments, cannot be ignored. But today it is fashionable to suggest that class formation was at best fragmented and localized, that the new industrial cities were not really that large, and that, in any case, most people still lived in Barsetshire. For Briggs, the major impulse to improvement and progress was the rising and ever more influential middle classes, who were the carriers of the notion of improvement, and whose demands resulted in political and administrative reforms. But now it is more frequently asserted that the middle classes were economically weak, and that such reforms as there were may best be explained in terms of high political manoeuvring rather than as responses to popular pressure.

As Briggs himself remarks, 'the sense of the past shifts in each generation,' and the sense of Britain's recent, industrial past is not, in 1985, what it was in 1955 or 1965. Briggs's past is no longer the fashionable past because the contemporary world which gave it meaning, and to which it in turn gave historical validation, is not what it was either. The great provincial cities, whose exuberant civic pride Briggs so vividly evoked, and which were still so palpable in the 1960s, are now physically ruined, economically desolate, and politically threatened. The GLC, which is the direct descendant of the LCC, whose creation and early workings he so carefully analysed, is under sentence of death. The universities founded in the 1960s, of whose establishment and expansion he was so redoubtable a champion, are on the defensive. The BBC, whose Reithian ethos of public service and improvement he so fulsomely celebrated, seems interested only in ratings, and teeters on the brink of commercialization. And the Butskellite, Welfare State world of low unemployment and high government spending, of cultivated consensus and avoided confrontation, about which Briggs has written so ardently, is now no longer practical politics. The present and the past no longer interact in a Briggsian way.

Of course, Briggs himself is far too acute an historian, and far too sensitive to the passing of generations, to be unaware of this. 'The facts of twentieth-century life,' he notes, 'have been as important as changes in scholarship in changing perspectives.' And the facts of twentieth-century life today are very different from what they were ten years ago, by which time most of the essays in these volumes had been written. Put more bluntly, this means that the broad nexus of left-of-centre goodness, of low-tech decency, of middle-class improvement, which flourished from the steam-engine to the steam radio and beyond, and which has informed Briggs's life as an academic statesman and his work as an academic historian, is no longer the conventional wisdom, but has itself become a thing of the past. The Welfare State is not a way of seeing history any more: it *is* history. Attlee and Toynbee Hall, G. D. H. Cole and the Fabians, Lord Beveridge and the LSE, Harold Macmillan and the middle way, C. P. Snow and the two cultures, Harold Wilson and white-hot technology: all these politicians and pundits whose ideas and values so pervade Briggs's work are now yesterday's men with yesterday's modes. And, it is abundantly clear, Lord Briggs does not like this at all. The most recently-written of these essays, like the concluding chapter in his *Social History of England*, register a firm, compassionate and deeply-felt protest against the bleakness of the 1980s, the 'Thatcherite contempt for consensus', the cuts in public spending, the growth in unemployment, and the increasing polarization of public and political life.

There is, in all of this, a considerable and instructive irony, the force of which can hardly have escaped Lord Briggs's notice. In his life and work, Briggs has celebrated and epitomized many admirable qualities which might quite accurately be called Victorian values and Victorian virtues. Yet the advent of a prime minister who claims to be doing the very same thing, has turned Briggs's contemporary and historical worlds almost completely upside down. When he defines the Welfare State as 'organized power deliberately used through politics and administration to modify the play of market forces', it is abundantly clear that this is a world we are losing, even if it is not yet fully lost. And when he quotes the *Standard* recently, as saying that the great Victorian engine of Britain's prosperity 'has finally run out of steam', the enormity and significance of that admission, for a man like Briggs, hardly needs labouring. Whatever may be the provenance of Mrs Thatcher's Victorian values, it is certainly not Briggsian. On the contrary, as the Lord Macaulay of the Welfare State, Briggs is as out of step and out of sympathy with the contemporary, Thatcherite world as he is with the type of history which that world is now in the process of making and manufacturing for itself.

As with another great historian and public teacher, the march of events has thus transformed Briggs from being a conformist into a dissenter. When G. M. Trevelyan wrote his *English Social History*, it was as an elegiac lament for a world of patrician, liberal decency destroyed by the Second World War. Now, forty years on, Briggs's very different *Social History of England* may in turn already stand as a more robust requiem for the world of Welfare-State decency destroyed by Thatcher. Indeed, Briggs's very last sentence in that book – 'just as we have had more than one yesterday, so we can, if we choose, have more than one future' –

may perhaps embody his protest, not only against the way things are now going, but also against the way they are, increasingly, now deemed to have gone.

(1985)

NOTE:
1. Asa Briggs, *The BBC: The First Fifty Years* (London, 1985); idem, *The Collected Essays of Asa Briggs*, vol. I, *Words, Numbers, Places, People*; vol. II, *Images, Problems, Standpoints, Forecasts* (Brighton, 1985).

# Socialist History

One of the most noteworthy examples of intellectual *embourgeoise-ment* during the 1970s was the transformation of the history workshops held at Ruskin College, Oxford, from ephemeral, marginal and near-clandestine activities into a permanent, recognized and well-publicized part of the contemporary scholarly scene. The most significant evidence of this development was the publication of the *History Workshop Journal*, the first issue of which has already become something of a collector's item, and the launching of the history workshop series, of which seven volumes have so far appeared. With two such flourishing enterprises under way, with several of its most illustrious comrades established among the ivory towers and high tables of Oxbridge colleges, and with Raphael Samuel providing inspirational leadership in inimitable style, the history workshop movement seems set fair to follow the path already blazed by that earlier *enfant terrible* of historical inquiry, *Past and Present*, from subversive opposition to gentrified dissent.

Nevertheless, as befitted their rebellious origins, these two publishing enterprises were boldly and bravely prefaced by impassioned, strident, messianic manifestos, chastising and dismissing those who were not of the faith, while explaining and celebrating the innovative work which was to be done under this new and committed banner. In the best tradition of scholarly revolutionaries, the workshoppers were full of righteous indignation against the introverted élitism and middle-class mores of the existing historical establishment. 'History', we were rather grandly informed, 'is too important to be left to the professional historian', and should no longer be written 'from the vantage point of those who have had the charge of running other people's lives.' The subject must, they insisted, be made 'more democratic', and be brought 'closer to the central concerns of people's lives', by encouraging 'working men and women' to 'write their own history'. The result, they contended, would be a more relevant, more accessible and more humane version of the past, concentrating on 'the real life experience of the people themselves', which would thus emerge in its true colours as 'the record of resistance to oppression'.

In short, the work to be produced under the workshoppers' angry yet ardent auspices was to be (among other things) feminist, radical, aware, and supportive. As such, their declared objective was what might be termed Gettysburg history – of the people, by the people, and for the people. If those who undertook it were self-taught, had to pay their own way, did not have an academic job, and had been denied a grant by the SSRC, then so much the better. For suffering, not security, was to them the sure sign of scholarship and of sincerity. 'The manuscripts', we were warned, in a sentence at once fervent, disconcerting and unfathomable, 'line the passage ways, crawl up the stairs to sleep at night, and invade the children's bedroom.' And the object of this exercise in somnambulist scholarship was not to reinstate the old-style social history as defined by G. M. Trevelyan: the history of the people with the politics left out. On the contrary, it was to produce a new kind of socialist history: the history of the people with the politics emphatically put back *in* – provided, that is, that they were of an appropriate, acceptable and advanced kind.

If it is recognized that this is a road which it is both possible and worthwhile for historians to travel, then these two books[1] must be applauded for taking us some way along it. Both are concerned with working-class life in that area to the north and east of Liverpool Street Station, which extends in an arc from Bethnal Green via Spitalfields to Whitechapel, and which was famous in its day for such do-badding criminals as Jack the Ripper, and for such do-gooding enterprises as Toynbee Hall. More precisely, Jerry White's volume seeks to recover the fabric of Jewish life among those who lived in one East End tenement block between 1887 and 1920, while Raphael Samuel's book puts between hard covers the ordered reminiscences of Arthur Harding, a man described by the Royal Commission on Metropolitan Police in 1907 as 'a most slippery and dangerous criminal'. Both volumes are characterized by passion and compassion, and between them, they provide a vivid, horrifying, unforgettable picture of what it was like to be down and out in London during the last years of Queen Victoria's reign and the early decades of this century.

White's book is primarily based on the oral testimonies of sixteen former residents of the seven-storey, barrack-like Rothschild Buildings, the construction of which he accurately describes as 'the ugly offspring of a reluctant paternalism'. On the supply side, these dwellings were the product of local redevelopment which was first allowed by R. A. Cross's Artisans' and Labourers' Dwellings Improvement Act of 1875, but which only came about in the aftermath of the Ripper murders, when the first full revelation of the horrors of life (and death) in the East End led to demands that something must be done. On the demand side, this particular tenement building, largely financed by the Rothschilds, became home to some of those poor, artisan Jewish immigrants, who were fleeing by the thousands from the pogroms which were widespread in Eastern Europe in the 1880s and again in the 1900s. Many of them eventually settled in the seamier parts of London, and by the turn of the century, over ninety-five per cent of the thousand-odd residents of the Rothschild Buildings were Jewish.

Although White devotes some space to explaining the genesis of this ghetto-block, his chief concern is to people it with faces from the past, and to recover the texture and fabric of their lives. So we are given a detailed tour of the two-roomed homes which predominated, with their unavoidable overcrowding, their carefully-tended window-boxes, and their samovars for making Russian tea on special occasions. Of necessity, the shared experience of persecution and flight, the common language and lowly status of the occupants, and their dense residential propinquity, forged a strong and abiding sense of community. But at the same time, there were countervailing – if weaker – forces, especially the tensions engendered by excessive proximity, the competing loyalties of different Eastern European nationalities, and the inevitable inequalities of work and income. At one level, there was a co-operative struggle for collective independence, which found expression in strikes and flirtation with socialism. But at another, there was a competitive struggle for individual independence, as some artisans became and remained more equal than others.

This ambiguous sense of solidarity is further explored in an analysis of a nearby area of casual labour more typical of 'outcast London', which was located at the other end of Flower and Dean Street. Its lodging-houses, prostitutes, criminals and gang warfare are examined through the eyes of the residents of Rothschild Buildings, and their necessarily ambivalent relationship is carefully and cogently described. In one guise, this surging, sinister swell of Gentile poor was both a threat and an affront to the proudly respectable Jewish community at the opposite end of the road. But in another, it also provided an indispensable supply of casual labour to relieve overworked Jewish mothers of some of the more tedious and time-consuming domestic chores. Indeed, for the women as well as for the men who inhabited Rothschild Buildings, it was the drudgery of work which inevitably dominated their lives – whether running the household, in an emphatically subordinate and wifely manner, or spending twelve hours a day toiling and sweating in the rag trade, the tobacco industry, the boot and shoe business, or in furniture making.

Much of this world was once familiar to Arthur Harding, whose tape-recorded reminiscences, made by Raphael Samuel between 1973 and 1979, are largely concerned with his life in nearby Bethnal Green in the years before the First World War. He was born in 1886, and was one of the last inhabitants of 'the Nichol', the most famous criminal slum in London, located to the north of Spitalfields, and immortalized by Arthur Morrison in *A Child of the Jago* (1896). Harding's life divided into three distinct phases, the first of which, lasting until the turn of the century, was his deprived and delinquent childhood. His mother was a cripple, who drank; his father was an idler, who beat her. The family frequently moved house, its accommodation was invariably over-crowded, and it was only sustained by the earnings of Arthur Harding's elder sister. Apart from a brief spell in Dr Barnardo's, his schooling was distinctly limited, and as a young boy he learned how to steal from the market and pinch goods from the shops. He tried his hand at cabinet making, and even enlisted in the army when too young. But the pattern of his existence was really set when, in 1902, he first got into big trouble with the police.

The second phase of Harding's life – criminal, violent, and interspersed with spells in prison – lasted until the early 1920s. During this period, he moved from the petty crimes of thieving, pilfering, snatching and pickpocketing to more brutal robbery, gang warfare and persecution rackets, which culminated for him in two long spells in prison in the 1910s. Thereafter, despite occasional brushes with the police, Harding began to go straight, and his life entered its final phase. He married in 1924, and returned to the cabinet-making trade. When it seemed threatened by the slump, he moved into the second-hand clothes business, and in 1932 began buying old gold and silver. Insofar as the 'urge to excitement' remained, it was no longer indulged by criminal activities, but by organizing strike-breaking convoys in 1926, and in supporting Oswald Mosley in the 1930s. By then, in fact, respectability had beckoned, as Harding and his wife quit Bethnal Green for Leyton. 'All my family', he concludes, with evident pride, 'was brought up here. They changed from Bethnal Green kids to something a bit selecter.'

No brief summary can adequately convey the richness of this text, peopled as it is with an astonishing range of characters, redolent of Dickens or Mayhew: some crooked, violent and brutal, others brave, stoic and compassionate, the majority an uncertain and rather moving amalgam of sinner and saint. Once again, it is the contradictions of working-class life which emerge most forcefully, this time through the contradictions in Harding's own experience, character and outlook. He was a rough, brutal and dangerous man, yet he prevented prostitutes being 'interfered with', despised men who lived on immoral earnings, and condemned some of his neighbours for living like savage animals. He was a criminal who hated the police as corrupt, and who fought on several occasions (not always successfully) to prevent them framing him with false charges. But at the same time, cordial relations with the force were an integral – indeed a vital – part of underworld life. And although for much of his career he was a threat to law and order, Harding's political opinions were essentially the unthinking and unreflective conservatism of those who claim to have no politics.

There can be no doubt that, in conformity with the avowed aims of the history workshop movement, both of these books excel in depicting 'the real-life experience of the people themselves', raw, naked and vivid. But at the same time, they also exemplify the weaknesses as much as the strengths of this approach to reconstructing the past. For all their evocative excellence, these volumes remain intellectually insubstantial. In the case of White's book, it is exceedingly difficult to know what to make of the material he presents – sixteen oral accounts of life in a building whose inmates numbered over one thousand. Are these few people typical or not? We have no way of knowing, and nor, it seems, does White. There is also too much extended quotation, as points are needlessly laboured, repeated and rehearsed, with the paradoxical (but predictable) result that the unstructured surfeit of material is less vivid and immediate than it might have been had the evidence been selected more carefully and presented more discriminatingly. It is indeed a pity that, on his own admission, the author succumbed to what he rightly calls 'the indulgence of inch-by-inch reconstruction'.

The inevitable consequence of this is that no effort is made to place this undeniably fascinating material in any context which would make clear its broader intellectual significance. No real attempt is made, for example, to relate it to the important recent work which has been done on Jewish immigrant communities, on the late nineteenth-century philanthropy movement, or on the essentially conservative culture of the London working class. The author may feel that it is up to his readers to contextualize and evaluate his findings for themselves, to provide their own framework within which to assess their novelty and significance: but he is surely the best qualified person to do this, and it is much to be regretted that he does not. For as a result, a whole variety of important questions go unaddressed and unanswered. Why, for instance, has White assumed his subjects to be primarily working-class and incidentally Jewish, rather than the other way round? Why should his chapter on community, which constantly hints at great ambiguities in social relationships, be without a conclusion? And why was no attempt made to explore the long-term decay and disintegration of the Rothschild Buildings ghetto, for which, presumably, the evidence is so much more abundant?

Similar difficulties recur – but in a more exaggerated form – in Samuel's book. As proletarian autobiography, the life and times of Arthur Harding is gripping; but as serious history, it is quite simply unfathomable. Time and again, the reader is left wondering what to believe and what to doubt, and how to reconcile the many discrepancies with which the text is riddled. The same events are given different dates, the same episodes are recounted in completely irreconcilable versions, and the same people are assessed in bewilderingly inconsistent ways. When the footnotes are consulted, doubts only increase, as they regularly admit that stories cannot be verified, that individuals cannot be identified, and that incidents cannot be traced. Of course, memory plays tricks on any old man or woman, especially when recollecting a life as eventful as this over such a long period of time. And undeniably, some of the inconsistencies merely reflect with accuracy the ambiguities of Harding's own class position. But it is also difficult to avoid the conclusion that a character so well accomplished in deceit, and so obviously given to fantasy, may have been editing and embellishing his story for the benefit of a wider audience.

Although these doubts and difficulties derive directly from these two very particular and peculiar historical enterprises, they are also symptomatic of the more general problems which arise when self-styled socialist historians attempt to produce this particular brand of 'people's history'. As Eric Hobsbawm – hardly a scholar hostile to history written from below or from a left-wing view-point – recently pointed out, all too often, the output of the history workshoppers 'sacrifices analysis and explanation to celebration and identification'. Having rediscovered their particular piece of the proletarian past, they are too eager to publish it in its raw, original and unprocessed state, as if that were all there is to historical investigation. Yet this excessive reliance on fallible and unrepresentative oral testimony, the deliberate cult of disembodied 'experience' for its own sake, and the blinkered belief that amateurs write history better than the professionals, actually result in a finished product which is, ironically, exceedingly old fashioned in both its form and its limitations.

For these two books, like so much that has been published under the auspices of the history workshop, are not so much works of historical scholarship as editions of historical documents. And as such, they are as vulnerable to criticism as any of those medieval charters or court rolls or monastic accounts which were published at the turn of the century by equally curious and well-meaning country parsons. What was – and is – the justification for printing such documents? What was – and is – their intellectual, as distinct from experiential, significance? How should such material be evaluated? Why, indeed, is it worth knowing about at all? The fact that the publishers of these documents are socialists in the 1980s rather than clergymen in the 1900s does not thereby release them from their necessary obligation to confront these questions and undertake these tasks. In their own defence, the workshoppers may assert that it is better to study the working class through their own eyes than through the distorted lenses of middle-class observers, whether contemporaries then, or historians now. But in practice, this merely replaces one brand of evidential distortion with another, which requires equally careful handling and interpretation. It is not only the bourgeoisie whose sources are suspiciously subjective.

It may be the case that politically, the antiquarianism of the left is preferable to the antiquarianism of the right: but historically, professionally, and intellectually, there is in practice no more to be said for the one than there is for the other. The claims advanced here – that these two books both exemplify 'working men and women writing their own history', and that as such they 'restore' to the proletariat their 'own' history which has somehow been 'lost' – sound so appealing that it seems churlish and ungenerous to question them. But at best, all we are given here is the history, not of people in general, but of persons in particular: of sixteen Jewish elders and one London criminal whose 'experience' can be of little relevance to any contemporary reader, of whatever social background. And at worst, the result is little more than a misguided exercise in ancestor-invention. For the only people to whom this history really 'belongs' are those who actually made it – first time round. Moving, immediate, zestful this material may be, but as presented here, it has no revealed significance or general relevance beyond itself.

Ironically, then, people's history and socialist history, as represented by these two volumes, needs to confront the very same challenges which most types of historian, and most types of history, must inevitably face. If their work is to be of wide appeal, and carry intellectual conviction, it must be concerned with broad perspectives, general explanations and big questions as much as with particular episodes, specific detail and evidential richness. Indeed, if the 'programmatic' editorial to the first issue of their journal is any guide, some of the workshoppers realize this only too well. History, they rightly point out, needs to be enriched by 'a more complex understanding of historical processes, more caution in handling the sources, more boldness in extending the boundaries of inquiry', and by 'a greater effort to achieve clarity of presentation'. Few historians – proletarian or bourgeois, socialist or capitalist – would contest the truth of these remarks. But on the basis of these two offerings, the workshoppers have a long way to go before they come near to realizing any of these objectives in their own publications. Perhaps that is the price you have to pay for letting the manuscripts crawl up the stairs.

(1981)

NOTE:

1. J. White, *Rothschild Buildings: Life in an East End Tenement Block, 1887–1920* (London, 1980); R. Samuel, *East End Underworld: Chapters in the Life of Arthur Harding* (London, 1981).

# Elite History

One reason why most historians don't write very much is that they have a full time job keeping up with the massive output of those few who do. Among these prodigy-producers, whom it would be more impolitely accurate to call Cliomaniacs, Lawrence Stone stands out particularly distinguished, partly by the sheer range, quality and audacity of his work, and partly because of the impassioned and varied responses which it invariably and deliberately provokes. His major books comprise four mammoth volumes, which together add up to over two thousand five hundred pages – a million words on a millennium of English history. Any averagely ambitious, energetic and intelligent historian would be happily contented with completing one of these weighty works: but even four such monsterpieces does not exhaust Stone's tireless energy. In between there have appeared another four books, amounting to a further thousand words; three edited volumes, in two cases with substantial contributions by Stone himself; dozens of articles and essays, some of very considerable length; and scores of coruscating, combative and controversial reviews.

Stone's historical universe is not only large and full of matter; it is also an exciting – if dangerous – place to be. The past of which he writes is one of great events and constant action: of rise and fall, change and crisis, evolution and revolution. There are always at least ten causes for this, seven consequences of that, and five reasons why most other historians have got it wrong. His admirers, and there are many, see him as Cliomagician, and acclaim his energy, his originality, his breadth of vision, his ebullient vigour and high spirits. His curiosity about the past is endless and insatiable; his interest in sociology and statistics, economics and anthropology, is irrepressible; his determination to tackle large and important topics ('the big *why* questions') is an inspiration; his openness to new ideas, new subjects and new approaches is exemplary; and his books are always brilliantly organized, written in lively and lucid language, and abound in firm and crisp judgments. And all this has been accomplished while shouldering formidable burdens of teaching and administration. At Princeton University, he presides over the Davis Center for Historical Studies, which puts on the best and bloodiest gladiatorial shows in the profession; he is one of the most influential and long-serving members of the editorial board of *Past and Present*; and he is an assiduous, inspiring and intimidating supervisor of graduate students, to whom he is known as 'the Pope of Princeton'. Cliomogul might be a more apt description.

But to his enemies, and there are also many, he is closer to being Cliomonster: cavalier in his use of sources, unsound in his statistical calculations, speculative in his generalizations, and irresponsible in his polemics. Indeed, his list of adversaries is nearly as long, and at least as distinguished, as his own list of publications. Those who are on the scholarly right, but wrong, include H. R. Trevor-Roper, G. R. Elton, J. P. Cooper, J. P. Kenyon and Conrad Russell. And those who are on the left but are not right include Peter Laslett, Alan Macfarlane, Edward Shorter and Michel Foucault. Of especial interest is Stone's long-running battle with Geoffrey Elton, his only real rival in the early modern historians' war of words. For forty years they have been slugging it out, in books and articles, lectures and reviews, each utterly convinced that the other has had a totally bad influence on historical scholarship, and both sublimely unaware of just how much like each other they actually are. Both are emigrés anxious to be more native than the natives in their adopted country; both are passionately devoted to the study of the English past; both believe that narrative history is the best way of doing things; both work astonishingly and compulsively hard; both love being controversial; and both are – in different ways – marvellous historians.

Whether exhausting the superlatives of his admirers or the venom of his critics, Stone's history is clearly not for the faint-hearted, the slow-witted or the lukewarm. History as he practices, preaches and provokes it is a high-risk, high-pressure, high-temperature enterprise. He loves stirring things up, even on occasions at considerable cost to himself. Hugh Trevor-Roper's demolition of his early work on the gentry was a terrifying piece of scholarly destruction, and his recent book on *The Family, Sex and Marriage* has been savaged in certain quarters as a 'disaster'. But Stone's self-assurance survives it all; his thirst for battle remains unquenched; and his determination not to mince his words is undiminished. In Oxford, he tells them how to do the history of the university better; in Cambridge he tells them how to do the history of the family better; and in Paris he tells the *Annales* school how to do the history of everything better. Constitutional history, he claims, is 'sterile and meaningless'; psychohistory is 'largely a disaster area'; economic history is merely 'a mopping up operation'; and Cliometricians are 'statistical junkies'. Not many historians, Stone breezily concludes, are 'possessed of true intellectual distinction'. So it is hardly surprising (although in fact both regrettable and wrong) that his colleagues declined to elect him President of the American Historical Association.

Curiously enough, Stone's history as practised in his substantive works is never quite the same as the history he preaches in his more polemical pieces. Constantly, tirelessly and evangelically, he exhorts his colleagues to study crime and deviance, witchcraft and popular culture, slaves and peasants, workers and paupers. Yet he himself has very rarely done any of these things. On the contrary, the realm of the past which he has made indisputably his own is the history of the English élite: its education, religion and culture, its minds, morals and manners, its houses, gardens and churches, its wealth, status and power. What makes this all the more remarkable is that, as a competitive meritocrat and compulsive worker, Stone has frequently made it plain how much he detests this 'antipathetic group of superfluous parasites'. One can only marvel at the sustained will power he has successfully exerted over nearly forty years to subdue these outraged feelings in the interests of dispassionate scholarly inquiry. This latest book is but further proof of his life long attachment to England and its élite.[1] One important change, however, must be recorded. While Lawrence Stone conceived this project and wrote the book, most of the elaborate research and computing which it required was undertaken or organized by his wife, who is thus fittingly acknowledged as the book's co-author. Instead of being a closed élite of one, Lawrence Stone is now half of an open élite of two.

What, then, is the Stones' book actually about? Ostensibly, and indeed substantively, it investigates English country houses and their owners, a subject much in vogue in recent years. But those who eagerly anticipate another piece of nostalgic, reverential history, a sort of *Brideshead Revisited* with footnotes, will be sadly disappointed. A book with chapter headings such as 'drop outs' and 'intrusions', 'strategies' and 'ruptures', can hardly be expected to treat country houses as ivy-clad dream homes bathed in perpetual sunshine, still less their owners as amiably and agreeably eccentric characters. On the contrary, the Stones view English country houses matter-of-factly as machines for the English power élite to live in, and so it is altogether appropriate that they themselves have resorted to a great deal of machinery in the course of their researches. As Jeanne Stone explains in an elaborate appendix, the core of the project was the collection, codification and manipulation of the statistical data of country-house ownership and building over a 340 year span. And to display their findings, the authors produce fifty-three graphs and sixty-four tables, on which the text of the book is essentially a commentary. The result is the first statistical study of what has hitherto been an impressionistic and anecdotal subject.

But the Stones' purpose is much more wide-ranging than merely introducing some welcome quantitative precision into the woolly and wistful world of Waugh and Wodehouse. Their fundamental aim is to test the oft-repeated view that, from the Reformation to the late nineteenth century, England's ruling élite possessed a unique capacity for survival and renewal, as successful men from trade, business, the law, the armed forces and government office bought their way into the ranks of the landowners. For contemporary commentators from Marston to Cobden, and for generations of historians thereafter, this picture of frequent and easy upward mobility by self-made men into the ranks of the landed élite has been a self-evident truth, which not only explains the exceptional and essential stability of modern English history, but also such major and specific happenings as the development of the most efficient agricultural system in Europe, the making of the first industrial revolution, the creation of a uniquely stable yet flexible political system, and the onset of economic decline through a failure of entrepreneurial zeal. In short, as the Stones rightly observe, 'a great deal of English social, economic, cultural and political history over the last four hundred years is riding the truth of a single paradigm.' Their book puts this truth to the test.

How? One obvious approach would be to trace the careers of successful men of business and affairs, to see how many used their wealth to buy their way into landed bliss. This is not the Stones' method. Another, to which they give some brief attention, would be to see whether younger sons of landowners were downwardly mobile into business, trade and the professions. A third approach would be to consider the problem from the standpoint of the élite, by quantifying and analysing its composition, so as to discover the degree and methods of infiltration by new blood into its ranks. It is with this aspect that their book is primarily concerned. The justification for approaching it by counting country houses is that the ownership of such a property is seen as an essential qualification for membership of the local landed élite from which the national ruling class was recruited. To make the project of manageable proportions (and it has taken them twenty years even so), the Stones have studied country houses and their owners in three carefully-chosen English counties: Hertfordshire, which was so close to London that it felt the pulse and pull of the great metropolis from the earliest times; Northamptonshire, which was in the depths of the country, a stable, rustic, isolated county; and Northumberland, which was as far as possible from London, and also semi-industrial, with coal mining and ship building centred on Newcastle. In each case, the local élites are exceptionally well documented, and between them these counties encompassed the widest possible variety of economic and social experience.

The Stones begin their study with the owners rather than the houses, by describing the strategies of marriage and inheritance evolved by established families to preserve their property and position. For any élite family, they argue, the great aim was to perpetuate their name, their titles (if any), their house, their heirlooms and their lands, and to keep them together. But such desires were constantly threatened by the hazards of biological failure, especially in the century from 1650, when the combination of reduced nuptiality, declining fertility and rising mortality brought about a major élite demographic crisis, which remains difficult to explain. Indeed, for the whole of the period from the sixteenth to the nineteenth century, most families were unable to transfer their inheritance from father to son in regular sequence for more than one hundred years. And yet, despite all this, the sale of a country house was an extremely rare event. If there was no direct male heir, there were usually distant male cousins to carry on the line, and if even this failed, there was always indirect inheritance through the female line which, combined with substitution or hyphenation of surnames, gave the impression of unbroken descent in the male line. As a result, most seats and principal estates remained unsold for centuries; there was 'an extraordinary degree of family continuity'; and the opportunities for self-made men to buy their way in were correspondingly limited.

Put another way, this meant that the number of owners who obtained their country houses by purchase rather than by inheritance was never more than a tiny proportion of the total. The popular picture of venerable country families overcome by disaster, and heartbrokenly selling house and land to some thrusting and acquisitive parvenu is simply not borne out by the Stones' figures. What is more, of those few who *did* buy in, the majority were lawyers, military men, government office holders, great London merchants and retired Indian nabobs, rather than manufacturers, industrialists and entrepreneurs as conventionally understood. Even in Hertfordshire, so close to London, there were never enough self-made purchasers to swamp the old and durable landed élite, and further away from the great metropolis, the newcomers were even less significant. No single Birmingham businessman bought his way into nearby Northamptonshire in 340 years, and in Northumberland, the county's industrial development from the eighteenth century had little effect on élite composition. What is more, and again contrary to popular belief, the few men who did buy their way in tended not to stay. Far from founding family dynasties to perpetuate their names, it was the purchasers of country houses, rather than the inheritors, who were the most likely to sell out.

So much for the owners: what of their houses? As Noel Coward once explained, the stately homes of England were built to prove the upper classes had still the upper hand. As such, they were multi-functional monstrosities: symbols of dignity and authority, centres of power and administration, and pleasure domes for sport, recreation and leisure. In terms of style, the Stones trace the evolution of country-house architecture from Jacobethan asymmetry through Palladian restraint to Victorian profusion. In terms of setting, they discuss the demise of the geometrical Elizabethan garden and the eighteenth-century rise of the picturesque. In terms of function, they stress the growth of privacy, made possible by the development of the corridor and the construction of separate quarters for the servants. In terms of scale, they show that, on average, country houses were becoming bigger throughout their period of investigation: indeed, between 1540 and 1840, they were undoubtedly the largest, most complex and most expensive buildings put up in the country. And in terms of construction, they discern three major phases: from the 1570s to the 1610s, when the great prodigy houses like Hatfield and Audley End were put up for royal accommodation; from the 1680s to the 1720s, when the Whig oligarchy was establishing itself in power and in its power houses; and the century from the 1780s, when the growth of servants and segregation required massive extensions, although rarely completely new building.

This examination of country houses and their owners makes it possible for the Stones to provide the first long-term historical profile of the landed élite as the ruling class of England. It was created and consolidated between 1540 and 1660, an amalgam of survivors from the late medieval nobility, of Tudor and early Stuart men of business like the Cecils, of local squires and gentry quietly extending their holdings, and of occasional men from trade, the law and the armed forces buying their way in. By 1660, this landed élite was established, and for the next hundred years, its power, influence and self-assurance were so great that it turned in on itself, preferring pleasure and leisure to work or office-holding. Then in the late eighteenth century, there was a revival of the ethos of service to the state, and a massive expansion of landed participation in politics and local government. But at no time was there much intrusion or penetration from the new rich. They were rarely wealthy enough and, in London as much as in the great provincial capitals, opulent merchants preferred to keep them-selves to themselves rather than set up as country gentry. Indeed, in the century after the Industrial Revolution, which offered an entirely new way for self-made men to make money, the landed élite became *more* closed and caste-like than ever. Less than ten per cent of all major landowners in 1870 were newcomers since 1780, and only a tiny fraction of them were industrialists. So, the Stones triumphantly conclude: 'the traditional concept of an open élite – open to large scale infiltration by merchant wealth – is dead'.

This leaves them, however, with two problems. The first is to explain the longevity of the myth of an open élite: how, when manifestly wrong, has it survived so tenaciously and ubiqui-tously? Partly, they suggest, because a few atypical examples were given undue prominence, and partly because endless repetition gave it such credibility that it took on a life of its own regardless of the facts. The second problem, more difficult and more im-portant, is to explain the survival, not of the myth, but of the élite itself: if not because of constant renewal, then how? Partly, the Stones argue, because the amount of movement in English society was much lower than is often supposed: instead of being rejuven-ated by self-made men frequently moving in, the élite was rein-forced precisely because there were so few who could or did.

Partly, too, it endured because the élite was very good at keeping going, regardless of the economic, political, social or demographic crises which threatened it: in family matters, it steered a safe and sensible course between the dangers of profligacy and parsimony; in social relations it trod a narrow path between excessive generosity and unacceptable ruthlessness; and in political affairs, it struck exactly the right balance between being too grasping and too concessional. And partly it continued because the lower and middle classes were captivated, not by the territorial, but by the *cultural* embrace of the landowners: they wanted all the trappings of gentility without the land, and that is what they got. So the élite survived, more rigid than renewed. As the Stones put it: 'if the concept of *"histoire immobile"* is applicable to any sector of English society, the landed élite is the most promising candidate'.

Have they got it right? Certainly, there is a considerable amount of circumstantial support for the Stones' thesis. For example, all of the profound consequences which were taken to flow from the supposed open élite have themselves been increasingly questioned in recent years. The whole notion of heroic agricultural improvers, largely recruited from the ranks of recently established landowners, who thus retained their profit-maximizing instincts, is now under attack. The idea that thrusting entrepreneurs, men of humble social origins, anxious to achieve the ultimate social goal of landed respectability, were the creators of the Industrial Revolution, is also much less fashionable than it once was. The growth of English political stability, at least for the century after 1688, has for some time been explained in terms of a closed oligarchy rather than an open élite. And the picture of late nineteenth-century economic decline, resulting from absentee and incompetent businessmen, besotted with the pleasures of country-house life, now seems altogether too crude to convince. In short, since the four riders have already very largely quit the paradigm, perhaps it is time the paradigm itself was dispensed with as well.

Nevertheless, this act of historical demolition inevitably means that other scholars get hit by some of the falling masonry. Historians of seventeenth-century country communities are rebuked for giving insufficient attention to other, competing foci of loyalty; E. P. Thompson is chided for ignoring the middle classes in his analysis of eighteenth-century society; Harold Perkin's picture of early nineteenth-century landowners as irresponsible and self-absorbed is totally rejected; and Mark Girouard is taken to task for overestimating the amount of new country-house building which took place in the Victorian period. But in a very real sense, the most sustained and significant victim of this book seems to be Lawrence Stone himself, not only because (as he handsomely admits) he had previously accepted uncritically the myth of the open élite, but also because the subject and substance of this work is oddly at variance with the kind of history he has written before. 'If history is not concerned with change', Stone once wrote, 'it is nothing.' Yet here is a book entirely devoted to continuity. The massive crisis of the aristocracy which Stone previously discerned in the late sixteenth and early seventeenth centuries now seems but a ripple on an essentially calm surface. The Civil War, hitherto depicted by Stone as the first modern revolution, a cataclysmic event in the making of our world, gets barely a mention. And his three-stage model of élite family revolution seems to have precious little bearing on the sinews and substance of élite survival. Viewed from the top, very little seems to have happened in England between the Reformation and the onset of the Agricultural Depression at the end of the nineteenth century.

Ironically, this is a very Eltonian conclusion to have reached by very non-Eltonian methods. And the similarity of their views (which, of course, neither of them will ever admit) should at once put us on our guard against accepting this argument too uncritically. For this book does have its problems and its pitfalls. Those who regard Lawrence Stone's statistics as by definition suspect will not be reassured by the uncertainties, conjectures, assumptions and subjective judgments which have of necessity gone into the collection and processing of the data. And those who believe that Cliometrics is the be-all and end-all of history will be equally disquieted by the authors' candid admission that 'the intellectual production of this book failed to make full use of the most up-to-date computer technology'. More prosaically, the brief

discussion of bourgeois self-perception seems altogether too impressionistic to be conclusive. It is simply ridiculous to dismiss
Lord Liverpool, Tory Prime Minister from 1812 to 1827, as an
'arch-reactionary', as any perusal of the most elementary text
book on nineteenth-century English history would have shown.
One is also bound to wonder how far these findings would have
been modified by a different or broader sample. Would there have
been so few industrialists buying in if Lancashire or Yorkshire or
Staffordshire had been chosen? And, since the myth of the open
élite is customarily held to apply to *Britain* and not just England, it
would be interesting to know whether studies of Welsh, Scottish
or Irish counties would corroborate their conclusions.

There are also some more fundamental problems about concepts and counting. The central assumption of this book is that the
owners of the country houses were the ruling élite: to study their
homes is to study the people. At first sight, this seems both
operationally understandable and eminently plausible. But in fact
it depends on getting satisfactory answers to two crucial questions: what is a country house? and did the country house owners
own the land? It is possible, for instance, that some of the authors'
conclusions might have been substantially modified if more small
houses had been included. And at one point in the book, the
authors seem to be dealing with members of the élite who owned
at least 3,000 acres, when it would have been more realistic to have
included all owners of 1,000 acres and above. It is, after all, at the
very edge of the landed élite that interaction with self-made men
was most marked, which means that the exact level at which the
line is drawn is crucial. It may be that in this book it has been
drawn too high. Finally, after all the graphs and tables and pages of
computer printout, it still remains a little unclear just how novel
this book's argument actually is. At the end of it all, we are left
with a middle class which was beguiled, deferential and assimi-
lated; with a few men of affairs and even fewer men of business
who bought their way into the ranks of the élite; and with an élite
itself which was resourceful, resilient and adaptable. As the Stones
coyly admit in their conclusion, what their book really boils down
to is not that there was no open élite in England, but rather that

there has been a fundamental misperception of what an open élite actually means.

There is, then, much more work to be done in the light of this book; which is no doubt precisely what the Stones intended. For what is really impressive and important about *An Open Elite?* is the authors' breadth and bravery in taking on the whole of post-medieval English history. The sheer cleverness of the original idea; the energy and virtuosity displayed in collecting and computing the data; the ingenuity with which the study of country houses and their owners is made to prise open a much larger and more important historical problem: all this compels and commands admiration and applause. Arcane and technical subjects like strict settlement and demography are infused with life, relevance and interest. The mass of data, which in lesser hands would have made for a boring read, is brilliantly presented, and is constantly illuminated and enlivened with well-chosen examples and case studies. The organization of the book into parts, chapters and sections, simply could not be bettered. At the very least, *An Open Elite?* provides the first quantitative basis for analysing the landed classes of England in their years of wealth, power and glory. More broadly, it is offered as a major reassessment of the social, political and economic history of England since the Reformation. Either way, it is the most important, exciting and original book on the English landed élite to have appeared since *The Crisis of the Aristocracy*. And there can be no higher praise than that.

(1984)

NOTE:
1. Lawrence Stone and Jeanne C. Fawtier Stone, *An Open Elite?: England, 1540–1880* (Oxford, 1984).

# PART FOUR

# GENERALITY

# Time

As someone once said, although we do not know exactly when, time is of the essence. It can be given or taken, saved or spent, borrowed or beaten, kept or killed. There are old timers and egg timers, time bombs and time tables, time signals and time machines. There is half time and fuii time, short time and over time, standard time and local time, the best of times and the worst of times. There is a time to be born and a time to die, a time to break down and a time to build up, a time to reap and a time to sow. There is the time of your life and time out of mind; there is peace in our time and there are times of troubles; there is no time like the present and there are times that try men's souls. Time cures all things yet it corrodes all things; it flies never to return but creeps along with leaden feet; it is on our side although it waits for no man. As Gollum explained to Bilbo in one of the few plausible pages of *The Hobbit*, there is a lot of it about:

> *This thing all things devours:*
> *Birds, beasts, trees, flowers;*
> *Gnaws iron, bites steel;*
> *Grinds hard stones to meal;*
> *Slays king, ruins town,*
> *And beats high mountain down.*

But if time is of the essence, what is the essence of time? 'I know what time is,' St Augustine said, 'but if someone asks me, I cannot tell him.' Physicists and philosophers have much the same problem: when pressed for time, they have no easy answer. Nor do historians. But they *do* have a powerful sense, if not of its nature, at least of its passing. Whether narrative or analysis, a multi-volume epic or a terse and trenchant article, all works of history implicitly begin with the words 'once upon a time'. For historians, any particular event, person, work of art or scientific discovery, is time bound and time specific. In that sense, as Goethe explained, historians serve 'the clock whose hands are forever stopped'. But since history is also a story, an unfolding process, one damned thing after another, it is equally important to get these damned things in the correct order, to know which came first in the womb of time, the chicken or the egg. The description, analysis and explanation of events, in time and over time, is the historian's main task, and the ability to use the time dimension skilfully and perceptively distinguishes the good historian from the bad. *Pace* H. G. Wells and Dr Who, it is historians who are the first and foremost time travellers: for them, 'Time, gentlemen, please' is not so much a publican's exhortation as a scholarly injunction.

Yet although history is largely a matter of time, the history of time itself has been remarkably little studied. The concept of time may be hard to grasp, but the measurement and perception of it have been fundamental to all civilizations, and especially to Western Europe, the most time-conscious society of all time. Along with the stirrup, gunpowder and the printing press, the mechanical clock ranks as one of the great inventions in the history of mankind, with momentous economic, social, political and cultural consequences. Yet neither the artifact nor its impact has received much historical attention. Now, in two splendid and complementary books, the first attempt has been made to rectify these omissions.[1] In a characteristically versatile display of cultural, technological and economic history, David Landes looks at the evolution of the clock as a machine, and at the triumph of public time as a discipline. And in an exceptionally wide-ranging foray into intellectual history, Stephen Kern explores the ways in which private notions of time (and space) were profoundly altered and extended in the thirty years before the First World War. The scope of these books is very different: one straddles the centuries; the other delves into decades. But between them, they make the history of time tick as it has never ticked before.

★

The first panel of Landes's timely triptych considers why mechanical clocks were invented in Europe rather than China, where the auguries were in many ways so much better. In medieval times, China was the undisputed scientific and horological leader; master craftsmen like Su Sung built splendid and elaborate water clocks between the tenth and twelfth centuries; and yet the next obvious step, the construction of weight-driven, mechanical clocks, was one which the Chinese resolutely refused to take. Quite simply, Landes suggests, there was no demand: the Chinese did not need time badly enough to measure it precisely. The workers who laboured in the fields regulated their lives by the rhythms of nature; and the Imperial Court was more concerned to track the movement of the heavenly bodies than to measure the passing of earthly time. Calendar dates might matter: but hours and minutes did not. In Europe, by contrast, they did: first in the monasteries, where the services had to be said on time, night and day, hour by hour; and then in the towns, where there was no natural sequence of tasks to provide the rhythm of the day. So, unlike China, the West needed pervasive, public time: with the clock as with everything else, necessity was the mother of invention.

Thus was the mechanical clock invented: how was it perfected? Between the fifteenth and the nineteenth centuries, it evolved from being massive, crude, weight-driven and highly approximate in performance, into the compact, portable, dependable, precise and sophisticated clock or watch. In retrospect, this development seems clear and inevitable: each improvement posed new challenges by bringing to the fore problems which had previously been relatively small enough to be neglected. But at the time, the competing claims of greater miniaturization and more elaborate ornamentation remained strong; the search for greater precision only slowly came to dominate invention and development; and even then there were many false trails and blind alleys. Landes's account of coiled springs, pendulums, minute and second hands, and jewelled bearings makes fascinating reading, and is peppered with a rich array of crackpot ideas, unscrupulous plagiarists, disputes about priority, unhonoured genius and the like. The path to true time did not run straight or smooth.

In the final, and largest, section of his book, Landes considers the making and manufacture of clocks in the seven-hundred-year period which extends from invention to obsolescence. He follows the clock-making coterie across Europe, from Italy to Germany to France to England and Geneva and then on to the Swiss Jura where, despite strong American challenges from the mid-nineteenth century onwards, productive pre-eminence remained for as long as the clock continued to be the best way of telling the time. Of all these shifts in production location that Landes describes, the most interesting took place in the early nineteenth century, when the British, who had been supreme clock-makers for nearly a hundred years, yielded pride of place to the Swiss. Landes's account of British decline has a dismal and contemporary ring to it: high costs, conservative styling, obsolescent techniques, entrepreneurial complacency and resistance by labour to innovation. But the reasons for the sustained and spectacular success of the Swiss are less easy to discover. Culture and religion no doubt had a great deal to do with it, but as the author admits, there is no easy or simple explanation. Perhaps Glynis Johns came nearest to the truth when she allegedly remarked: 'I think the Swiss have sublimated their sense of time into watch-making.' For a century and a half, they remained supreme at their craft, and when they were undone, it was not by rival manufacturers of better or cheaper clocks, but by the quartz revolution: when the ticking had to stop.

Admirers of Professor Landes's work will have no difficulty in recognizing all his hallmarks in this book. There is the tone of cosmopolitan sophistication, of a man at ease in the auction rooms, galleries and universities of the western world; the sure mastery of the history and languages of most European countries; the ability to write of technology, machinery and gadgetry with authority, enthusiasm and finesse; the unshakable belief that cultural values are a prime determinant of entrepreneurial and hence economic performance; and a resolute scepticism about the determinist theories which underpin so much of the recent New Economic History. Throughout its pages, the text scintillates with wise and witty aphorisms: 'fashion abhors bulges'; 'there is no better way to consign something to oblivion than to put it in a *Festschrift*'; 'nothing has more power to stir French genius than the prospect of beating the English'; 'the essence of every con game is the victim's eagerness to get something for nothing.' The evocation of eighteenth-century London as a great maritime and commercial capital is beautifully done; and the mock-heroic account of 'The Case of the Cryptic Clock' could not be bettered. Early in his account, Landes notes that clocks are the product of 'ingenuity, craftsmanship, artistry and elegance': so is this book.

There are, of course, difficulties. As Landes candidly admits, his book is 'only a prologue', and cannot avoid some of the pitfalls of the pioneer. The early chapters in both the first and second sections, which deal with the medieval world, are necessarily very speculative. The author writes with such assurance that it all sounds extremely plausible: but much of it is little more than inspired conjecture. Of necessity, too, the vocabulary is often very technical: constant talk of clepsydras, escapements, gear trains and oscillatory motion becomes a trifle wearisome. And sentences like 'the atomic clocks of the national observatories use quartz crystal oscillators with frequencies of some 2.5 megacycles per second, checked by cesium-beamed resonators vibrating at 9,192,631,770 ± 20 cycles per second,' are not easy to assimilate. Above all, this is very much a supply-side story: about invention, technology and entrepreneurship. This is probably the only way the subject can be realistically handled; but it would be good to know more about who bought the clocks and watches, and why. In the end, it seems to come down to our old friends the triumphant middle classes, who would never have risen without the clock. And, although there is much on the culture that produced the clock, there is less on the impact of the clock on culture. The diffusion of time awareness throughout society and around the world still awaits extended treatment.

In one sense, Landes's book ends on what for him is obviously a sombre note – the demise of the clock as the supreme means of measuring time. But in another, it is more of a success story, which finishes with the triumph of time: public and uniform, universal and irresistible. Clocks may stop, but time goes on. Indeed, since the late nineteenth century, local time has been inexorably killed, as global time has become all-conquering. In 1883, largely under pressure from the railway companies, the United States adopted a system of time zones. In the following thirty years, World Standard Time was established virtually throughout the globe, with Greenwich universally recognized as the noughth meridian. No wonder the demand for clocks, so largely met by the Swiss, was unprecedented. But this was not the only development on the time front that took place in these years. For, as Stephen Kern is at pains to point out, the very period which saw the establishment of public time brought about a reaction in thinking about private time (and space). As the measurement of time became more public and precise, so the perception of time became more private and pluralistic. Not for nothing did Conrad's secret agent set out to blow up the Greenwich Observatory, the supreme symbol of standard time.

Perception of past time, for instance, was fundamentally transformed in the three decades before the First World War. The development of the phonograph and the cinema meant that the past was no longer something finished, separate and discrete, but actively persisted into the present in a new and immediate way. There was also a reaction against the public past of history towards the private past of the mind. It was there that Freud sought the sources of individual neuroses; he stressed the crucial importance of childhood experience in influencing later life; and he argued that all subsequent experiences, too, left traces in the mind that shaped future responses. In an allied manner, Proust explored the preservation of the past in our bodies in the form of memory, which only needed some apparently random stimulus to awaken it. For Proust, as for Freud, the personal, private past was both good and important: they disagreed as to whether it could be rediscovered by active or passive means, but they were at one in seeing it as the best way to a happy future. Others were not so sure: Nietzsche and Ibsen saw the past as bad and burdensome, as did Joyce, who, in *Ulysses*, argued that history was the nightmare from which Stephen was trying to awake. There was, in short, no consensus about the past inside your head – except that it mattered more than the past anywhere else.

As the past was privatized and explored, so perceptions of the present underwent changes. The wireless telegraph, the telephone and the cinema all extended the present spatially, making possible simultaneity of experience across distance, most famously illustrated in the sinking of the *Titanic*, where many people far removed from the scene were able to experience the disaster directly, at first hand, as it happened. In the creative arts, the same development in public time was privately investigated through simultaneous poetry and music, and most famously in Joyce's more advanced books, which were montages of many simultaneous events rather than in traditional narrative form. The present was also extended temporally, as its sharp edges were blurred and its brief duration was lengthened, to include parts of the past and fragments of the future. Philosophers debated the nature and duration of what we experience as 'now'; Virginia Woolf explored in her novels heightened moments of the extended present; and the cinema 'thickened' the present into slow time, by prising open and expanding particular moments and events. The present ceased to be ephemeral and instantaneous, and merged imperceptibly into the flowing stream of time.

Both the past and the present were publicly extended and privately examined and the same was true of the future. In some ways, it was incorporated into the global present; in others, it was explored individually, imaginatively and intuitively. The whole pace of life speeded up: trains and steamships went faster than ever before; bicycles, cars, trams and aeroplanes enhanced the inexorable sense of speed; business transactions were more rapid, thanks to the telephone and the telegraph; and the cinema was an appropriately dynamic art-form to reflect and record this new dynamic age. Imperialism was another way of rushing forward, as politicians saw in it a way of 'pegging out claims for the future'. More privately and less acquisitively, the next world was explored artistically and poetically in the works of the Futurists, while H. G. Wells speculated on what might happen next in a string of Science Fiction novels: *The Time Machine*, *Anticipations*, *The Shape of Things to Come*. Most of these prophets viewed the future with enthusiasm. But not all: Spengler gazed into the future with as much pessimism as Ibsen peered into the past.

So it is not easy to generalize. But Kern's essential point stands out: in the late nineteenth and early twentieth centuries, even as public time coalesced, private time fragmented. The one became more absolute, while the other became more relative. And this is only part of the story: for there were similar and simultaneous changes in perceptions of space as well. The demise of Euclidean geometry and the rise of relativity meant that, spatially as well as temporally, nothing was absolute any more. Matter was no longer either stable or separate: X-rays could pierce it, and what they showed suggested it was no different from void. The new technology killed remoteness: national boundaries were crossed by planes; the telephone pierced privacy; the global village was at hand. The first space-invaders were earth-bound not extraterrestrial: the last frontier was closed in the United States; Africa was partitioned; nowhere was remote any more. Art reflected this, or developed unawares along parallel lines: there was a multiplication of points of view, and after the Cubists, homogeneous three-dimensional space was never the same again. Space, like time, was everywhere in flux.

From all this to the First World War was but a short step, well illustrated by the crisis of July 1914. The telegraph and the telephone so accelerated the pace of events that there was no opportunity, as in the old days, for delay to wield its ameliorating influence. In other ways, too, the nations involved were obsessed with time: members of the Entente, secure in their national pasts, looked to the future with guarded optimism; but the newer nations of the Alliance felt much less at ease. Appropriately, Europe rushed headlong into war, amidst a flurry of telephones, telegrams and timetables – ragtime on a grand scale. As with its origins, so with its actuality, the war was largely about time. In some ways, it homogenized it: there was no scope for private time; synchronized operations were the order of the day; every soldier needed a watch. But in other ways, it changed time out of all recognition. Life at the Front seemed so utterly bizarre that there was no connection whatsoever between it and what had gone before: the present and the past were completely separate. And so were the present and the future: here and now was all that there was; death was just around the corner; perhaps Spengler had been right all along.

This exciting book brims with ideas and insights, evidence and examples, and provides the most comprehensive account of the life of the mind in these crucial decades before the First World War, when so much of our modern civilization was formed and fashioned. Kern's command of art and literature, painting and architecture, philosophy and psychology, physics and technology, is astonishing: he moves from Proust to Picasso, Einstein to Stravinsky, with consummate ease and unquenchable enthusiasm. Unavoidably, in a book of such ambitious scope, there are sins of omission and commission. There should have been something, for instance, on the rise, dissemination and impact of professional history, of that public past against which the proponents and explorers of the private past were allegedly reacting. And the chapters on the First World War, although they round off the book well, do not always seem consistent with, or relevant to, some of what has gone before. The stress on homogenous time, for instance, seems to contradict much of the earlier discussion on the growth and proliferation of private time; while the discussion of how the major combatants viewed the past, the present and the future seems neither fully convincing nor wholly relevant.

In truth, the period Kern treats was so complex, creative and bewildering that no single book, however accomplished, can do full justice to it. Here, on occasions, the great names rush by at such frenzied speed that it is hard to take it all in. The attempts to relate public and private time, time and space, culture and technology, do not always come off: the developments were not always in the same direction, and it is not always clear what, if any, were the connections. Above all, one must ask just how many people, even in the West, let alone the rest of the world, were really influenced, in this period, by the developments Kern describes. How many ordinary people read Freud, heard Stravinsky, used the telephone, or went flying? For the majority of people between the years 1880 and 1914, it was probably the triumph of Landes's public time, rather than the fragmentation of Kern's private time, which was the more remarkable and all-pervasive development. Many of the changes of which he writes did not make a major impact on western society as a whole until the interwar years at the earliest, and reached the third world much later still. But for most people, the things of which Kern writes were more the shape of things to come than the way we live now: another time, perhaps.

No one who has read these two fascinating books will be left in any doubt as to the daunting difficulties involved in writing the history of time. Clearly, measurement of it is one thing; perception of it quite another. The history of public time leads inexorably in one direction; that of private time proceeds along a bewildering variety of contradictory paths. The treatment of time by thinkers and inventors, scientists and entrepreneurs, is relatively easy to deal with: but the diffusion of time, the adoption of its discipline by the majority of people, is much less easy to pin down. Such is the whirligig of time which Landes and Kern have sought to slow and study, bringing together history and horology, Clio and the clock, in two pioneer works which will surely stand the test of time. They deserve a big hand (and perhaps a little hand too).

(1984)

NOTE:
1. David Landes, *Revolution in Time: Clocks and the Making of the Modern World* (London, 1984); Stephen Kern, *The Culture of Time and Space, 1880–1918* (London, 1983).

# Sex

'Historically,' Karl Marx once wrote, 'the bourgeoisie has played a most important part.' Indeed, there was a period in historical writing, roughly coincidental with the first half of the twentieth century, when it seemed to play virtually the *only* part, credited as it often was with most of the major developments in the making of the modern world: from the growth of towns, the decline of feudalism, and the waning of the Middle Ages, via the Renaissance, the Reformation, and the scientific revolution, the consolidation of absolutist states, the English civil war and the Enlightenment, the Industrial, the American, and the French Revolutions, to 1848, the new imperialism and the growth of bad taste, and beyond. No wonder the middle classes were the ever-rising soufflé of history: they had a great deal to be rising about. Having travelled hopefully and arrived punctually at some crucial time and place in the unfolding historical drama, they did what they were supposed to do, and then moved onwards to the next engagement. Whenever history needed a helping hand, the middle classes were always there, ready, willing, and able to provide it.

Today it all looks rather different. Whatever the middle classes were doing in the past, there is a widespread belief that they are no longer rising now, and since their contemporary circumstances give increased cause for anxiety, so the easy certainties and confident generalizations made about their trajectory and their accomplishments in previous centuries have in turn been eroded and undermined. After two decades of intense and sceptical scholarship, it is no longer fashionable to believe that all historical change must be explained by the movements of social classes, and the middle class of Marx has been the most significant casualty of this shift in historical thinking. Figures once eagerly recruited into the burgeoning bourgeois fold, all the way from Queen Elizabeth I to Queen Victoria, are now more usefully and realistically placed in other categories. At best, many historians now maintain that the middle classes may indeed have risen, but they never really got to the top. And at worst, the once-triumphant bourgeoisie has been relegated into an inert, residual category: the history of the people with the patricians and the plebs left out, and everyone else left in. What was once the motor of historical change has now become the trash can of historical taxonomy.

For the nineteenth century, Marx's century, the picture of a triumphant bourgeoisie was painted first and challenged last. But even here, the safe citadel of middle-class supremacy has been undermined from without and eroded from within by recent scholarship. For Britain and Germany in particular, and more speculatively for Europe as a whole, it has become increasingly fashionable to argue that, however hopefully the nineteenth-century bourgeoisie was travelling, it never actually arrived. Internally divided, and insufficiently self-conscious, it failed to achieve economic pre-eminence as a class, social dominance as a status group, or supreme power as a political movement. A petty clerk like Mr Pooter and a bloated financier like Augustus Melmotte might both share the designation 'bourgeois,' but as the qualifications 'petite' and 'haute' implied, they shared very little else. Capitalist did not equal bourgeois, because the former antedated the latter; nor did entrepreneur, because many middle-class men were not in business but in the professions or government service. As Peter Gay candidly (if coyly) observes at the outset of his fascinating book, there was no such thing as a typical bourgeois: the unscrupulous entrepreneur, the ingenious engineer, the timid grocer, and the pedantic bureaucrat could all be sheltered beneath the very umbrella that was itself a misleading symbol of a spuriously uniform bourgeois culture.[1]

Such candour is an agreeable, if not altogether auspicious, way for Peter Gay to begin what promises to be one of the major historical enterprises of the decade, a five-volume history of the nineteenth-century bourgeois cultural experience. Not surprisingly, after offering these important introductory disclaimers, he adroitly sidesteps such contentious and unpromising topics as class formation, economic characteristics, and political accomplishments. For the nineteenth-century bourgeoisie that Gay seeks to put back at the centre of modern history is not that of Marx, but of Freud. Drawing extensively on private diaries and family correspondence, medical texts and household manuals, religious tracts and works of art, from Britain, France, Germany, and the United States, he aims to investigate the part played by sexuality, aggression and conflict in the middle-class experience from the early nineteenth century to the First World War. In this particular book sexuality is at the centre (with love, we are told, to follow in the second volume). Here he is concerned with the middle classes as dreamers rather than as doers, in bedroom and bathroom rather than in boardroom or bourse. Boldly going where (almost) no historian has gone before, he takes us on a voyage of erotic exploration, into the private world, private lives and private parts of the nineteenth century's most private class.

The result is a book which should offend puritan moralists and conservative historians in approximately equal numbers. Those who condemn fashionable or faddish scholarship, who regard psychohistory as megabunk, will find much to accelerate their pulse rates here. As if to forestall such criticisms, Gay argues that this is not so much a work of psychohistory as of history informed by psychoanalysis. But this is a fine and improbable distinction: a work that seeks to explore the inaccessible domains of the nineteenth-century unconscious, and the inner recesses of bourgeois erotic fantasy, is surely psychohistory if it is anything. And it is undeniably couched in the language of the couch: 'her transfigured incestuous investment had extensive cultural reverberations,' etc., etc. Beyond doubt, Gay lays bare not only the mind, but also the body of the nineteenth-century bourgeoisie as never before. This is not just a history of *mentalité* but of *sensualité* as well. In more than four hundred closely packed pages, we are taken on a breathless, steamy tour of castration complexes, Oedipal traumas, penis envy, and wet dreams, not forgetting erections and excrement, ovaries and orgasms, masturbation and menstruation, prostitutes and pornography. For the prude, this book will be distressing; for the prurient, it will be irresistible. Either way, Clio and the clitoris have never been so close.

The serious and scholarly purpose of this work is to investigate how the Victorians – mainly English and American – went about discovering sexuality for themselves, what they knew about it and what they repressed, and how outside pressures and experiences impinged upon their erotic lives. More polemically, the book is conceived as a weighty and explicit corrective to the popular and tenacious misconceptions concerning Victorian sexuality – the 'dominant, derisive, little-challenged perceptions' that have prevailed for so long. One of these is the belief that middle-class Victorian men were devious and insensitive hypocrites, who presented to the world the image of good family men, but who in private satisfied their lusts by keeping mistresses, frequenting brothels, or molesting children. Another is that middle-class Victorian wives were competent housekeepers, doting mothers, and erotic disasters, who preferred saucepans to sex, and directed all their love and warmth into housekeeping and child rearing. Terrified, ignorant, and unsuspecting, they were reputedly given the advice on their wedding night to 'Grit your teeth and think of England.'

But Gay accepts none of this. 'The nineteenth-century middle-class wife who pours all her affection into her children and denies her husband all sexual warmth,' is, he insists, 'largely a myth', derived not from the experiences of women themselves, but from the writings of a few moralists, like Dr William Acton, whose books misled many nineteenth-century readers and many twentieth-century historians. Gay, by contrast, begins with a fascinating case study, based on the late-nineteenth-century diary of Mabel Loomis Todd, who not only had a good time in bed with her husband, but also conducted (with his active connivance) an ecstatic affair for over a decade with Austin Dickinson, the treasurer of Amherst College and brother of Emily Dickinson. Nor was she alone among bourgeois women in her enjoyment of sex. Another half-dozen cases yield similar conclusions, and these are more widely corroborated by material drawn from some late-nineteenth-century surveys of female sexuality, Kinsey Reports before Kinsey. Accordingly, the conclusion seems clear: a high proportion of middle-class women enjoyed sex, took pleasure in marital sexuality, and regarded it as a healthy and wholesome pursuit. That works of nineteenth-century literature argued to the contrary merely shows the wide gap that can separate experience and expression. And of course, it was Freud who bridged it, by formulating the view that women were sexually as alive and passionate as men.

Viewed in this light, male blustering about nineteenth-century sex can be seen at last for what it really was: not a description of female frigidity, but a symptom of male anxiety about sex and male fear of women. Throughout history, women have been depicted by men as evil, powerful, mysterious temptresses, all the way from Eve in the Garden of Eden to Alexis in the episodes of *Dynasty*. Men never recover from their early and total dependence on their mothers, or from their fear of castration by voracious vaginas. Woman as vampire, man as victim is a well-known stereotype, which was given added force in the nineteenth century as women made real and successful attempts to improve their sexual and secular circumstances by divorce-law reform, the campaign for the vote, the expansion of jobs, and the extension of educational opportunities. In public and in private, Gay concludes, nineteenth-century women were a threat, and in this war of the sexes, the man had to retaliate. One riposte was to try to keep them out of higher education, ostensibly because the tensions of menstruation meant that they were not up to the physical and mental demands of university life, but in reality in the hope of keeping them in their 'proper' calling: the home. Another was to deny women any erotic desires, which effectively meant that the man was good enough in bed however well or badly he performed. In view of these reactions, the contemporary literature that claimed that women did not enjoy sex can be seen for what it really was: not as a description of women's experience, but as a buttress for threatened male egos. In bed or out of it, the man must be kept on top.

What does all this add up to? Nineteenth-century bourgeois attitudes, Gay argues, were formed towards sexuality by the interplay of the public domain of discussion and the sheltered sphere of personal life. In public, there was indeed much reticence and circumlocution, just as in private there was much sexual pleasure and satisfaction. But this does not make the Victorians self-conscious hypocrites, saying one thing (that sex was bad for your health) and doing the other (enjoying it even so). On the contrary, Gay suggests that the 'fortifications of the self' which the nineteenth-century bourgeoisie constructed were not to *deny* sensuality, but to provide a haven, a shelter, where sexuality might be enjoyed and where modern romantic love could flower. For the Victorians, sex was to be between consenting adults in private. Repression, reticence, reserve, and 'hypocrisy' were the means whereby space was created for the bourgeoisie to live out their private, sensual lives. The middle classes cultivated their passions, like their gardens, behind high walls.

As Gay generously acknowledges, much of this argument, especially as it concerns the sexual potentialities and performances of middle-class Victorian women, has been made before, and it is a pity that he seems more concerned to traverse this old ground than to open up new territory. Much space, for example, is lavished on analysing women's sexuality; but the erotic lives and needs of men receive rather less attention. If, as the author implies, the majority of middle-class men were either insecure or tender, or both, then who actually read the pornography or visited the prostitutes, which were such an all-pervasive part of the Victorian world? Nor are the chronological divisions as finely drawn or convincingly explained as they might be. We are told that there is a fundamental change in bourgeois attitudes during the second half of the nineteenth century. But since most of the material is culled from this later phase, it is rather difficult to see how things differed earlier, or how they changed thereafter. Nor is it clear how a bourgeois attitude came into being in the first place, or how or when middle-class women lost the ground (what ground?) that Gay claims they were trying to regain since the 1870s. And there is a sense in which this all appears as a teleological tale, showing that the history of the bourgeoisie leads inexorably to Freud and the women's movement. Perhaps it does; perhaps it should. But it all seems a little too neat for comfort. In writing about sex, it is probably better to be Whiggish than priggish; but it is arguably best of all to be neither.

Having looked at the unconscious as an influence on middle-class sexual conduct and sexual politics, Gay turns, in the middle section of his book, to consider how the pressures of the real world liberated or limited sexual practices and attitudes. Pregnancy, for example, was an ordeal and a danger for middle-class mothers throughout the nineteenth century. Despite all the cant about the need to fulfil women's maternal urges, childbirth was always painful and often fatal, to the mother, the child, or both, and this necessarily detracted from the pleasures of sex, as that instrument of life could become an instrument of death. For much of the nineteenth century, too, the deaths of young children were commonplace in middle-class families: biology was destiny, to be accepted with submission and resignation. Only in its closing decades did the improvement in contraceptive methods bring some sense of mastery over the natural world, as the age of control superseded the age of conscience. But even this was an ambiguous gift, and Gay finds its impact on bourgeois sexuality hard to assess. In some ways, it diminished middle-class freedom, as sex became more self-conscious and guilt-ridden. But in others, it enabled middle-class couples to avoid biology's most stringent decrees while enjoying its most delicious gifts.

As all this implies, the Victorian bourgeoisie's attitude towards sex was a curious amalgam of awareness and ignorance. They actually had a great deal of carnal knowledge; but at the same time, there was much they did not know and did not choose to know. There were intimations of immorality to be found everywhere in the Victorian world which it was impossible to ignore: lurid newspaper accounts of crimes and deaths, government reports on working-class life, Mrs Beeton on blood and bones, free trade in pornography, smutty schoolboy jokes, and ubiquitous nude paintings and statuary. All these meant that it was unlikely that anyone would grow up in Victorian England completely ignorant of bodies or sex. Yet there coexisted with this a remarkable amount of ignorance, some of it unavoidable, much of it deliberate: ridiculous euphemisms, evasions and circumlocutions like 'the love that dare not speak its name' (homosexuality), 'an interesting condition' (pregnancy), and 'the birds and the bees' (the facts of life). And at a time of unprecedented progress in science and medicine, many doctors, teachers, and clergy mounted sustained and censorious campaigns against the evils of excessive sexual indulgence and masturbation, for which there was absolutely no medical support. In many ways, the bourgeoisie suppressed very well, better than it knew. As Gay puts it, 'road maps to orgasm were hard to come by in the bourgeois century'.

Although this book is as fine an example of the psychohistory of a social group as I have read, this does not mean that it has avoided the pitfalls necessarily associated with the form. As Gay sensibly admits, 'the reticence of the bourgeois century raises intractable questions about its erotic life' which cannot convincingly be answered by perusing the pages of a handful of erotic diaries. They may be the best evidence available; but they are really not good enough. They are a bewildering amalgam of fantasy and candour, pride and shame, embarrassment and self-advertisement, which defy all attempts at rigorous historical analysis and make it impossible to transform what are essentially Freudian case histories of the dead into Weberian ideal types. How typical of her time, for example, was Mabel Loomis Todd? We do not know; nor does the author. On one occasion he tells us that she was 'in most respects wholly at home in the nineteenth-century middle class'. But elsewhere he is less sure: 'I am not suggesting,' he later remarks, 'that her erotic experience was in any way commonplace.' The most measured conclusion that can be reached is that, in the light of the evidence deployed here, it is now impossible to maintain that all Victorian middle-class women were 'erotic disasters'. But it cannot be argued instead (and Gay does not try to do so) that all nineteenth-century bourgeois women were sexually passionate and fulfilled beings, happily cloistered with their husbands in some suburban love nest. All that can safely be hazarded by way of generalization is that no generalization is possible.

The real problem, as Gay wisely admits, is that in sex as in everything else, 'there was no bourgeois experience in the nineteenth century or in any other: only bourgeois experiences'. And if anything, these were even more diverse and varied than Gay allows. To be bourgeois in 1789 was in many ways fundamentally different from being bourgeois in 1815 or 1848 or 1870 or 1914, and the common emotional experiences of these successive generations often cut across the bounds of class solidarity. And to be Catholic or Jewish or Protestant, or English or French or German or American, only makes the category of the bourgeoisie even more chimerical. In an attempt to pull this bourgeois experience together, and to justify (one suspects) the high proportion of late-nineteenth-century American material in the book, Gay suggests that the United States was the leading influence on Western European bourgeois values. But this does not seem entirely convincing, especially when it is juxtaposed with another comment, that nineteenth-century bourgeois culture 'varied markedly across time, place, rank and hence in attitudes'. It is, in short, hard to see how there could be a sexual attitude specific to the bourgeoisie when it is so hard to show that there is a specific bourgeois class. If there is no Marxian nineteenth-century bourgeoisie, there is hardly likely to be a Freudian one, either.

Nor is this the only difficulty. For while, in some ways, the bourgeois experience was diverse and fragmented, in others it was so commonplace and universal as to be virtually indistinguishable from nineteenth-century experience *tout court*. As Gay rightly points out, the 'bourgeois century' was an age of steam, of movement, of migration, of great cities, of declining religion, of progress and optimism, upheaval and chaos. But none of this was exclusive to the bourgeoisie: to a lesser or greater extent, almost the entire population of the western world was affected by these developments and these moods. So it is not at all clear how 'under external pressure, the nineteenth-century bourgeoisie generated common styles of thinking' about life in general or about sex in particular. For even those features of the external world that helped to educate the bourgeois sexually were a common part of the nineteeth-century experience. There was nothing specifically characteristic of a class in pornography, nude statues, birth control, or prostitution. And if, as Gay argues persuasively, some middle-class women in the nineteenth century did indeed enjoy sex while others did not, then how does this differentiate them from the women of any other class – or of any other time?

Insofar as it was defined by the external world, then, it is hard to accept that there was a homogeneous bourgeois class or a unique bourgeois experience, of sex or of anything else. But of course, there was also the inner world of the bourgeois mind, both conscious and subconscious, on which these perceptions of reality impinged, and to which it in turn responded. Perhaps there was, after all, something distinctive about this nineteenth-century bourgeois mind so that, however commonplace its perceptions, and however varied its circumstances, this still meant that there really was a specific, identifiable bourgeois attitude to sexuality. But Professor Gay will not allow himself such a luxury. 'I have constructed my volumes,' he notes, 'on the fundamental building blocks of the human experience – love, aggression, and conflict.' For him, Freudian assumptions are not specific to the period and the class he seeks to describe, but are timeless and universal. 'The essential ingredients of human nature,' he suggests, 'are both very simple and very tenacious'; it is characterized by 'timelessness and ultimate simplicity'; and so the bourgeoisie has shared its psychological development 'with all mankind'. To try to conjure up 'a distinctive bourgeois style in sexuality' out of a timeless mind exposed only to varied and commonplace experiences of reality is a daunting enterprise indeed.

Notwithstanding his title, Professor Gay is correct in his feeling that there was no such thing as *the* nineteenth-century bourgeois experience. There were many experiences, many conflicts, much ambivalence, and in this book he has succeeded in bringing some of these vividly to life, with learning and humanity, in a way that no historian has ever managed before. Of necessity, as the bourgeois experience is made more vital and varied, so the bourgeoisie whose experience it was becomes more faded and fragmented. But this is unavoidable: the more we know about the bourgeoisie, the less we know that there was a bourgeoisie. Certainly, this book does much to reinforce the current view that, historically, the bourgeoisie has played a less important part than was once supposed. But it also provides ample material for reworking Marx's mistaken maxim into a more fittingly Freudian formulation: historically the bourgeoisie has most importantly played with its parts.

(1984)

NOTE:

1. Peter Gay, *The Bourgeois Experience, Victoria to Freud*, volume I, *The Education of the Senses* (London, 1984).

# 21

# Food

During the twelve days of Christmas, most of us will no doubt eat more than is good for us, and a great deal more than we usually do. As well as the roast turkey and the cranberry jelly, the brussels sprouts and the chipolata sausages, the plum pudding and the brandy butter, the mince pies and the Christmas cake, there will be crystallized fruits and liqueur chocolates, Stilton cheese and assorted nuts, all washed down with wine and spirits in abundance. Those who monitor our health will tell us that so much indulgence is bad for our bodies: too many calories and too much cholesterol. Those who monitor our morals will tell us that it is bad for our souls: when the third world eats so little, how can we possibly eat so much?

Some, but not many, will be susceptible to these Yuletide exhortations to abstinence and penitence. But most of us will eat on regardless: in our post-Christian civilization, there can be a festive season without religion, but not without food and drink. And for those who seek to defend their seasonal gluttony, or assuage their seasonal guilt, here is a comforting thought. Even the most gargantuan Christmas dinner of the 1980s is but a light snack compared with the massive meals consumed by the Edwardian upper classes – not only on the twenty-fifth of December, but throughout the year; not only at dinner, but throughout the day. An Edwardian time traveller, contemplating the average Christmas meal of today, would not condemn us for eating so much, but censure us for consuming so little.

To a quite unusual degree, late nineteenth- and early twentieth-century Britain was obsessed with food – almost as much as we are, but in a very different way. Some wanted food; some achieved food; some had food thrust upon them. One third of the population was still in poverty: their problem was that they didn't have enough to eat. By contrast, the better off members of the working class were enjoying a broader and more wholesome diet than ever before. For them, this was the period of the retailing revolution, of the rise of the chain store, from which they bought unprecedented amounts of bacon and eggs, cheese and butter. And the middle classes did even better for themselves, as a glance at the later editions of Mrs Beeton's *Book of Household Management* will serve to show. Some, indeed, got the best of all these worlds, like the Rowntrees, who surveyed the poverty of the deprived, purveyed chocolates to the better off, and became comfortably rich themselves in the process.

But of course, it was the upper classes who ate the most. 'Not since Imperial Rome', J. B. Priestley once remarked, 'can there have been so many signposts to gluttony. The Edwardian breakfast alone would make our Christmas dinner seem meagre.' And he was quite correct. Between eight o'clock and ten-thirty, the weekend visitor to an Edwardian country house would be offered a selection of food to boggle the mind and bloat the body. To begin with, there would be porridge, cream, tea (both Indian and China) and cold drinks; then there would be a hot selection of scrambled and poached eggs, bacon, ham, sausage, devilled kidneys, haddock, kippers and kedgeree; then there would be a cold table including pressed beef, ham, tongue, gelatines, pheasant, grouse, partridge and ptarmigan; then there would be melons, peaches, raspberries and nectarines; and finally there would be scones, toast, marmalade, honey and imported jams.

And all this was merely limbering up before the main gastronomic events, which took up most of the remainder of the day. Lunch, at one-thirty, would consist of eight courses, at the very least. Then there was afternoon tea, which was not just a drink, but included toast, scones, a variety of sandwiches and a selection of cakes, to say nothing of lobster salad if King Edward VII happened to be staying. Then there was dinner, which might be anything up to twelve courses. And, for those who were still feeling peckish, there would be a late supper table laid with sandwiches, cold meats, devilled chicken and a selection of spirits and mineral water. All day, from morning to night, it was food, glorious food. As one Edwardian *bon vivant* explained to Consuelo Vanderbilt (herself no stranger to the good things of life), 'considering that it is the only pleasure one can count on having three times a day every day of one's life, a well-ordered meal is of prime importance'.

No one believed this more emphatically than King Edward VII himself. From the time when he was an undergradute at Oxford, and entertained his tutors and professors, he had acquired an insatiable passion for very large amounts of very rich food, and age only augmented both his appetite and his waist line. Quite simply, King Edward VII was a glutton: he ate anything and everything, and he ate it very quickly. All day, every day, day after day, he ate, with only brief interludes at Homburg or Marienbad or Baden Baden to rest his digestion and reduce his avoirdupois. Somehow, it was altogether appropriate that the man understandably known as 'Tum-tum' to many members of the country-house circuit was forced to postpone his coronation because he was suffering from appendicitis.

While out shooting or when going to a race meeting, King Edward liked to start the day well. Breakfast would include poached eggs, bacon, haddock, chickens or woodcock. Lunch, too, was always a substantial meal, as at Ascot in June 1908, when it consisted of fourteen courses. And dinner was normally on the same grand scale, as in 1910 when, just before leaving Biarritz for the last time, the ageing and failing monarch still managed to eat his way through turtle soup, salmon steak, grilled chicken, saddle of mutton, several snipe stuffed with foie gras, asparagus, a fruit dish, an enormous iced concoction, and a savoury. Just for a change, he always consumed roast beef and Yorkshire pudding on Sundays, so as to remind himself how the other half ate. But for the rest of the time, he preferred such rich fare as caviare, quail, grilled oysters, or pheasant stuffed with snipe – which was itself stuffed with truffles.

★

The most conspicuous feature of this astonishingly lavish style of eating was the enormous amount of meat consumed. So, part cause, part effect of this passion for birds and beasts was that the rearing – and the slaughtering – of feather and fur assumed a major dimension in the life of late Victorian and Edwardian country houses. Their inhabitants were as obsessed with guns as with butter, with shooting as with eating. Railways and motor cars made it easier to assemble the guests and the guns for the weekend. Improvements in firearms during the second half of the nineteenth century, including breech loading and smokeless powder, made it much easier to shoot. And the rearing of semi-tame birds, driven towards the guns by brave and obliging beaters, brought the sport, and the quarry, within the range of anyone who could hold a gun and pull the trigger.

The result was the Edwardian shooting party, as quintessential a feature of early twentieth-century high life as the breakfast blow-out, and which provided, in J. G. Ruffer's memorably exact and evocative phrase, 'the opportunities of a Vimy Ridge machine-gunner with an infinitely better lunch'. Great houses like Chatsworth, Holkham, Blenheim and Elveden were renowned for the excellence of their shooting. And the big guns themselves were legendary figures: Sir Ralph Payne Gallwey travelled 7,725 miles in 1891–92 in search of wildfowl; Lord Ripon once killed twenty-eight pheasant in one minute at Sandringham; and Lord de Walsingham once slaughtered 1,070 grouse in a day. Indeed, in the hands of such master mass murderers, the killing of birds reached a level that was barely sporting.

For King Edward, who possessed neither the shape nor the temperament for fox hunting, but who wanted to be considered a sportsman even though he took no exercise, shooting was the ideal activity. When he bought the Sandringham estate in the 1860s, much of its attraction lay in the shooting potential. The head of game killed there was gradually but inexorably increased from seven to thirty thousand a year; the clocks were put forward half an hour throughout the house to allow more daylight for shooting during the winter months; and when the partridge and pheasant gave out, there was always the grouse and the deer at

Balmoral. Although he was never a particularly good shot, Edward VII enjoyed both the extravagance and the exclusiveness of the pursuit; and his enthusiastic and well-advertised patronage did for the shooting of birds what the Prince Regent's had done a century earlier for the hunting of the fox.

Compared with King George V, however, Edward VII was but a novice. For George V, when he wasn't sticking in stamps, sailing his yacht, listening to music-hall songs on the gramophone, or just being plain philistine, was obsessed with shooting to a point where even the long-suffering Queen Mary was heartily sick of it, and where even his most devoted servants and courtiers disapproved and despaired. The passion got the better of him in the 1890s, and thereafter, it never left him. Shortly before he acceded, he visited Lord Burnham at Hall Barn. Sustained by a light lunch of turtle soup, snipe, pudding and truffled turkey, the party slaughtered four thousand birds in one short December day, one thousand of which fell victim to Prince George's own gun. As he coyly admitted to his eldest son on the way home, 'perhaps we went a little too far today, David'.

But this was an ephemeral and uncharacteristic moment of remorse. In December 1912, after a particularly energetic round of shooting at Sandringham, Lord Lincolnshire regretfully calculated that 'seven guns in four days killed ten thousand head. The king one day fired 1,700 cartridges and killed one thousand pheasants. Can this terrific slaughter last much longer?' The answer was an emphatic yes. Although he continued to use hammer guns long after they were out of date and out of fashion, George V was recognized to be one of the best six shots in the country. And he stayed in practice throughout his life. To the very end of his reign, by which time the great Edwardian shooting passion had moderated somewhat, he tramped his Norfolk coverts, and stalked stags and shot grouse at Balmoral.

For those prepared to travel further afield, the game was bigger and more exotic. As the world contracted during the late nineteenth century, and with the new imperialism in the ascendant, the white hunter emerged as the international edition of the domestic big shot. From the Andes to the Arctic, from India to

Brazil, and from eastern to southern Africa, the pursuit of big game became big business. Companies were set up to arrange the travel, to provide the clothes, and to look after the ladies. Books were published on where to go, what to shoot, and how to do it. And although the trophies from such expeditions never found their way to the dinner table, no Edwardian big house was complete without its tiger rug, its stuffed lion, or the polar bear standing in the hallway.

Once again, it was the two kings who lead the field. Edward VII shot (as he ate) everything and everywhere: bears in Transylvania, boars in Albania, crocodile in Egypt, elk in Sweden, deer in Hungary, and tigers in Nepal – where, needless to say the shooting party dressed for dinner every night. And George V, after the fatigue and pageantry of the Delhi Durbar, insisted that he, too, should go to Nepal for a little recreation. Six hundred elephants and fourteen thousand servants were provided to help the proceedings go with a bang, which they emphatically did. After two weeks' shooting, the total bag was thirty-nine tigers, eighteen rhinos, and four bears, of which the king himself potted nearly half. 'It is a misfortune,' sighed Lord Crewe, 'for a public personage to have any taste so strongly developed as the craze for shooting is in our beloved ruler.'

Judged by today's more austere and aware standards – of cholesterol-conscious cooking, of the World Wildlife Fund, of Save the Whales, and of the Animal Liberationists – this extreme self-indulgence at the dinner table and on the grouse moor seems not only bizarre, but also offensive. However much we consume this Christmas, it will not be as much as these bloated Edwardians ate every day, and the odds are that, unlike many of them, we shall not have killed our own poultry. So how, exactly, should we explain this quite extraordinary efflorescence of destructive self-indulgence? Why did so many Edwardians eat and shoot so much?

Inevitably, the answers to these questions can be little more than conjectural. But here are three suggestions. Perhaps it was a virility symbol for those many obese and inert males (of whom, of course, Edward VII himself was the prime example), who tried to prove their manhood by shooting their way through game once, and then by eating their way through it yet a second time. Perhaps it was a last great fling of conspicuous and competitive consumption, as parvenus and plutocrats tried to establish a new and opulent lifestyle of which King Edward approved, but with which many old-established but now-impoverished landed families could no longer compete. And perhaps – at least in retrospect – it was an ominous foretaste of that even greater slaughter which was soon to come, not on the grouse moors of Scotland, but on the battle fields of Flanders.

But however it is explained, the killing of so much life and the consumption of so much food by the Edwardians was both violent and excessive. Perhaps it is not altogether surprising that so many members of CND are vegetarians.

(1984)

# 22

# Poverty

Divine authority and empirical observation are, by definition, rarely in accord, but they do at least agree on this: that the poor are always with us. Chastity may have gone the way of all flesh, and obedience may have been banished from the marriage service, but poverty – grinding, inexorable, ineradicable – remains even today the commonplace circumstance of humanity: not a state voluntarily embraced on the road to salvation, but a condition unavoidably endured with little prospect of relief. It may well be, as George Bernard Shaw once put it, that 'the greatest of evils and the worst of crimes is poverty', but it is even easier to express outrage at its existence than to raise pious hopes as to its eradication. The history of the world is the history of many things, but in most places, at most times, and for most people, it was and is as Thomas Gray described it in 1750: 'the short and simple annals of the poor'.

So far so good. But if poverty is promoted from a platitude to a problem, things become much more difficult. For the problems of poverty are simple yet complex: what is poverty? And what is the problem? Is poverty, like beauty, in the guilty eye of the beholder, or in the empty belly of the sufferer? How are poverty levels compared, across centuries and cultures, continents and countries? Is there an absolute standard of poverty, and if so, what is it? Or is it all relative, since the poor man only feels deprived when at the gate of the rich man's castle? What is the difference between the deserving and the undeserving poor, between those who labour but earn insufficient reward, and those who are impoverished because they cannot work? And how is poverty to be treated: by realistically diminishing desires, or by seeking to satisfy demands? And if the latter, then again, how: by indiscriminate giving, by systematic aid, or by the promotion of economic development? As the questions multiply, the answers dissolve. Defining poverty has always been difficult, and eradicating it has thus far proved impossible.

For the policy makers and the pundits, these are the central issues. But for historians, the crucial question is rather different: not, *what* is the problem of poverty, but rather, *when* did poverty become a problem? Since the poor are, indeed, always with us, why is their presence accepted in some societies and at some times, yet deemed to be intolerable in other places and at other times? For most of recorded history (and in many places still, alas, today) poverty was not a problem at all: it was a fact of life, an inescapable condition which was, accordingly, either ignored or ennobled, fatalistically accepted or randomly relieved. Only in the western world, during the last two hundred years, has it been upgraded from an insuperable and 'natural' condition into an intolerable but soluble problem, as the Industrial Revolution has held out, for the first time, the prospect of the more abundant life, not only for the élite, but for humanity as a whole. Only when its eradication became possible did poverty become a problem. We may not have gone far towards solving it in practice (*vide* Ethiopia) but in theory, at least, the West has the power to abolish all forms of human poverty, just as it has the power to abolish all forms of human life.

Arguably, it was the Industrial Revolution in England which brought about this fundamental change in circumstances and attitudes, as the years from the 1780s to the 1850s saw not only the first great phase of self-sustained economic growth, but also the first great phase of self-sustained discussion about poverty. Throughout this period, the poor, the tired and the huddled masses forced themselves on public attention in greater numbers and with greater urgency than ever before. And historians have been equally anxious to give them their due, even if they have disagreed as to how to do it. Of course, there was a great deal of poverty. But, as the 'standard of living' controversy has shown, it may have been getting less (or it may not). Undeniably, the condition of the people was bad. But, as the debate on government growth has suggested, the state may have been becoming more interventionist (or it may not). Much less studied, however, has been the contemporary and conventional wisdom about the poor people of the proletariat. Who, exactly, thought about the poor, and what, precisely, did they think? When was poverty first perceived as a problem? And what influence did those who thought about the subject exert on those who tried to do something about it? It is to the answering of these fascinating and fundamental questions that Gertrude Himmelfarb has devoted her most recent, most ambitious and most important book.[1]

Even so, in terms of its subject and its approach, this is a quintessentially Himmelfarbian performance. In this book, as in her others, she is primarily concerned with the study of *minds* – a key word in her historical vocabulary, and the prime constituent of her historical universe. Her first book, on Lord Acton, was a history of his mind rather than a biography of his life. Her study of Darwin was primarily an account of his thoughts and his theories: it was the mind not the man who mattered. Her collected essays, revealingly published under the title *Victorian Minds*, presented a throng of thinkers, in a celebration of cerebration. And her analysis of John Stuart Mill suggested that different states of mind might dwell within the same body. The result of this approach is a particularly rich and unusual brand of intellectual history: concerned with scientists and historians, publicists and novelists, as much as with great thinkers; more interested in the typical and representative second-rate figure than with the transcendent philosopher out of sympathy with his time; strong on individual minds but sceptical of free-floating ideas; and all this written about with a grace and elegance which makes her books compulsive reading.

But there are difficulties with this approach, in part deriving from her wholly admirable desire to see the mind as the link between those who think and those who do. To the purist historian of political thought, she is too eclectic and inconsistent in her methodology (as instanced by the savaging Alan Ryan gave her book on Mill); while to hard-nosed historians of political action, she seems altogether too preoccupied with ideology (as shown by the severe criticisms of her attempt to analyse the passing of the Second Reform Bill in these terms). For the first group, her head is insufficiently in the clouds; for the second, her feet are insufficiently on the ground. What is more, almost all her writings are pervaded by strong neoconservative convictions. Her study of Acton showed not only that he was a liberal, but also that he was a pessimist. Her account of Darwin presented him as an inadvertent consolidator of a *conservative* revolution – a phrase which she also used in *Victorian Minds* to describe Victorian England. Her essay on the passing of the Second Reform Act implied that the Tories beat the Liberals because their ideology was somehow better. And her analysis of Mill concluded with a swingeing attack on the evils of contemporary society.

Not surprisingly, then, this latest book offers a biographical treatment of those who thought about poverty, not an impassioned evocation of those who experienced it. Her first concern is to trace the late eighteenth-century shift from moral to political economy. On her reading, Adam Smith appears more under the first than the second of these banners: *The Wealth of Nations* was as much about the poor as about the rich; although a proponent of laissez-faire, Smith favoured state education and the retention of the Poor Law; and he optimistically saw in the contemporary economic changes the prospect of progress and improvement for the labouring masses as a whole. His disciples were illustrious, eccentric and divergent in their views: Burke, Pitt, Eden, Bentham and Paine each claimed Smith as their authority and inspiration, yet they disagreed violently as to the causes, nature and treatment of poverty. Then came Malthus who, according to Himmelfarb, did not perfect Adam Smith but did away with him, by undermining his optimistic view of the future, by demoralizing political economy, and by arguing that the laws of population meant that for most people life would always be nasty, mean, brutish, short, and poor. Only in the second edition of his famous *Essay on Population* did Malthus soften his tone somewhat, and tentatively admit that Smith may have been right. But by then he had already set the bounds of the debate on poverty for the next half century.

In her second section, Himmelfarb takes up the story in the 1830s, and examines the making and provisions of the 1834 Poor Law Amendment Act, which introduced the fundamental (if flawed) distinction between the able bodied and working poor, who did not deserve relief, and the indigent paupers, who did; and which propounded the principle of 'less eligibility', whereby relief in the workhouse should be so meagre and unattractive that only the indigent would seek it. Almost everything written about poverty in the next decade or so was in some way or another a response to this measure. The Tory opposition (such as it was) saw this as the negation of paternalism and humanitarianism; the Tory radical, Carlyle, could not make up his mind one way or the other; the radical populist, William Cobbett, was unequivocally opposed, on the grounds that the new law took away the last property rights of its intended beneficiaries; *The Poor Man's Guardian* and the Chartists subsumed poverty in more general considerations about the political and economic conditions of the working class; while Engels concluded that poverty as endured by the new urban proletariat was both quantitatively and qualitatively worse than that suffered by the pre-industrial poor.

From Engels' Manchester, Himmelfarb shifts her focus to Mayhew's London, the world metropolis of pauperism, with its unique amalgam of very rich and very poor. As she persuasively shows, Mayhew's notion of poverty was cultural rather than economic, and was derived from his almost Hogarthian picture of London street life, about which he began to write from the late 1840s. Although ostensibly investigating the poor as a whole, his melange of facts and figures, images and impressions, anecdotes and interviews, was neither systematic nor consistent. It was undeniably vivid in imagery and well-disposed in intention. But by concentrating on the street life of mid-nineteenth-century London to the virtual exclusion of all else, Mayhew not only failed to treat the new urban and industrial poor, but also depicted the people he *did* investigate with such repellent verisimilitude as to evoke feelings of revulsion rather than of compassion. Although he began writing at almost the same time that the Public Health Act was passed, he had no real influence on government policy; and although he was something of a best-seller, his stress on the street life of London ultimately led him down a blind alley.

In her last section, Himmelfarb changes tack once more, and takes us on a tour through the fiction of the 1840s – but with a difference. For she is, quite rightly, as much concerned with low and bad fiction as with those great works subsequently deemed to be high and good. Her analysis of W. H. Ainsworth's *Jack Sheppard* and of G. W. M. Reynolds's *The Mysteries of London*, brilliantly demonstrates both the horrific picture painted of the poor in popular literature, and also its close relationship to such serious writers as Dickens and Thackeray. Dickens himself is honoured with an entire chapter, as the incomparable creator of a multitude of poor people so teeming and diverse as to defy any simple categorization. Disraeli makes an obligatory appearance for his two nations, but it is instructive to learn that his poor were as much agricultural as industrial, and that the former were much worse off than the latter. And Mrs Gaskell brings the book to a symmetrical conclusion, as the first real optimist since Adam Smith, whose novels were full of hope for reconciliation between north and south, capital and labour.

Beyond any doubt, this book bears all the hallmarks of Himmelfarb's work at its best and most vigorous. It is, again, a piece of rightish writing, although she grinds fewer contemporary axes than in her book on Mill. She vigorously reasserts the merits of studying the history of those below from the perspective of those above; she is sceptical of such modish notions as 'social control'; she is noticeably less reverential towards historians of the left, from R. H. Tawney to E. P. Thompson, than of the right; and she tartly rebukes radical literary critics from George Orwell to Raymond Williams for their limited vision and sympathies. More positively, this leads to some important re-evaluations of major figures: Adam Smith and even Malthus are presented in a more attractive and humane light than is customary; Mayhew gets fewer marks than usual as a social observer; Disraeli is taken rather seriously as a theoretician of aristocratic paternalism; and the tight-lipped Mrs Gaskell is reborn as a ray of sunshine.

But Himmelfarb is far too accomplished a historian, and far too well aware of the complexities of her chosen problem, to be merely polemical. To begin with, she writes, once again, with remarkable grace and finesse, so that, even while transforming the annals of the poor from being short and simple into being long and complex, she never loses the reader's interest. She has read astonishingly widely on the subject, from the great thinkers and established authorities to penny dreadfuls and unstamped and illegal newspapers; the ease with which she moves from economic to political to sociological to literary material is enviable and admirable; her reappraisal of such major figures as Adam Smith is compelling and provocative; and her analysis of the writers and writings of the 1840s ranks among the best things she has done. Never before has the sense of so much thought about so much poverty been so vividly conveyed. Just as *Victorian Minds* showed how many Victorians had minds, so *The Idea of Poverty* shows how many of their immediate forebears had ideas about poverty.

Whether, as the publisher claims, this also amounts to a 'fundamental re-definition of the subject' is, however, rather less clear, since even after 500 pages of arresting prose, the subject has not really been convincingly delineated, let alone re-defined. *The Idea of Poverty* is a beguiling title, but an amorphous notion, neither strong nor sharp enough to unify what is, essentially, another collection of Himmelfarbian lives of the mind. We are told, for example, that the book's concern is thought about poverty in England from the 1750s to the 1850s. But why, in that case, are the works of Tocqueville, Engels and Marx given such extended treatment, when they only became available in translation much later? Why do Paine, Carlyle and Cobbett merit so much discussion when, on the author's own admission, they were not very much interested in poverty? Why devote chapters to *The Poor Man's Guardian* and the Chartists when most of what is said about them is, understandably, hardly relevant to the subject? Why lavish an entire section on Mayhew, when he was only concerned with the marginal, atavistic street-folk of London, and not with the contemporary, industrial proletariat? And why give so much space to fiction, when most creative writers – even Dickens – were not primarily concerned with the poor?

All this is merely to say that many historians of ideas will have as much difficulty with this book as with Himmelfarb's previous works. And so, for rather different reasons, will the historians of political behaviour. For it still remains unclear just what influence those who thought about poverty actually exerted on those who tried to do something about it. Of course, in a general sense, the problem of poverty, like the practice of politics, is essentially the art of the possible. And in both cases what is possible is in part determined by what is thinkable. But only in part; and, in the case of poverty in Britain between 1750 and 1850, it seems only to have been a very small part. As Himmelfarb herself admits, Smith had little influence on Malthus, and Malthus in turn had little influence on the New Poor Law. Insofar as the 1834 Act owed anything to ideology, it was to those 'countless pamphlets, tracts, sermons, articles, speeches and reports' which Himmelfarb mentions but does not discuss. And, in the same way, it is not at all clear that Carlyle or Mayhew, the Chartists or the novelists, had very much influence on the government reports or parliamentary legislation of the 1840s.

Of course, poverty is by definition a protean problem, and any work on the subject is bound to result in rather a protean book. But this is especially so if it is concerned with the *idea* of poverty rather than the actuality. Undeniably, part of the essential reality of any historical subject is, as Himmelfarb claims in self justification, what well-informed people thought about it at the time. But there is much more which must also be considered and which, in her rather tangential approach, Himmelfarb regrettably ignores. The social and political changes of the period are only lightly sketched in. The poor themselves receive rather less explicit discussion than they should. Although the thinkers on poverty get their due, the complementary subject of *wealth* gets no treatment at all. Yet, as R. H. Tawney once put it, 'what thoughtful rich people call the problem of poverty, thoughtful poor people call the problems of riches'. Above all, there is little sense of how truly bizarre, unprecedented and incomprehensible contemporaries found that group of astonishing changes we retrospectively but inadequately call the Industrial Revolution.

The real problem for Himmelfarb is that, if her pundits and ideologues were placed in this broader historical context, they would be so much diminished in importance as to undermine the whole enterprise. For most of them either did not understand what was going on, or did not influence what was going on, or both. There may, indeed, have been links between those who thought and those who did something about poverty, but it is quite astonishingly difficult to show how, exactly, this happened, or whether it mattered, if it did. And even if there *were* such connections, it is equally unclear whether those in government who tried to deal with poverty had much, or the major, impact on it. On the contrary, insofar as the problem of poverty *was* both recognized and resolved in this period, it was not because the politicians had read Malthus, or because of the provisions of the 1834 Poor Law, but because the Industrial Revolution increased aggregate prosperity and individual wealth even as population exploded. Never mind the minds: it was the matter that ultimately mattered. For all its very real insights and interest, it is difficult to avoid the conclusion that *The Idea of Poverty* is neither the best way into the history of ideas nor the best way into the history of poverty.

(1985)

NOTE:
1. Gertrude Himmelfarb, *The Idea of Poverty: England in the Early Industrial Age* (London, 1984).

# Secrets

Paradoxical though it may seem, the most well-known department of the British government is probably the organization known as Her Majesty's Secret Service. But it is better known in fiction than in fact, thanks to the popular stories which have firmly established a particular image of it in the public mind, many of them actually written by former undercover agents. Some, like William Le Queux, John Buchan and Ian Fleming, have created a world of breathless excitement and daring adventure, in which the patriotic endeavours of a few brave and resourceful heroes change the course of history – invariably to Britain's advantage. Others, such as Somerset Maugham, Graham Greene and John Le Carré, have evoked a more reflective mood of monotonous routine, detached boredom and cynical disenchantment which, nevertheless, has its own particular brand of downbeat romance. Yet it may well be that these very open and optimistic secrets provide the most effective and misleading cover for the real work and identity of the British intelligence community, partly by making it seem more successful than it actually is, and partly by implying that more is known about it than is in fact the case.

For the reality is both less confident and more confidential. In the first place, the British intelligence network seems not so much invincible and impregnable as incompetent and incontinent: a secret service which leaks its own secrets. Since the Second World War, it has been undermined and discredited by a succession of sensational scandals, exposing moles and traitors, defectors and double agents, from Burgess and Maclean, via Vassall and Lonsdale, to Philby, Blunt and beyond. By comparison, the triumphant world of James Bond is not just fiction: it is pure

fantasy. Yet in addition – and despite all this – successive governments have consistently sought to stifle public discussion and
parliamentary debate on the dubious grounds that total confidentiality is vital to the Secret Service's efficient functioning. Its
archives remain indefinitely closed, even for its earliest years; the
rules governing the publication of the official histories of its
wartime activities are inconsistent and unnecessarily restrictive;
only in the late 1970s did the British government officially admit
that the peacetime secret service actually existed; and the Thatcher
administration has resolutely refused to allow any detailed parliamentary investigation into its operations.

There are, then, two crucial questions which need to be asked of
the British Secret Service. First: how good is (and was) it at finding
and keeping secrets? Second: how far should its own existence and
operations be kept secret? During the last ten years a Cambridge
historian, Christopher Andrew, has been burrowing for the
answers, with all the diligence of a latter-day mole. The non-
availability of the intelligence archives has obliged him to track
down fragmentary evidence which has escaped government
censors or has turned up unexpectedly in the wrong departmental
file; to use private sources of information, both written and oral,
which cannot always be disclosed; and to resort to conjecture and
speculation more extensively than some austere historians might
like. Above all, he has had to come to terms with the bizarre world
of secret service mentality, where the difference between truth and
falsehood, fact and fiction, right and wrong, is often far from
clear, and where self-deception and self-dramatization are unavoidable occupational hazards. Yet he has triumphantly sur-
mounted these difficulties, and produced a history of the Secret
Service which is as exciting as any spy novel, and which also
makes the most powerful case yet for greater public accountability.[1]

Andrew's history is divided into six major phases. He begins in the
last quarter of the nineteenth century, with the establishment of
intelligence departments in the Admiralty and War Office, and the
setting up of the CID and the Special Branch, largely in response

to growing international tension and fears of domestic subversion (especially from the Irish). But as was so often to be the case, the politicians were rarely interested, there was insufficient coordination and inadequate funding, and little was achieved by such amateur agents as Baden-Powell, who thought spying a 'jolly lark', and who enjoyed dressing up. Appropriately enough, the government was only forced into more resolute action in the 1900s, by the massive proliferation of deluded and fantastical 'invasion scare' literature, which began with Erskine Childers's *Riddle of the Sands*, and was carried to even greater extremes of farcical paranoia by Le Queux and E. Phillips Oppenheim. The result was that in 1909, a sub-committee of the Committee of Imperial Defence recommended the setting up of a Secret Service Bureau, whose home and foreign departments were the direct forerunners of MI5 and SIS (which later became MI6).

During the First World War, these diverse and makeshift British intelligence services were active in three major spheres of operation. The least important was the home front, where imaginary fears of German spies, and the elaboration of extravagant conspiracy theories, created far greater difficulties for MI5 and the Special Branch than the few authentic German agents who were easily picked up, and the threats of labour unrest in the aftermath of conscription which were (as usual) greatly exaggerated. On the Western Front, intelligence was gathered about German train and troop movements using aerial reconnaissance, collaborators in occupied territory, and agents in Holland and Switzerland, and was often sent home in carrier pigeons. But on the whole, this was not a success: the rival intelligence networks rarely co-operated, and were often infiltrated by the enemy, while Douglas Haig, the British commander, was uneager to use the material which was made available to him. But there was one outstanding triumph: the interception and deciphering of German naval and diplomatic communications by 'professor types' recruited to Room 40 of the Admiralty, which not only anticipated the later achievements in the Second World War at Bletchley, but also made possible the discovery and publication of the Zimmerman telegram and the successful countering of the German U-boat menace.

By the end of the war, it was Bolshevik Russia, rather than Imperial Germany, which was seen as the greater threat, and on which the intelligence services concentrated their now much diminished resources. Clandestine attempts to prop up the Kerensky government, to persuade Lenin to fight on against the Germans, and to support the White Russians in the Civil War, were all equally unsuccessful. In India and in Britain itself, there were renewed fears of civil unrest and of widespread subversion, this time seen as part of a worldwide Comintern plot. But once again, they were wildly exaggerated: the armed services remained loyal, the trades unions wanted higher wages not revolution, and Indian national protest owed much more to Gandhi than to Lenin. As in the war, it was the codebreakers who obtained the most valuable secrets, by successfully intercepting Russian diplomatic communications between 1920 and 1927. But this knowledge was put to dubious and ineffectual use. In 1924, the publication of the (apparently genuine) 'Zinoviev letter' helped to bring down the Labour government. And three years later, when the Conservative government broke off diplomatic relations with the Soviet Union, it foolishly revealed its sources of information, whereupon the Russians promptly changed their codes, which were thereafter unbreakable.

Beyond doubt, the period from the late 1920s to the outbreak of the Second World War was the low point in the history of British intelligence. For much of the time, the politicians starved it both of money and attention. Those on the left believed – with ample justification after the 'Zinoviev letter' affair – that the Secret Service was their enemy, and those on the right were on the whole too gentlemanly or too lethargic to be bothered. At home and abroad, government security was virtually non-existent, which made possible the first, fatal infiltrations by the Cambridge moles; and this, combined with continued inability to decipher foreign codes meant that the Germans, Italians and Russians knew much more about British intelligence in the 1930s than Britain did about theirs. Not surprisingly, the conduct of British foreign policy was bedevilled by contradictory information from the Secret Service and by confused responses from the politicians. At each stage on the road to war, from the occupation of the Rhineland and the Munich settlement, to the invasions of Czechoslovakia, Poland, Norway and the Low Countries, most of the available British intelligence was faulty, and that which was not was usually ignored.

Yet, in a manner reminiscent of those many spy novels where victory is clutched from the jaws of defeat at the eleventh hour, Andrew's story reaches a triumphant climax during the Second World War. Indeed, the hero of this book turns out to be Winston Churchill himself, the first Prime Minister with an insatiable appetite for secret intelligence, who relied heavily and wisely on the information it provided, whose leadership moulded its disparate departments into a unified community, and who insisted that resources be lavished on an organization hitherto inexcusably starved of funds. This made possible the improvised recruiting of so many Oxbridge undergraduates to MI5, SIS and Bletchley, whose numbers increased fivefold in the space of eighteen months. On the debit side, this resulted in the appointment of men like Blunt and Philby, who should never have been let in. But it also led to the breaking of the Enigma machine ciphers, which enabled the British to intercept German military communications for most of the war. And the intelligence thereby acquired made it possible to stop Rommel reaching Cairo, to win the Battle of the Atlantic, and to deceive the Germans about the location of the D-Day invasion. This may not have changed the final outcome of the war, but it certainly shortened it, and thereby saved millions of lives.

Once again, in the aftermath of victory, the Secret Service was run down, most of the 'professor types' returned to their ivory towers, and the unified control and *esprit de corps* of wartime both evaporated. And, although there was no return to the austerity of the 'thirties, subsequent changes in the pattern of international relations and in the technology of intelligence have again fundamentally undermined the position of the British Secret Service. The loss of great power status, combined with the advent of the computer and the communications satellite, has turned Britain into a junior partner in the intelligence field, heavily dependent on the resources, goodwill and tolerance of the United States. There were some notable successes in the retreat from greatness in Malaya and Iran, but some equally notable disasters in Albania and Egypt. In recent years, the wheel has come full circle, as secret service activity has once more been concentrated on the battle against Irish terrorism and communist infiltration of the trades unions. The interminable succession of spy scandals has severely damaged morale and understandably undermined American confidence, while the Thatcher government's handling of the GCHQ affair, and the Geoffrey Prime and Michael Bettaney cases, has been singularly inept. Unlike most fictional spy stories, this book does not have a happy ending.

But what it does do is to demonstrate the real value of treating a sensational subject in a serious and scholarly way. In the first place, it clearly makes good the claim that any study of modern British foreign and defence policy which 'leaves intelligence out of account is bound to be incomplete'. Jellicoe's behaviour at the Battle of Jutland seems altogether more credible now we know that the intercepted signals of the German navy were not forwarded to him in time. Churchill's attacks on government defence policy in the 1930s appear in a new light when we learn that he enjoyed access to intelligence information throughout this period, and that this was officially sanctioned by MacDonald, Baldwin and Chamberlain, the very men who bore the brunt of his well-informed criticisms. And it is a supreme and well-documented irony that the Chamberlain government finally accepted the inevitability of war with Germany in early 1939, not because of the threatened invasion of Czechoslovakia, but because of faulty intelligence predicting an attack on Holland.

To this extent, the Secret Service has probably been more important than the fictional accounts of it may suggest. But in other ways, it is clear that the romances of Buchan and Fleming exaggerate and mislead. For most secret service work is much more concerned with the humdrum and routine collection of intelligence than with the high living and spectacular adventures of a few glamorous men with licences to kill. There are occasional

James Bond types to be found in these pages, like Sidney Reilly in Russia and Mervin Minshall in the Balkans, and there are some glorious moments of high farce when the antics of men like Baden-Powell and the delusions of fanatics like Le Queux are described. But their achievements were rarely significant, and were never remotely as important as they themselves were inclined to believe. For all its bravura and panache, this account is emphatically the history of Smiley's people. And as such, it conveys with total conviction the downbeat reality of secret service life.

It also eloquently demonstrates the real limitations to such activity. For it is in the collation and analysis of intelligence that the greatest difficulties are to be found, and where the greatest mistakes are usually – and often unavoidably – made. With so many competing agencies, it has rarely been possible to gather all the relevant material in time. And it is never easy, and sometimes quite impossible, to distinguish between intelligence that is true or false, important or insignificant. As a result, both the military and the mandarins tend to believe what they want to believe, and make decisions about intelligence based on essentially strategic or political criteria. So, in the First World War, Haig took note of the optimistic intelligence reports and resolutely discounted the rest; and in the 'thirties, Neville Chamberlain refused to credit the information produced by the anti-appeaser Vansittart, even though it was usually more accurate, because it did not fit in with his own policy preferences. Above all, this history reminds us that, however accurate and reliable the intelligence may be, it still remains exceedingly difficult to predict the political and military intentions of a foreign power on the basis of it.

But one of the many delights of this book is that its contents make it possible to predict fairly safely what some of the reactions to it will actually be. Both inside the service and out, those of the far right will find much in it and about it which will confirm their paranoid tendencies and conspiracy theories. They will see it as a book which exposes the Secret Service to sustained and unfair criticism, which makes heroes out of the long-haired intellectuals of Bletchley, which constantly belittles the achievements of its regular operators, which deliberately understates the threats to national security that these brave and gallant men have so often overcome, which mischievously sacrifices official secrecy for scholarly sensation, and which thereby undermines both the credibility and the importance of the whole operation. Indeed, from this perspective, Andrew's book will no doubt be seen as the supreme example of Cambridge treachery towards the Secret Service: for there is only one thing worse than a mole subverting the organization from within, and that is an intellectual ridiculing it from without.

Those on the left will view things rather differently. They will be impressed by the evidence which Andrew marshals of the narrow social background, the highly reactionary sympathies, and the limited intellectual resources, of so many of the Secret Service's personnel. Much of this book reads more like a history of the Drones Club than of an intelligence outfit: names such as 'Fido', 'Nobby', 'Blinker', 'Bubbles' and 'Pink Tights' abound; many agents sport such disguises or necessities as glass eyes and monocles, spats and wooden legs; and they become involved in ludicrous and implausible adventures, but with no Jeeves to pull them through. Equally clear is the evidence of the service's political partiality: in the 'twenties it was irresponsibly hostile to Labour and excessively well disposed to the Conservatives, while in the 'thirties its hatred of communism and admiration for Hitler meant that it gave one-sided support to the policy of appeasement.

But in writing this book, Andrew himself has a broader and more urgent concern, which is to attack the 'ancient and irrational taboo' that strict confidentiality is the necessary precondition for successful undercover operation. For on the contrary, it is his belief that the British Secret Service is far too secret for its own good, and that this is more the fault of the politicians than of the intelligence community itself. In part, this is because most ministers have been confused about their responsibilities, and have viewed it with indifference or suspicion, thereby only reinforcing the service's innate tendency to paranoia, introversion, self-perpetuation and distrust of politicians. But in addition, by obstinately refusing to concede any adequate form of public scrutiny, successive governments have allowed the very real problems of insufficient funding, casual recruitment, incompetent leadership and lack of unified control to accumulate and to go untreated for generations. What is urgently needed, Andrew concludes, is a system of parliamentary scrutiny resembling the Congressional Committees of Inquiry into the US intelligence community which were set up in the aftermath of Watergate.

In short, Andrew's cure for the past and present ills of the British Secret Service is *more* public accountability, not less. Of course, this is an argument which cannot be proven. Many of the shortcomings which his book catalogues – mistakes in recruitment, conflicting intelligence reports, the dangers and difficulties of dealing with double agents, and the incorrect evaluation of data by the military and the politicians – are no doubt to some extent intrinsic to the enterprise. Furthermore, it is by no means clear whether the United States secret services – for all their greater accountability – are all that much better than the British. Above all, the scale and significance of British Secret Service operations has dwindled so dramatically and so drastically since the halcyon days of Bletchley that it may be positively anachronistic to suppose that the remedies of the 'thirties will be appropriate for the very different circumstances of the 'eighties.

Nevertheless, the evidence advanced here, of an organization lamentably deficient in historical perspective, and dangerously isolated from the very national community which it is in existence to protect, suggests that something should be done and can be done. Short of appointing Andrew himself as the head of the secret service, some limited but effective form of parliamentary scrutiny does indeed seem to be the next best thing. At the very least, the case made here is so cogent and so compelling that it demands and deserves attention: the British Secret Service would keep its secrets better if it was forced to be less secretive about itself.

(1986)

NOTE:

1. Christopher Andrew, *Her Majesty's Secret Service: The Making of the British Intelligence Community* (London, 1986).

# Nostalgia

The stately homes of England seem set fair to reconquer the
United States for Squire Western, the Duke of Omnium and Lord
Marchmain. That, at least, is the impression conveyed by this
splendid exhibition, which has recently opened in Washington,
devoted to 'The Treasure Houses of Britain'.[1] Thirty-five
thousand square feet of gallery space have been given over to it;
more than seven hundred works of art from over two hundred
houses are on display; the Ford Motor Company alone has sub-
sidized it with a sum in excess of one million dollars; and 700,000
visitors are eagerly and confidently expected before the exhibition
closes. Not surprisingly, media attention has been intense; a bevy
of British aristocrats was flown in to lend a tone to the opening;
and the Prince and Princess of Wales have appeared to give the
show a suitably spectacular start. Now that these inaugural festivi-
ties are over, this may be an appropriate opportunity to take a
closer and more critical look, not only at the exhibition itself, but
also at the broader British background to it, and at the real aims
and objectives of those responsible for staging it.

It has become a platitude of modern British history that one of its
most significant themes is a profound and pervasive hostility to
industry and to urban life. By the late eighteenth century, men and
women came to feel that they had largely mastered the natural
world, and this, combined with the major impact of the industrial
revolution on the landscape, led to a profound shift in attitudes to
the countryside. People of all classes no longer saw it as a wilder-
ness to be tamed, but increasingly as a Garden of Eden –
threatened, not so much by the serpent as by the dark, satanic mill

– which must be preserved. At all levels of society, from the Chartists to the Fabians to High Tory paternalists, a veneration for green fields, village communities and high mountains became commonplace, as reflected in the paintings, the prose and the poetry of so many creative figures during the last two hundred years. Indeed, this cult of the countryside seems set to supersede the rising middle classes as the favourite all-purpose explanation for modern British history: for the economic growth of the Industrial Revolution no less than for the economic decline which followed; for fox-hunting at one extreme and for Animal Liberationists at the other.

One way to treat this subject more precisely is to look at the timing and tone of these romantic, rural impulses as embodied in the cult of the country house during the last hundred years. Since the 1870s, the British economy has experienced three major downturns, each one known to contemporaries as the 'great depression': during the last quarter of the nineteenth century; between the end of the First World War and the beginning of the Second; and in the long, lean years after 1974. Like all historical happenings, slumps never repeat themselves exactly, but these three depressions share many common characteristics: unacceptably high levels of unemployment, both cyclical and structural; the loss of overseas and domestic markets to international competitors; complaints that entrepreneurial effort was insufficient and that worker productivity was inadequate; renewed awareness of the blight, poverty and deprivation in big cities; hunger marches, riots, strikes and other expressions of urban unrest; and a widespread sense of unease, pessimism and anxiety, which hardly needs labouring in the aftermath of Handsworth and Brixton.

But these three recessions have also had a much broader impact on the country. In politics, they have in each case coincided with a significant shift to the right: from Gladstonian Liberalism to the age of Lord Salisbury, from Asquith and Lloyd George to the era of Baldwin, and from Wilson's 'New Britain' to the hegemony of Thatcher. In part, this is because depression divides the left, and so lets the Conservatives in: Salisbury profited from Liberal disarray in the aftermath of Home Rule; Baldwin from the inter-war confusion engendered by Liberal decline and Labour's infirmity; and Thatcher from an opposition vote split between Labour and the Alliance. But there are also more positive reasons why recession in Britain seems to favour reaction rather than revolution. Economic crises make most men and women increasingly cautious and conservative; safety first becomes a more appealing slogan than the new frontier; retrenchment, self-interest and conformity triumph over expansiveness, openhandedness and dissent. It was, after all, the undergraduates of the prosperous 'sixties and early 'seventies who aspired to change the world; today, their successors are more concerned to get good grades so they can get good jobs.

But there is also a distinctive cultural climate engendered by each of these depressions in turn. It is hardly coincidence that the late nineteenth century was the time when Elgar was composing his most elegiac music, when Lutyens was designing his most romantic houses, and when a variety of conservationist bodies and pastoral publicists like the National Trust and *Country Life* were coming into being. In the inter-war years, the Council for the Preservation of Rural England was set up; writers as diverse as G. M. Trevelyan, P. G. Wodehouse and Hugh Walpole were hymning and hyping the hedgerows; and Stanley Baldwin appeared as Lord Emsworth incarnate, puffing his pipe, poking his pigs, and telling everyone that the true spirit of England was the sight and sound and smell of the countryside. And in our own time, the same sentiments have re-emerged: witness the bestselling books of Mark Girouard on English country houses and the extraordinary success of *Brideshead*; the hue and cry raised by the preservationist lobbies over Mentmore (in vain) and Calke Abbey (much more successfully); and the passing of the National Heritage Act and the raising of the Mary Rose, the latter acclaimed by some as a triumph almost comparable to regaining the Falklands.

All this adds up to a recognizable and distinctive public mood, which has twice come and gone, and which is now firmly entrenched in Britain once again: withdrawn, nostalgic and escapist, disenchanted with the contemporary scene, preferring conservation to development, the country to the town, and the past to the present. And, not surprisingly, the version of the past which catches and crystallizes these sentiments is itself as conservative as the prevailing political climate. No one would have described Elgar or Trevelyan as rabid revolutionaries. The committees of the great preservationist societies were – and still are – groaning beneath the weight of great grandees. The very idea of a 'national' heritage, which is somehow 'threatened', and which must be 'saved', is often little more than a means of preserving the artifacts of an essentially élite culture, by claiming – in most cases quite implausibly – that it is really everybody's. At best, the outcome is a highly value-laden version of the past, not so much history as establishment mysterification, in which there is no room (and no need) for dissent, opposition or an alternative point of view. And at worst, the result is a neo-nostalgic, pseudo-pastoral world of manufactured make-believe, a picture-postcard version of Britain and its past, titillating the tourist with tinsel 'traditions'.

So, between the economic upswings of the last hundred years, there have been these three inversely correlated waves of conservative and escapist sentiment, each – like the depressions that have generated them – arguably more intense than the one before. And, just as business cycles need the helping hand of entrepreneurial endeavour, so these nostalgia booms require their own inventors of tradition and peddlars of dreams to get them going. Consider the image of England at present purveyed in American newspaper advertisments: Burberry raincoats, Laura Ashley dresses, Pringle sweaters, Liberty fabrics and Scotch wool tartans, all exploiting nostalgic and snobbish Anglophilia in the interest of British exports. And in England itself, tourism is now the country's biggest foreign currency earner after North Sea oil and the export of automobiles, providing jobs for 1.3 million people, with a predicted 50,000 a year being added for the rest of the decade. Is it any wonder that a recent headline in *The Times* ran as follows: 'Minister puts history at peak of new strategy to attract more tourists'? In the rapidly de-industrializing Britain of the 1980s, nostalgia and escapism are big business. Indeed, if the economy continues to decline at its present rate for much longer, they may soon be the country's *only* business.

★

It is in this long-term perspective of Britain's recurrent economic crises and regular swings to conservative cultural values that this country-house exhibition in Washington may best be understood. But what of the display itself? Its avowed purpose is to celebrate and to publicize five hundred years of upper-class patronage and collecting since the advent of the Tudors first made the art world safe for aristocracy. To contain the remarkable assemblage of paintings, miniatures, sculpture, furniture, porcelain, silver, tapestries, armour and books that have thus been brought together, seventeen rooms have been specially designed and constructed within the East Wing of the National Gallery, some of which vividly suggest the feel of country-house interiors, rather than the antiseptic impersonality of an art museum. There is also a massive and magnificent catalogue, which reproduces in colour every item on display, provides the fullest possible documentation and analysis, and is further enhanced by a set of lively essays filling in the historical background.[2] And for those who want a more vivid sense of the country houses themselves, Gervase Jackson-Stops has provided an admirable introduction, accompanied by some outstandingly beautiful photographs specially taken by James Pipkin.[3]

The first section of the exhibition traces the development of country-house collecting from the period of the fortified medieval castle, via the outward looking 'prodigy houses' of the Elizabethan and Jacobean periods, to the sumptuous Baroque palaces of the late seventeenth and early eighteenth centuries. Here, in one broad sweep, we see the rise and reign of superior secular patronage in the aftermath of the dissolution of the monasteries. We begin with a quite magical room devoted to the Tudor Renaissance, which achieves its effect by bringing together some outstanding pieces never before seen side by side. There is the Lumley horseman from Sandbeck, the earliest known equestrian statue in the history of English sculpture; there is the sea dog table from Hardwick, with its inlaid walnut top, supported by four carved dogs with dolphins' tails, themselves resting on the backs of tortoises; and there is the Rainbow Portrait of Elizabeth I from Hatfield, so rich and suggestive in its iconography that its precise meaning remains a subject of contention among art historians. There are suits of armour which remind us that this was still an unsettled time; there are tapestries which were as much to warm the walls as to decorate them; and there are some exquisite miniatures by Nicholas Hilliard and Isaac Oliver.

From this great chamber, we proceed into a Jacobean long gallery, appropriately modelled on the background to Daniel Mytens' painting of the Countess of Arundel, which is itself on display, as is the companion study of her husband, arguably the first great aristocratic patron and collector. Here are assembled fifteen paintings of Tudor and Stuart worthies, ornately dressed, proudly posed and poised, works of propaganda no less than of art. This is followed with a more intimate section devoted to the gentry houses of the Restoration, with their French furniture, their Dutch-influenced interiors, their Kneller portraits, their cabinets and their sconces. And this in turn is brilliantly contrasted to the later exuberance of the Baroque, when the Vanbrugh palaces set new standards of country-house luxury which are well captured here. A Grinling Gibbons carving of dead game from Kirtlington Park reminds us that hunting, shooting and fishing were an integral part of upper class life, both for recreation and for nourishment; the magnificent silver wine cooler from Burleigh House, weighing over 3,400 ounces, gives some indication of their capacity for alcohol; and the silver-framed looking glass, silver candle stands and silver-covered table from Knole, forming a richly-decorated suite of bedroom furniture, almost beggars belief.

The second section, concerned with collecting inspired by the eighteenth-century Grand Tour, covers a shorter span, and so achieves a greater cumulative impact. It begins, predictably, with a room devoted to Lord Burlington, Chiswick House, Inigo Jones and the Palladian Revolution. This prepares us for a display of contemporary Italian topographical paintings, including Canalettos of the Doge's Palace and the Grand Canal, and for an ingeniously created sculpture rotunda, full of those ancient marbles, bronzes and vases which many English aristocrats acquired at bargain prices in their travels to the Mediterranean. A room devoted to Augustan taste illustrates the beginnings of Old Master collecting, with a particularly fine Titian from Garrowby, and Van Dyck's *Betrayal of Christ* from Corsham Court. There is an intimate show of Dutch art, in a room where the arrangement of the paintings is inspired by Zoffany's portrait of *Sir Lawrence Dundas and His Son* from Aske Hall, which is itself on display. And the perspective is then broadened once again, with a gallery devoted entirely to landscape, including Claude's famous *Landing of Aeneas* from Anglesey Abbey, and English works by Gainsborough, Richard Wilson and Joseph Wright of Derby, paintings which often provided the inspiration for those great parks and rural vistas which country-house owners were at that time creating.

The climax of the exhibition is a section devoted to 'The Gentleman Collector, 1770–1830', a period which saw the high point of country-house patronage and acquisitiveness. British aristocrats were at that time the richest and most secure in the western world, and since many European monarchs and land-owners were obliged to unload their treasures in the aftermath of the Revolutionary and Napoleonic Wars, there was more than ever for them to buy. Their interest in books, prints and drawings is shown in a room devoted to the country-house library; there is some splendid Oriental porcelain and Chinese Chippendale furniture; there is Meissen from Alnwick Castle and Sèvres from Harewood House (although it might have been more advantageously displayed on a dining table); the early eighteenth-century four-poster state bed from Calke Abbey, complete with its magnificent Chinese hangings, is on show for the first time; and there is a selection of sporting pictures and silver gilt. Once again, the close connections between leisure and patronage are well displayed, as in the Stubbs *Mares and Foals Without a Background*, painted for the second Marquess of Rockingham in 1762, and in the four race cups won by Lord Scarbrough's horse Catton in the 1810s.

But it is the tripartite Waterloo Gallery which creates the most overpowering impression of aristocratic opulence and acquisitiveness. The room itself, with its columns, its top-lit ceiling, and its pictures double-hung on the walls, is convincingly evocative of early nineteenth-century galleries, as shown in Charles Robert Leslie's study of the Grosvenor family. The centre-piece of the display is Canova's *Three Graces*, commissioned by the sixth Duke of Bedford for the Woburn sculpture gallery. There are furniture and fittings showing Egyptian influence, as in a settee and arm chair from Buscot Park. Here, too, are gathered works by the great British artists of the time, such as Gainsborough's full-length study of the third Earl of Bristol, and Romney's double portrait of Sir Christopher and Lady Sykes. And here, also, are some quite outstanding Old Masters, including Rubens' spectacular and newly-cleaned Marchesa Caterina Grimaldi from Kingston Lacey, a vivid indication of what could be bought at this time, even by relatively poor landed families.

Those who believe that aristocratic taste went rapidly downhill during the remainder of the nineteenth century will find their views amply – perhaps excessively – corroborated by the rest of this exhibition. One section is devoted to Victorian sentimentality and the cult of the Scottish Highlands. Predictably, there are two Landseers, with stags not quite at bay; there is a vast Winterhalter of the Duchess of Sutherland looking rather coarse; and there is some quite excruciatingly hideous furniture from Osborne, supported on stags' legs, and adorned with antlers. The Pre-Raphaelites which follow are few and familiar, like Burne-Jones' *Love among the Ruins*, from Wightwick Manor; there is a rather beautiful silver claret jug designed by William Burgess for the Marquess of Bute, which provides temporary relief and uplift; and a room enticingly entitled 'Edwardian Elegance and the Continuing Tradition' turns out to be little more than a selection of John Singer Sargent's family paintings, dominated by the famous Marlborough family group from Blenheim, and the beguiling portrait of Lady Rocksavage from Houghton. But on the whole, this is a downbeat finale to a dazzling display. The organizers seem rather to have lost interest, and their waning enthusiasm shows through.

For all its undeniable splendours, no exhibition devoted to this theme and mounted on this scale can be without its flaws. It is not clear why some works have been included, and others left out. The distinctions between patronage and collecting, between functional and decorative art, seem inadequately made and explored. The exhibits are assigned their chronological places in rather an inconsistent way: some by date of acquisition, others by date of completion. And the effect is sometimes to mislead as to the real extent of aristocratic collection, especially in the early period. By displaying only magnificent objects, many aspects of upper-class collecting go ignored: there are no cases of stuffed birds, no stags' heads, no elephants' feet, which clutter so many country houses. The personalities of the greatest patrons do not really emerge: even Lords Arundel and Egremont seem little more than names. There is no great Holbein exhibited. And it seems strange that there should be but one work by Turner, arguably the greatest ornament and beneficiary of country-house patronage. Above all, these works of art give only the cosiest view of the landed classes' world: there is but one picture of a prison, one of the Industrial Revolution, and one of the poor. It is not just fine art that is on display here: it is very refined art indeed.

Put less mellowly, that means that 'The Treasure Houses of Britain' may be justly acclaimed, not only for the overall high quality of the objects and the installation, but also for providing a popular and saleable image of English upper-class life. But that is not all which needs to be said. One rather obvious and important point is that the private collections and public galleries of North America already contain massive amounts of such English country-house art. Between them, the Frick Collection, the Huntingdon Gallery and the Yale Center for British Art alone would yield a harvest of paintings not much inferior to those now on display in Washington. It cannot, therefore, be plausibly maintained that this exhibition shows things in America of a kind and of a quality that have never been seen before. So what, exactly, is the point in temporarily transporting these treasures across the Altantic, when so much that is so similar, and has been seen by so many, is already in the United States for good?

In the first place, it is clear that this exhibition is not just concerned to evoke admiration for country-house art. It also seeks – on the principle of veneration by association – to elicit feelings at least as ardent and well-disposed on behalf of the country houses themselves, and even more so on behalf of their owners. How else is one to explain the highly emotive, value-laden language which pervades the accompanying literature? It might just be acceptable to call stately homes 'treasure houses', but to describe them as 'vessels of civilization', as 'temples of the arts', seems altogether excessive. And when we are further informed that they are 'the envy of the rest of the world', this seems little more than meaning-less hyperbole. Even worse are the descriptions offered of the owners: 'wealthy and privileged, but also well-read and well-travelled', characterized by 'culture and humanity, scholarship and lack of pomposity'. The best that can be said about this is that it is the language, not of scholarship, but of sentiment; more accurately, it appears that those in charge of this exhibition have lost all sense of proportion or historical perspective.

Indeed, two of the essays contributed to the catalogue by people who know better, show plainly just how naive and overstated these wild claims really are. In his account of British landowners as collectors, Francis Haskell puts their activities so crushingly in perspective that he comes close to demolishing the whole notion that they were ever paragons of patronage. As he explains, they bought few paintings in or of the Italian Renaissance; there were not many outstanding country-house collections in being even by the early eighteenth century; the portraits (if any) commissioned by most landed families were limited in number and poor in quality; it was only in the aftermath of the French Revolution that the really great accumulations of Old Masters came into being, and in any case, most of these were initially displayed in London; and from the 1880s onwards, landowners were more active in selling works of art than in acquiring them, as the one-way traffic across the Atlantic so vividly serves to show.

In fact, Haskell's rather deflating argument may be pushed even further. For, as the catalogue itself demonstrates, most works of art cost very little, even in the more robust currency of the time: £50 for the Leconfield *Aphrodite*, and only double that for the

Van Dyck *Betrayal of Christ*. They were not yet precious and priceless objects in the way that they have since become. So it is hardly surprising that country-house owners often treated their collections in a cavalier manner: they blithely cut tapesteries to fit odd and irregular spaces; they regularly relegated out-of-date pictures and furniture to the attics; and the magnificent Calke state bed was never even unpacked after its delivery. As this suggests, most aristocrats and gentry were more likely to be philistine than cultured, indifferent to art rather than well-disposed. Compared with the minor princelings of Germany or the city states of Italy, what is really remarkable is not that they spent so much of their wealth on art, but that they spent so little.

In practice, as Mark Girouard – another catalogue contributor with his feet firmly on the ground – makes plain, the greatest aristocratic expenditure on the arts was usually on the mansion itself and the park: the outward and visible signs of wealth, status and importance. For, as he goes on to argue, country houses were not fetish objects, inhabited by implausibly nice and exquisitely civilized people: they were fundamentally machines for a power élite to live in. Look at the faces which gaze out of the pictures on display: proud, tough, assured, haughty, confident; they are men and women who know precisely their place in the nation, and their nation's place in the world. These were people who enjoyed income, not just from agriculture, but from East India trade, London building estates, coal mines and canals, harbours and railways. They endured damp, draughty and insanitary houses; they could stay for hours in the saddle; they condoned man traps, employed game keepers, and favoured the death penalty for poaching. Above all, they stood for oligarchy, hierarchy, in-equality and exclusiveness: all the things against which the Americans rebelled in 1776, and which even the British have, in the last hundred years, come to regard as increasingly un-acceptable and indefensible.

But this exhibition has a second, and arguably more insidious purpose, which follows on inexorably from the first. If the works of art are so magnificent, if the houses are so magical, and if the owners both past and present are so wonderful, then surely paintings, palaces and patricians should be allowed to remain together in the future? Here, it seems, is the real object of this exercise: to argue not just for the preservation of the 'total' country house, but also for continued aristocratic occupancy. Once again, the cascade of emotive language is turned on, to present a highly-coloured account of recent aristocratic plight and pluck. During the last hundred years, country houses have been 'threatened' by democracy, death duties, two world wars, and more recently by 'swingeing' capital transfer tax. Even Hugh Dalton, a Labour Chancellor of the Exchequer, felt 'anguish at the prospect of the great estates breaking up'. In the 'fifties, country houses were 'embattled fortresses, powerfully resisting the hand of the de-molisher and the developer', appropriate symbols for 'a post-war Britain too inclined to accept the idea of progress for its own sake'.

But, we are told, the position is now fortunately much brighter. Thanks to the inspiration of that 'radical politician' (?) Lord Lothian, the National Trust has allowed many families to remain in their homes, so that they continue 'loved and lived in', and are not 'simply museums'. In 1974, the Victoria and Albert Museum staged an exhibition on the destruction of the country house, which 'struck an emotional chord'; the National Land Fund now offers 'succour' to mansions in distress; and recently it has even become possible to retain works of art *in situ* after they have been accepted by the Treasury in lieu of death duties. 'It is', we are told, 'of the greatest importance that this principle should be extended.' And why? Because it will enable owners to continue to fill their historic role, of 'sharing their houses with the public, and main-taining them as heirlooms in trust for the nation at large'. For that, we are reminded, is what they have always done: since the eighteenth century, great owners have readily welcomed visitors to great houses; the stately homes of England are thus 'the oldest and longest running museums in the world'; and this is how they should be allowed to remain.

Clearly, to question an argument couched in such impassioned and emotive terms runs the risk of seeming ungrateful, philistine or even radical. But since that is no doubt part of its polemical purpose, it is important not to be swept along into unthinking acceptance. To begin with, it is not at all clear that those in today's stately homes business are simply carrying on an old tradition in opening their houses to the public. The few tourists let in long ago were the beneficiaries of *noblesse oblige*; but now it is the owners who benefit from the thousands who go through the turnstiles, partly from the revenue thus acquired, and partly from the tax concessions thus enjoyed. Moreover, it can hardly be coincidence that the last hundred years, which have seen the self-conscious elaboration by the aristocracy of their role as guardians of national culture, has also been the century in which they have themselves been most under threat. And so, by demanding – and getting – special treatment as patrons of the arts, they have been able to hold on to their paintings, their houses and their way of life, in defiance of the social, economic and political trends of the time. Paradoxically, but deliberately, the art collections have thus increasingly become the means of ensuring aristocratic survival. Once it was the country-house culture which was parasitic on the country-house élite; now it is the élite which is even more parasitic on the culture.

Yet as the need to resort to these elaborate stratagems only serves to show, the British aristocracy is in many ways an anachronistic group in decline. Do the government and the tax-payers really have a duty – even in the name of art – to prop it up indefinitely? There are already more than one hundred country houses in the expert care of the National Trust: just how many more do we actually need? And besides, this argument necessarily involves a double standard. The British aristocrats who ransacked Europe in the eighteenth century are acclaimed by their descendants for their discerning collecting and for augmenting the national heritage. But now their successors are obliged to sell to the new rich of the United States, this is decried as a national tragedy. Yet this seems not only inconsistent but also unrealistic. Ultimately, taste and culture are a function of economic relations: art follows cash. When Britain was a rich country with a rich élite, great treasures were acquired; now the nobles and the nation are poor, they are up for sale again. And, with Britain's economy in the state it is, what else is it reasonable to expect?

★

Viewed from such a standpoint, 'The Treasure Houses of Britain' is not so much an exhibition as a rhetorical exercise, displaying works of art, tugging at the heartstrings, appealing to snobbery and nostalgia, all in support of an idealized view of the country house and its owners, which is as historically unconvincing as it is politically reactionary. The real problem, with art no less than with aristocracy, is to get a sense of proportion. Among country-house owners, there have always been terrible philistines, and there have always been those with a genuine love of beautiful things; there have always been those who calculatingly viewed family heirlooms as assets to be realized, and there have always been those who see them as a trust to be treasured. And in the professional world of museums and conservation, attitudes to country-house collections are almost as varied. There is no doubt a case to be made for keeping some of these intact. But there is also an argument – in the name of art but not in the name of artistocracy – for displaying many of these things in galleries, open and accessible to all, and shorn of the emotional baggage and élitist connotations which seem inseparable from the cult of the country house.

Indeed, in at least two ways, the exhibition itself powerfully undermines the very case which its sponsors and organizers want it to make. In the first place, while celebrating country-house collecting, it will probably further country-house dispersal. Many things on show here are still in private hands, and their public display will surely stimulate more rich Americans to acquire additional items of Britain's 'national heritage'. But more importantly, the very nature of this marvellous museum display is a quite devastating riposte to the claim that works of art are always best kept *in situ*. Many country houses are inaccessible, open rarely, contain at best indifferent works of art, and show them badly and inexpertly. Yet here are gathered together the most outstanding gems from two hundred mansions, in near-perfect conditions of display and access. In terms of making the artifacts of élite culture available to a broader public, this exhibition does incomparably more for the national heritage than any number of country houses.

But, to state the obvious, it does so overseas, in a great

American gallery, and with generous American funding. From the British standpoint, however, this only serves to highlight another problem. For the argument in favour of museums rather than country houses as the best medium of display presupposes that English art galleries are in a position to acquire and to show such beautiful things in surroundings and conditions comparable to those available in Washington. But that, of course, is rarely and decreasingly possible. Many British museums are almost as shambolic and uninviting as the most rundown country house: their funds inadequate, their lighting unsatisfactory, their galleries only intermittently open. The Thatcher government is not much concerned about this: the idea that works of art may elevate the mind and lift the spirit, and that they should be freely and easily available for all, is not something which seems to concern her administration very much. And as long as this remains the case, and British museums continue pitifully under-funded, then country houses may become more important as 'vessels of civilization', not less.

But of course, Mrs Thatcher herself is no better disposed to the country-house world which is so valued and vaunted in this exhibition. She may approve of the tourist trade as a dollar earner, but her personal brand of radical and petty bourgeois conservatism has no time for the escapist syndrome, which she sees as anachronistically irrelevant to the Britain of 1985. Her heroes are self-made men (and self-made failures) like Clive Sinclair, Freddie Laker and Cecil Parkinson; they are not traditional Tory gentry like Francis Pym or grandees like Lord Carrington. She hates the idea of Britain as a museum society, intent on embalming itself, whether the impulse comes from the left (in the shape of Scargill and the miners) or from the right (in the form of country-house owners and their propagandists). If told, by the organizers of this exhibition, that Britain possesses the finest country houses in western Europe, she would reply that Britain also has the worst and the weakest economy. One does not have to be a Thatcherite to concede that these things may, perhaps, be connected. We may leave this exhibition dazzled; but we should certainly not leave it blinded.

(1985)

NOTES:

1. National Gallery of Art, Washington, 'The Treasure Houses of Britain: Five Hundred Years of Private Patronage and Collecting', 3 November 1985 to 16 March 1986.
2. Gervase Jackson-Stops (editor), *The Treasure Houses of Britain: Five Hundred Years of Private Patronage and Art Collecting* (London, 1985).
3. Gervase Jackson-Stops and James Pipkin, *The English Country House: A Grand Tour* (Washington, 1985).

PART FIVE

# BIOGRAPHY

# The Dictionary of National Biography

'Mr Stephen is editing a little dictionary', a friend explained to a clergyman foolhardy enough to ask whether Leslie 'did any writing'. The enterprise in question was the *DNB*, one of those grandiosely conceived and indefatigably executed works of late nineteenth-century self-regard, comparable to the *Victoria County Histories* and the *Survey of London*. Year after year, at three-monthly intervals, sixty-three volumes plopped from the press, from Jacques Abbadie in 1885 to William Zuylestein in 1900, containing some thirty thousand pages on which six hundred and fifty contributors recorded the details of thirty thousand lives. And, as with the painting of the Forth Bridge, once this great Victorian monument was completed, it was time to start all over again. In 1901, a three-volume supplement appeared, repairing important omissions from the original work, and adding in those worthies who had died since its appearance. Ten years later, another three volumes followed, spanning the decade from the death of Victoria to the demise of Edward VII.

Although he remained a regular and prolific contributor, Stephen had long since abandoned his editorial connection with the scheme by then. For an enterprise initially conceived with almost jaunty vagueness ('I have been thinking a great deal', he recorded airily in the autumn of 1881, 'about biographies, universal and otherwise'), had proved to be an unexpected treadmill, as the trials and tribulations of editorship tyrannized and tormented him. Contributors were constantly difficult, insanely verbose, excessively pedantic, obtusely antiquarian; suggestions for inclusion sometimes bordered on the absurd, as when a clergyman submitted a list of 1400 'important' hymnwriters; the labour of reading, writing, checking, co-ordinating, corresponding and proof-reading was prodigious; and the regular deadlines every three months loomed inexorably and inescapably ominous. 'Accursed', 'hideous', 'damned', 'diabolical', 'uninteresting', 'repulsive', 'infernal', were some of the adjectives Stephen employed to describe his labours or his contributors. Eventually, in 1891, wifely protest combined with ill-health forced Stephen to relinquish the editorship to Sidney Lee, who had been his assistant since 1883, and it was under his equally indefatigable auspices that the original scheme was completed along with the first two supplements.

Their combined labours produced an enduring monument to national greatness and national enterprise. No other country, as Stephen and Lee frequently boasted with evident relish, could rival the *DNB* in scale, scope or speed. Austria, Germany, Holland and Sweden had all initiated similar schemes: but they had taken conspicuously longer, produced conspicuously less, and were all conspicuously incomplete. Moreover, by narrowing its scope from universal to British and imperial biography, the *Dictionary* could satisfy the 'commemorative instinct' of the nation, providing as it did a uniquely comprehensive monument to past greatness. Rhetoric, sentiment and panegyric may all have been eschewed ('No flowers, by request', as Alfred Ainger put it), but it remained the *DNB*'s purpose 'to do the state some service' by 'helping the present and future generations to realize more thoroughly than were otherwise possible the character of their ancestors' collective achievement, of which they now enjoy the fruits.' Furthermore, the *DNB* was a monument to entrepreneurial zeal. Elsewhere, similar schemes were often state aided which, it was clearly implied, was one of the reasons why they had failed. But, thanks to the willingness of the publisher, George Smith, to lose £70,000 on an outlay of £100,000, the *DNB*, 'in accord with the self-reliant temperament of the British race', was 'the outcome of private enterprise and the handiwork of private citizens'.

Thus conceived and completed, embodying 'the fruit of conscientious industry combined with the power of vivid and coherent deliniation', the *DNB* was established as an abidingly useful and incomparably wide-ranging work of reference. But it also reflected the limitations of its age and the prejudices of its creators. Written at a time when there was no established or institutionalized school of historical research, it was riddled with errors and inaccuracies, especially in the early volumes. Stephen's anticlericalism ensured that religion received short measure in the early stages (Keble only merited three and a half pages, and St Alban and St Asaph had to wait until the supplement to get in), while Lee's liking for literati (his first question about a potential subject was 'what did he write?') meant that authors were over-represented towards the end. Considering that the venture had been made possible by private enterprise, there were astonishingly few businessmen commemorated, and the number of women was negligible. And moral judgments came thick, fast and firm: there was to be 'much discretion in dealing with a life's moral disfigurements', and only 'occasionally' was 'the admission of sinners to the biographic fold' allowed.

The first, heroic phase of the *DNB*'s life closed with the completion of the second supplement, and with the deaths of Stephen, Smith and Lee. Since then, six single-volume supplements have appeared, commemorating the great and the good who died in each decade from the 1910s to the 1960s. As such, they reflect both the abiding influence of the original conception, and also the changes which circumstances have forced upon it. In a less spacious age, the scale of the enterprise has necessarily been reduced: each decade now gets one volume instead of three, and the number of lives has been pruned from a thousand to seven hundred and fifty. Longer lives have been shortened, while shorter lives have been lengthened. The treatment of George V and George VI was almost perfunctory compared with Lee's lengthy laments for Victoria and Edward VII, and the twenty-two pages accorded to Churchill in this volume are miserly compared with the fifty allotted to Gladstone half a century before.[1] On the other hand, the average length of each life has advanced from a page to a page and a half, so that even the most obscure receive enhanced recognition. As supplement has succeeded supplement, the number of industrialists, scientists and women has grown, while the cohorts of writers, lawyers and divines have declined, although neither of these trends has been as pronounced as it should have been  With the demise of Smith's publishing house, no other private business would take over such a costly venture, so that this monument to entrepreneurial zeal is now accommodated in the institutional hands of OUP, which may also explain why the editorial chair has migrated westward, from the Cambridge of Stephen and Lee to the Oxonian and imperial portals of Rhodes House.

More fundamentally, the character of the *DNB* has changed completely, as what began as a piece of historically-conceived inquiry has evolved into an end-of-decade report. In the old days, personal acquaintance did not matter: one completed and distant life was very much like another. But now, when private information and individual recollection must often be the substitute for archival research, personal knowledge is of the essence. So, ostensibly authoritative biographies of the long-since departed have been superseded by interim studies of the recently-deceased. And as a result, the number of contributors has increased as much as the style of their contributions has changed. Over half of the original *DNB* was written by thirty-four regular authors. In this volume, there are nearly as many writers as subjects. As a result, the role of the editor has changed as well. Stephen and Lee were Botham-like all-rounders, as much contributors as editors, producing between them well over a thousand articles. But their successors have increasingly become non-playing team captains, co-ordinating the efforts of others, as in this volume, where Sir Edgar Williams restricts himself to two brief lives and the extended study of Churchill.

Despite these developments, there is much of this latest volume which is directly in the tradition of Stephen and Lee. The writers, the lawyers and the clergy may still be on the run. But the politicians and proconsuls, civil servants and administrators, generals and admirals, remain in dominant abundance. Predictably, they are joined by a whole generation of scientists and technologists, engineers and experts, to whom the Second World War has given enhanced status. Together, these old and new men form the great majority, and it is their world, of committees and research terms, of mandarins and boffins, as depicted in the novels of C. P. Snow (the original for at least one of whose characters is in this book) and in sundry Sampsonian *Anatomies of Britain*, which is commemorated in this volume. Here is an official prosopography of official Britain: civil servants write about civil servants, scientists write about scientists, diplomats write about diplomats, and Speakers write about Speakers, all accepting, implicitly, the values and methods of their chosen profession. As a result, the book's centre of gravity is markedly to the right. There are very few trades unionists, and one of their number, William Gallacher, is revealingly described as a 'working-class agitator and politician.' On his ennoblement, Marshal of the RAF Lord Douglas of Kirtleside admitted to being 'a moderate socialist' which, as his biographer explains, made him 'a somewhat unusual member of the higher military hierarchy'. There also seems to be much more space devoted to practitioners of golf, cricket, rowing and fox-hunting than to professional footballers.

By the time we reach the letter B, the tone of the volume is unmistakably established in two scrupulously mandarin pieces by Lord Trend on Bridges and Normanbrook, his predecessors at the Cabinet Office. Here, elegantly catalogued and lucidly unfolded, are the qualities which are continually enumerated, acclaimed and celebrated thereafter: stamina, resilience, fortitude and endurance; tact, reticence, loyalty and discretion; the capacity to draft cogent memoranda, master difficult agendas, write lucid minutes; to assimilate information, chair committees, create and control administrative machinery. Those men were quiet, careful, cautious, pragmatic, orderly, logical and unemotional. To their colleagues they appeared strong, stern, shy and silent; they took work home at night and at weekends; they had time for few hobbies or recreations; they jealously guarded their private lives; but in the select company of those who knew them well, they were warm-hearted, charming, kindly and generous. Indefatigable, relentless, remorseless, formidable, indomitable: they sound like the Grand Fleet at anchor at Spithead. In such company, it is clear why a man like Dowding ('his vision was intense but narrow') never made it to the top.

It is also revealing that Bridges and Normanbrook were relatively long-lived, as were most of the men in this book. Over one third were born in the 1880s, and sixty per cent were born before 1890. They survived the First World War, and came to greatness in the Second: they are the lost and found generation, the exact contemporaries of the *DNB* itself. All day, every day, day after day, night after night, they worked, researched or administered. Youthful illness, permanent disability, personal tragedy, were all conquered. And great were their rewards on earth: honorary doctorates and fellowships from their Oxbridge colleges; smooth progress up the Establishment ladder from a C to a K to a G; inexorable advance from FRS to a Nobel Prize to PRS to OM. The way to get to the top, this book makes clear, is to work harder and live longer than your rivals and contemporaries. The wayward Mervyn Peake, living on 'this desperate edge of now', and the mercurial evanescence of Jim Clark and Joe Orton, counts for little in the scales of achievement when weighed against such elephantine stamina and titanic endurance. This book is, unashamedly, perhaps inevitably, a monument to the loneliness of the long distance runner, rather than a paean of praise to meteoric fame or youthful success.

This stress on the sustained, orderly transaction of business, and on the smooth workings of the government machine does mean, however, that a variety of other equally admirable and important qualities receive rather less than their due. One of those is versatility. There are some memorably described polymaths, such as 'professional violinist and economist', 'schoolmaster, cricket historian and administrator', 'eye surgeon, missionary and philanthropist'; but in the main, it is those who plough a single furrow who receive the fullest attention. Genius, flamboyance, audacity, intuition, romanticism, high colour: all seem slightly suspect. Even Churchill, who is given ample and unstinted praise for most of these attributes, is presented as the exception which proves the rule: for he is shown to have been a greater man because his wayward, unstable, intuitive fertility was tamed and disciplined by the mandarin and the military, Bridges and Ismay. His achievement as the inspirer of the British people receives much less attention than does his success in kicking the government machine into top gear. Improvisation, flexibility, anticipation, a sense of opportunity: all these qualities which flowered in wartime and are equally necessary in peace, seem rather lost sight of.

So it comes as no surprise to discover that, despite the general improvement which has taken place since the 1900s, commerce and trade – where these qualities are presumably even more important – are still underrepresented. The illustrious and the industrious are amply commemorated; but the entrepreneur and the industrialist get much shorter shrift. Bankers, financiers, company chairman and shipowners are there in some profusion; but businessmen such as Clarke, Nuffield, Bowater and Rootes are decidedly thin on the ground. Women are another group who seem peripheral to this male and mandarin world. In explaining why there were so few of them in the earliest volumes of the *DNB*, Lee noted that 'women's opportunities of distinction were infinitessimal in the past, and are very small compared with men's at the present moment'. Here, too, little seems to have changed. In the first supplement, women were some four per cent of the total; here, the figure is nearer seven. Most come from relatively comfortable, upper and upper-middle class backgrounds, and succeeded in professions without any formal or hierarchical career structure. So, the majority are actresses (Elsie and Leigh), academics (Cam and Darbishire), artists (Bell, Cohen, Knight) or authors (Allingham, Blyton, Compton-Burnett, Sackville-West and Sitwell), topped off with occasional politicians (Astor, Bonham-Carter and Lady Lloyd George) and royals (Princess Marina, Queen Victoria Eugenie, the Princess Royal). Vera Brittain, Ivy Williams ('the first woman to be called to the English bar'), and Rachel Crowdy (she 'belonged to a generation when women had to possess very obvious strength of character if they were to attain recognition'), are the only ones who might be described as noteworthy, self-consciously, propagandizing feminists. 'Women will not, I regret', concluded Lee, 'have very much claims on the attention of the national biographer for a very long time to come.' That may not be right; but it still seems to be true.

Because so much of this book is about the great and the good, the two major innovations in editorial policy are less exciting than might appear at first glance. The promise to be more candid about sex and scandal, spying and secrecy, represents a significant shift from the stern and unbending days of Stephen and Lee; but in practice, the result is rarely significant. Such revelations as are made about the private lives of Harold and Vita, Somerset Maugham, Joe Orton and E. M. Forster, add nothing that is new: they are informative but not titillating. On the other hand, the statement that Nancy Astor's friendship with Lord Lothian was 'always regarded as platonic' is merely salacious innuendo: it is titillating but not informative. The only real plum is Cecil Beaton's remarkable comment on Lily Elsie's anaemia – 'this was no doubt the reason for an unusually early menopause and for a certain frigidity' – which should be a winner for the *Guardian*'s 'Naked Ape' column. Nor do the revelations on secrets amount to much, with two exceptions. One concerns the life of Sir Stewart Menzies, wartime head of the Secret Intelligence Service which is, predictably, based on 'private information' and 'personal knowledge'. Yet, uniquely among all the entries, this contribution is unsigned. Is this sinister machination, or merely a proof-reader's oversight? The second is Anthony Blunt's account of Tomas Harris, whom he describes as 'artist, art dealer and intelligence officer'. What wistful, envious or remorseful sense of irony prompted Blunt to remark that Harris perpetrated 'the most successful double-cross operation of the war'?

It has always been a general, if flexible rule, that the writers of 'official' biographies should not contribute on the same subject to the *DNB*. The rationale of this remains obscure, and in this volume robs us of Nigel Nicolson on Alexander, A. J. P. Taylor on Beaverbrook, Martin Gilbert on Churchill, Jonathan Dimbleby on his father, John Pearson on Ian Fleming, P. N. Furbank on E. M. Forster, Philip Williams on Gaitskell, Sybille

Bedford on Aldous Huxley, Michael Holroyd on Augustus John, J. E. Morpurgo on Allen Lane, Ronald Lewin on Slim, and Christopher Sykes on Evelyn Waugh. On the other hand, we do get Jose Harris on Beveridge, James Lees-Milne on Harold Nicolson, O. S. Nock on Stanier, and Hugh Thomas on John Strachey. In such circumstances, where the great have already received the supreme accolade of official biography, there is little new to add. Much more interesting are the accounts of the otherwise unbiographied men and women of second rank, such as Scarbrough, Zetland, Ketton Cremer and Lord and Lady Iveagh, whose elegant, distinguished but unspectacular lives receive fitting memorial. As Stephen himself once remarked, 'it is not upon the lives of the great men that the value of this book really depends. It is the second-rate people that provide the really useful reading.' He would not have been disappointed in this volume.

It was also Stephen who noted that the real joy of the *DNB* lay in 'the great art of skipping', and here, too, little has changed. Some of the contributions are as dull as their subjects; but many scintillate and sparkle. What a delight it is to learn than Nancy Astor was 'a curious mixture of religious maniac and clown'; that to Lord Bridges there fell 'the immense responsibility of translating the inspired poetry of Churchill's directives into the plain prose of effective action'; that Cadogan 'played golf regularly, relentlessly, and rather badly'; that Joe Orton 'aspired to corrupt an audience with pleasure'; and that Vincent Massey 'could stroke even a cliché until it purred like an epigram'. Lord Annan notes that E. M. Forster's works 'were full of aphorisms', something on which he is rather an authority himself. Sir John Hicks sums up the issues between Keynes and Robertson with magisterial fairness and clarity. And Kenneth Rose reveals that Sir Frederic Hooper, the head of Schweppes, 'detested the fizzy drinks upon which the prosperity of his firm depended'. One can only agree with that 'poet, playwright, critic, editor, and publisher', T. S. Eliot (whose later life, Richard Ellmann informs us, 'became rather stately'): 'I did not know death had undone so many.'

★

When originally conceived, Lee observed that 'national biography must be prepared to satisfy the commemorative instinct of all sections of the nation'. His volumes did not meet up to that exacting requirement; nor does this one; nor, perhaps, could any. What it does do is to reveal the pinstripe, the stuffed shirt, the rolled umbrella, the bowler hat, the regimental tie and the lab coat, in their time of greatest trial and in their years of supreme achievement. For those who are captivated by this world, and who accept it at its own self-evaluation, as it is presented here, this book will make riveting reading, even if few will possess the stamina, fortitude, endurance, etc, etc to read it from cover to cover. In particular, high praise is due to the editor, who must have used many of Stephen's adjectives in the course of his task, and who merits many of Lord Trend's in having completed it. In 1900, when the original *DNB* was complete, Stephen surveyed it, and found it to be 'a good bit of work'. In its mandarin understatement, as much as in its appreciation of the book's real merits, the same phrase may fittingly be applied to this most recent instalment.

(1981)

NOTE:
1. E. T. Williams and C. S. Nicholls (editors), *The Dictionary of National Biography, 1961–1970* (Oxford, 1981).

# 26

# Lord Palmerston

The history of the world is no longer the biographies of great men. The Victorians, who needed heroes as an addict needs heroin, enshrined their worthies in multi-tomed tombs. Letters were reproduced verbatim, speeches were quoted at inordinate length, and eulogies were printed *in extenso*. If the public career was successful, the moral was ponderously pointed; if the private life was suspect, the veil was dutifully drawn down. Super stars like Disraeli, Albert and Gladstone were celebrated in six, five and three volumes apiece, and most cabinet ministers could usually count on at least two – especially if, like Lord Randolph Churchill, their reputation was safer in their son's hands than in their own. Although Lytton Strachey assailed such pious pomposity by showing that the slenderest of books could sometimes be the weightiest, and that eminence was not necessarily next to Godliness, these pantheons in print were still being constructed on a lavish scale until the Second World War: four volumes (and still unfinished) for Salisbury, three for Joseph Chamberlain (likewise then incomplete) and for Curzon, and a double-decker apiece for Asquith, Balfour, Campbell-Bannerman and Rosebery.

The second half of our century has seen a dramatic decline in the construction of these many-volumed vaults. In the United States, where resources are greater, sentiments stronger, and presidents *ipso facto* great men, the commemoration business has become even more luxuriant, as the metaphorical shrines have become actual, three-dimensional temples, housing the sacred relics of presidential papers: that for Kennedy in Boston stops short just this side of idolatry; that for Johnson in Texas goes well beyond it.

But in England, the old genre has withered and nothing new has emerged: there are no longer biographies of great men because there are no longer great men to biography, and there are no longer publishers to produce such works because there is no longer a reading public prepared to buy them. Among relatively recent cabinet ministers, only Ernest Bevin (two vols down, one to go) and Nye Bevan (canonized by Michael Foot) have received extended treatment, while the massive life of Churchill is unique in its Victorian dimensions. Today, the best way for a politician to guarantee this much-coveted form of life after death is to write it himself. And if he entertains pretensions to prolixity, it helps (as Harold Macmillan was the first to admit) if you own a publishing house as well.

This diminished celebration of the recently departed has been paralleled by a scholarly reaction against biographies of the more distantly deceased. The Victorians' confident vigour meant that they were fascinated by the impact of men on circumstances; in our less expansive age, we are more preoccupied with the impact of circumstances on men. Unlike the old, the 'new' history – economic, social, urban and demographic – explores people as categories, groups, statistics, abstractions, rather than as flesh and blood beings. 'Mere' biography is dismissed as attributing an unmerited significance to the trivial doings of trivial individuals. At best, it is a poor way of writing history – person rather than problem oriented, when no individual, however influential, has so dominated an age that it is sensible to write its history round him. Trends and tendencies, patterns and processes, *crises* and *conjonctures*, are what matter, not the vain protests of men, standing Canute-like in their impotent incomprehension, against the prevailing tides of history. We are all Marxists now.

Above all, there is the real danger for the professional historian that, if he writes an outstanding biography, it may become a best-seller. For biography still flourishes – albeit on a reduced scale and with diminished intellectual self-confidence – both within and without the walls of academe. In one guise, it has been reincarnated as prosopography, which stresses backgrounds rather than opinions, collective behaviour in preference to individual diversity, in the (usually vain) hope of discovering some historical laws of circumstantial determinism. In another, it has been resurrected as psycho-history, which seeks greater intellectual respectability by becoming evidentially more sensational, probing the intimate details of men's inner lives as lived in their bedrooms and bathrooms (and thereby shifting the mainspring of historical causation from Cleopatra's nose to Luther's lav). A third response has been to restate the view that men sometimes make events as much as events make men; that history does, after all, occasionally need a helping hand; and that even Marx was an individual not a process. We are all persons now.

The alternative is to argue that good biography may be bad history, but that it takes more than a good historian to write great biography. Like the historian, the biographer must be familiar with the contemporary stage upon which his hero acts: if biography does encompass the universal in the particular, it is important to know about the universe before studying the particle. But in addition to knowledge of the period, careful study of the sources, thorough acquaintance with the secondary literature, the posing of pertinent questions and the exercising of controlled imagination in answering them, the biographer must also display empathy, sensitivity, sensibility, intuition and, above all, be prepared to mortgage a large part of his intellectual and emotional life to understanding one particular, defunct figure. Cohabitation with the dead is not easy: Martin Gilbert has been living with Churchill for two decades, Dumas Malone has been communing with Jefferson for even longer. The demands of such single-minded scholarly devotion should not be underestimated. Bad biographies may be easy to write; but good ones are much more difficult.

This is especially true of the lives of major political figures. It is hard to strike the balance between public and private life; the day to day activities of politics and administration are frequently excruciatingly tedious; and past issues which once aroused passionate controversy often seem merely arcane and recondite today. As a result, only a few such studies have earned widespread critical acclaim: Plumb's *Walpole* (a grand opera, complete with overture, but still lacking its third act); Lady Longford's *Wellington* (her pen as mighty as his sword); Gash's *Peel* (a peerless study of a baronet); Lord David Cecil's *Melbourne* (one patrician beguilingly evoking another); Blake's *Disraeli* (champagne and epigrams all the way); and Marquand's *MacDonald* (*Fame is the Spur* stood on its head). But many prime ministers have fared less well: Chatham and Lord John Russell because there are few private papers; Gladstone and Salisbury because their careers were too long for any one writer to encompass comprehensively; C. J. Fox and Lloyd George because their passion to rule and their ruling passions are so hard to reconcile; and the younger Pitt and Baldwin because the weight of the times nearly suffocates the life.

Most of these difficulties lie in wait for the intending biographer of Palmerston. He was born before the American constitution saw the light, and lived to see the Great Republic's civil war: among statesmen of the first rank, only Gladstone and Churchill have exceeded his elephantine span as an MP, but he surpassed them both in the number of years he held government office. For some of his public career, there are few papers left, most tantalizingly for his formative, apprentice years as Secretary at War. Most of his remaining life was spent in foreign affairs, so that an account of his career can easily degenerate into a laundry list: the congress of X, the convention of Y and the treaty of Z. Despite the endless stream of speeches, official documents, memoranda and letters, he left behind few memorable phrases with which to lighten a flagging narrative. 'Civis Romanus sum' was cribbed, and his only quotable quote ('Die, doctor, that's the last thing I shall do', reputedly uttered on his death bed) is probably apocryphal. Above all, there is that constant tension between his private passions and his public life: a biography of Palmerston as a day worker is very different from a study of him on the night shift. So, it is hardly surprising that, as Kenneth Bourne disarmingly puts it in his preface, 'there is no satisfactory biography of Palmerston, and there probably never will be'.[1]

But this has not deterred a large number of writers from trying their hand. The great five-volumed mausoleum constructed by

Bulwer and Ashley was a running commentary on such letters as these two admiring friends were minded to publish, and gravely mummified Palmerston as a decorous Victorian statesman. In the 'twenties, Philip Guedalla (whose book Bourne revealingly describes as 'infuriatingly allusive rather than solidly informative') produced a piece of portrait sculpture rather than monumental masonry, which presented Palmerston in Stracheyesque terms as the last great figure of the eighteenth century. A decade later, writing against the background of Hitler, Stalin and Mussolini, H. C. F. Bell's doubledecker life depicted Palmerston as the embodiment of mid-nineteenth-century liberal nationalism, who established and safeguarded Britain's claim to moral pre-eminence in Europe. Shortly after the Second World War, Sir Charles Webster's study of his foreign policy portrayed Palmerston as a good European, the champion of constitutional government against despotism, and as a man whose sustained animosity to Russia afforded useful lessons at a time when the Cold War was blowing at its hottest. To celebrate the centenary of Palmerston's death in 1965, Donald Southgate reasserted the virtues of Palmerstonian patriotism in a decade of imperial demise and national self-doubt. But Jasper Ridley, writing most recently, was decidedly equivocal in his praise for 'the most English minister'.

It is a measure of Kenneth Bourne's achievement that, if he completes his study with a second volume on the scale of this first, it will not only supersede all these biographies of Palmerston that have gone before, but also make it unnecessary for anyone to do the job again. The scale of the book is Palmerstonian in its dimensions: more than six hundred pages of text, and over a thousand footnotes. And the industry and vitality displayed are equally Palmerstonian: over fifty manuscript collections consulted, including (for the first time) full and exhaustive use of the voluminous Palmerston papers themselves. Throughout these pages, the author displays an intimidating mastery of the personal and professional facets of Palmerston's life, seems as accomplished in analysing domestic politics as in unravelling foreign policy, and writes with equal authority about the functioning of government departments or on the mood of a parliamentary debate. The result is a book especially informative on Palmerston's crucial but neglected early years, which also contributes fundamentally to our understanding of most major political issues between 1807 and 1841, and which presents Palmerston himself more convincingly than any biography has done before. Without doubt, this is as authoritative a life of Lord Cupid and Lord Pumicestone as we are ever likely to get.

Palmerston was born with a silver-plated spoon in his mouth; but initially it came nearer to choking than to feeding him. He was heir to extensive estates in Ireland and England, and to an Irish title. His education at Harrow, Edinburgh and Cambridge Universities was relatively happy. He had a powerful and energetic political patron in Lord Malmesbury, who ensured his return as an MP at the age of twenty-two, got him a government job as a Junior Lord of the Admiralty in the same year, and arranged for him to be offered the Chancellorship of the Exchequer in 1809. But somehow or other it all went wrong. The death of his father in 1802 and of his mother three years later not only affected Palmerston deeply, but left him responsible for his siblings and for many more distant relatives. As a youngster, he was nervous, timid, and lacking in outward warmth of feeling. He was defeated three times at the polls before securing a seat in Parliament, and delayed almost a year before making his maiden speech. So, when the glittering offer came in 1809, he refused it, on the grounds that it was aiming too high, and accepted instead the more humdrum office of Secretary at War. One cannot imagine the younger Pitt or Disraeli or Gladstone or Churchill being so bashful.

Palmerston stayed at the War Office for the next nineteen years, which must surely rank as the longest and lowliest apprenticeship served by any major nineteenth-century political figure. And, although he succeeded in clearing off the arrears of regimental accounts, the job proved more of a dead end than a stepping stone. Palmerston was not a success in defending his department from parliamentary attack: his speeches were alternatively stammering and stuttering, hectoring and histrionic. He was too much the bureaucrat, immersed in detail, to be a good politician, and too much an autocrat, bullying his staff, to be a good administrator. He overstepped the bounds of departmental jurisdiction, which brought him into conflict with the Commander-in-Chief of the army at Horse Guards, and ultimately with both Wellington and the royal family. He broke with Malmesbury in 1812–13, but thereafter maintained a dangerous independence, which meant that he was constantly at risk of being sacrificed to the needs and ambitions of others. So faint had been the mark he made that the prime minister, Lord Liverpool, refused to back him in the general election of 1826, and dangled an English peerage and colonial governorships before him in the hope of getting him out of the way. In the short-lived ministries of Canning, Goderich and Wellington, which followed Liverpool's, there was still no promotion: he remained where he had begun, at the top of the heap of mediocrities.

Nor was his personal life particularly happy. A lunatic nearly shot him at the War Office in 1818. Even by the lax standards of the day, his private life was profligate and indiscreet. In 1808–9, he fell in love with Lady Cowper, a demanding mistress who was as unfaithful to him as he was to her. Only in 1837 did she at last become free to marry, thereby condemning Palmerston to a matrimonial waiting game even longer than the political apprenticeship he was simultaneously obliged to serve. In addition, there were dozens of lovers, several of whom refused him in marriage, and perhaps six illegitimate children. The result, for Palmerston, was exhaustion, recrimination, jealousy, heartache and blackmail. And the bastards had to be kept – either by finding them jobs in the War Office (which further aroused departmental resentment) or by buying them off (which further straitened his already straitened finances). His income was inadequate; his estates were heavily mortgaged; he invested rashly in unsound stock exchange ventures; he was taken in by knaves and swindlers. Undoubtedly, such extra-curricular activities further hampered his career: he seemed too unsound and insufficiently committed to be considered seriously for higher office; and with so many other demands on his time and his energies, it is hardly surprising that his parliamentary performances were so often below par.

The late 1820s brought a major and unexpected change in his political fortunes. By sheer effort of will, he ceased to be a nervous and diffident speaker, and became a leading parliamentary orator, giving major speeches on foreign affairs and Catholic Emancipation. He began to distance himself from the Tories in 1826, and resigned from Wellington's government in 1828. The deaths of Liverpool, Canning and Huskisson accelerated the break-up of the old Tory party, and in the fluid situation which ensued, Palmerston found himself courted by both the Tories (among whom he was now an important, if rebel, figure, almost by default) and by the Whig opposition (who, having been out of office since 1807 coveted his recent experience of government). Urged on by political hostesses like Lady Cowper and Princess Lieven, he behaved with uncharacteristic audacity, and threw in his lot with the Whigs. Like other such shifts of parliamentary allegiance, most notably Gladstone's and Churchill's, it was a shrewder move than ever he could have guessed. For he had abandoned the Tories at just the point when their hegemony was ended, and embraced the Whigs at the very moment when theirs was beginning.

But even during the Whig governments, which were almost continually in power from 1830 to 1841, his position was rarely entirely secure. He was the third choice for Foreign Secretary in Grey's administration; he was the only member of the Cabinet to lose his seat in the landslide election of 1831; he made frequent difficulties for his colleagues over the Reform Bill; and there were constant plots to oust him. When Melbourne took over in 1835, he was not at all sure that he wanted Palmerston back at the FO; he lost his parliamentary seat again that year; and the conspiracies to remove him continued. His old faults were not fully eradicated before new ones appeared. He was still not completely at ease in the Commons, his speeches were rarely memorable, and his attendance was irregular. He drove his staff too hard and kept unsociable hours. He was hated by the foreign ambassadors in London, and was slow to present papers to the cabinet and the monarch. He was not always scrupulous in the printing of diplomatic material, and he wrote for the press when he categorically denied it. He must have been an infuriating colleague.

But he *survived*, which was more than Castlereagh and Canning, his two most illustrious predecessors in the job, had done. His capacity for hard work was unrivalled, and was admitted even by his sternest critics. He habitually worked standing up at a high desk so that, if he literally fell asleep, the shock would wake him up. His marriage to Lady Cowper in 1839 was to make him more affable and less irritable (although no more faithful: it was, as one colleague explained, 'a marriage vow which they both know does not bind them'). He established an unassailable reputation for expertise in foreign affairs. His pragmatic grasp of Britain's material interests and his realistically flexible approach to the balance of power set him above Castlereagh, and his manipulation of conference diplomacy and his tactical skill in ensuring that Britain was never isolated were superior even to Canning's. His successes were substantial and undoubted: in the early 'thirties with his handling of the conference on Belgium and in recovering the entente with France; and at the end of the decade with the Opium War and the settlement of the Turco-Egyptian crisis. In the 'twenties, he had played the waiting game and rarely won; in the 'thirties, he played it and rarely lost.

By stressing so much of Palmerston's early life (half the book is gone before we reach 1830), Bourne makes him psychologically a more convincing figure than any of his predecessors. In his early years, he was shy, unsure and lacking in self-confidence, devoid of both political passion and real ambition. Even as Foreign Secretary, his policy was much more cautious and much less reckless than is often supposed. Insofar as he *was* driven, it was by financial need (an official salary was especially useful in the 1820s), by the desire to discharge his responsibilities to his family and dependants, by the pressures and demands of the politically involved women with whom he slept, and by the constant fear of failure. It was this need to prove himself to himself which explains his impatience of human frailty in others, his inability to delegate, and his compulsion to drive his subordinates as hard as he drove himself. Here, Bourne argues, is the real Palmerston, gnawed by inner self-doubt and uncertainty, and hidden from the world by a façade of rudeness, deviousness, lying and hypocrisy. There is little trace here of the genial, bantering affability, the cool and studied insouciance, the jaunty, cocksure showmanship, of earlier legend or later life.

Like all outstanding biographies, this life also illuminates the times. To describe convincingly Palmerston's views on free trade, slavery, Catholic Emancipation and parliamentary reform, contributes new insights to our understanding of early nineteenth-century politics. To explore the working of Liverpool's ministry, the crisis and chaos of parties from 1828 to 1830, and the functioning of the Whig ministries of the 1830s, does the same for our knowledge of early nineteenth-century government. The many pages devoted to the War and Foreign Offices convey with positively soporific vividness the tedium and time-consuming nature of much government administration. While there was political intrigue in plenty, there was less than some accounts of nineteenth-century high politics might imply: running the country just took up too much time. Above all, the book excels in conveying the feel of what it was like actually to govern. The problem of making foreign policy in the 1830s when, for much of the time, three other ministers thought they, too, should interfere; the need to win approval from the Commons, the Lords, the cabinet and the monarchy; and the difficulties in dealing simultaneously with foreign ambassadors in London and British ambassadors abroad: all this is brought out with (to use Bourne's favourite adjective) masterly authority.

The author's commendable determination to situate Palmerston so fully in his times, and to explore so many facets of his life, of necessity results in a book which does not always make for easy reading. Most of the chapters are more than fifty pages in length, and several are nearer a hundred. The interminable details of suppliants for War Office pensions, and of each new twist and turn in foreign policy, inevitably pall. On occasions, one wishes that the book were less infuriatingly informative and more solidly allusive. The five-year lag between the completion of the manuscript and its publication means that some of the conclusions on matters such as army flogging and the press have already been anticipated. Perhaps, too, Bourne's Palmerston – unsure, contorted, underhand – is in some ways as much a life for our times as were the grave statesman, the 'Lord Cupid', the moral crusader and the cold-war warrior for previous generations. And, because Palmerston emerges as a more complex and less agreeable figure than in some of his earlier incarnations, there is not the emotional identification between author and subject that would make this biography as satisfying a work of art as it is an outstanding work of scholarship. At the end of the day, the historian's distance has triumphed over the biographer's involvement.

But such cavils are relatively trivial compared with the magnitude of the achievement. In the introduction to his study, Donald Southgate predicted that 'Palmerston must long await his true memorial'. Stripped of the crenellations of Victorian hagiography, and reinforced by the concrete of twentieth-century scholarship, here it is. The history of the world may not be the lives of great men any more; but, if this biography is any guide, the great men of the world certainly still deserve the histories of their lives.

(1982)

NOTE:
1. Kenneth Bourne, *Palmerston: The Early Years, 1784–1841* (London, 1982).

# 27

# Lord Birkenhead

'There is', John Lord Campbell observed in his mid-Victorian, multi-volume *Lives of the Lord Chancellors*, 'no office in the history of any nation that has been filled with such a long succession of distinguished and interesting men as the office of Lord Chancellor.' A roll-call which included such illustrious history-makers as Wolsey, More, Bacon and Clarendon lent some credence to Campbell's unmeasured hyperbole. But since then, things have gone rather downhill, and most recent Lord Chancellors have been woolsacked worthies rather than eminent statesmen: grave, wise, sober, learned, venerable – and unmemorable. Names like Herschell, Loreburn, Buckmaster, Finlay, Cave and Caldecot trip off the tongue with about as much familiarity as the batting order of a minor counties cricket eleven. Indeed, during the last hundred years, only two Lord Chancellors have rivalled the renown and repute of Campbell's greatest hits: W. S. Gilbert's rich comic creation in *Iolanthe*, a susceptible insomniac who married a fairy; and F. E. Smith, first Earl of Birkenhead, whose appointment to the woolsack was denounced by the *Morning Post* as 'carrying a joke too far'.

F.E.'s life was shamelessly, successfully and simultaneously devoted to self-advancement, self-advertisement, self-indulgence and self-destruction, and he achieved more distinction in each of these fields than most men achieve in any. Driven by remorseless ambition, and aided by a first-rate brain of quicksilver speed, he amassed a remarkable tally of gongs, baubles and glittering prizes, at Oxford, in the law, and in politics. Endowed with a gigantic ego and towering self-confidence, he was the supreme right-wing demagogue between Lord Randolph Churchill and Sir Oswald Mosley, with mesmeric oratorical gifts of lightning wit, stinging retort and poisonous vituperation. And he was as reckless as he was rude: his magnificent carelessness, shameless hedonism and limitless extravagance betokened an inexhaustible appetite for life and pleasure; he squandered several fortunes on houses and horses, cars and cards, boats and brandy; he excelled at rugby, riding, golf and tennis; he burned all his candles at both ends; and he drank and spent as if there was no tomorrow. His consumption was conspicuous in every sense, and in the end he died of drink and left only debts. In one guise, F.E. was the classic exemplar of the rags-to-riches fable; in another, he was the sort of man who gets ambition a bad name. If Gilbert's Lord Chancellor had been played by Errol Flynn, the result might have been a passable imitation of Lord Birkenhead.

Such a Janus-faced judge presents daunting problems for any intending biographer. Indeed, when Birkenhead died, J. L. Garvin observed that at least two lives would have to be written about him: one covering his political career, which could be completed at once; the other, concerned with what might politely be called his personality, which could not be written for some time to come. Within five years of his death, Birkenhead's son produced a two-volume biography, which was revised, condensed and re-issued in 1959. Considering that F.E. was such a beastly father, this was a remarkable work of filial piety and affectionate loyalty, on a par with Winston's life of Lord Randolph for devotion and discretion. Then, in 1960, William Camp completed his 'unofficial portrait', which took its title, *The Glittering Prizes*, from one of Birkenhead's more controversial and offensive later speeches, and pulled no punches at all. As biographies, they were both eminently readable in style, yet quite contradictory in substance. The one depicted Birkenhead as generous, warm-hearted, brilliant, loyal and kind; the other stressed his arrogance, cynicism, extravagance, superficiality and ultimate failure. Now another John Campbell has tried to bring together the sober judge and the drunk lord, and in so doing has written the most fully researched and fully revealing life of this particular Lord Chancellor that we are ever likely to get.[1]

Or want: for, like many a definitive biography, this book is more the kiss of death to its subject than it is the life everlasting. At best, Birkenhead was never more than a political figure of the second rank: an MP for only thirteen years, a Cabinet Minister for barely ten, and dead and gone at fifty-eight. To lavish nine hundred pages on so brief and brittle a life seems indulgent in the extreme. All too often, Birkenhead himself disappears into a morass of wordy contextualisation, and there is far too much 'substantial quotation' from speeches, letters, essays and judgments. Had this been a vehicle for recounting new stories, offering new interpretations or developing new arguments, there might have been some justification for such lengthy exposition. But the only new insight which (no doubt unintendedly) results from such inexorable treatment, is that Birkenhead is made to appear rather boring. Indeed, there are moments when the book threatens to overwhelm not only its subject but also its author. The prose never flags, but it does occasionally sink to the level of journalese: 'the question was, could Lloyd George deliver?'; 'F.E. in 1912 had the Prime Ministership well within his sights'. It seems unhelpful and ahistorical to compare F.E. with President Kennedy or Enoch Powell. Some of the material is repetitive and overlapping. And it is odd that Campbell should speak of Birkenhead's 'sober dignity' as Lord Chancellor, and 'sober judgments' in Baldwin's Cabinets, when he was already hitting the bottle extensively.

At the end of this massive book, Campbell's Birkenhead remains the same bifurcated being to whom Garvin had drawn attention – lovable to some, loathsome to most, and baffling to virtually everybody. Despite his admirably extensive researches, Campbell is no more successful than his predecessors in reconciling the contradictions of Birkenhead's temperament. The result is a book lacking in evenness of tone or steadiness of viewpoint, a roller-coaster of admiration and criticism, which leaves the reader unsure whether this is by a biographer evoking a personality or a historian addressing a problem. For example, Campbell devotes much effort to depicting 'the real F.E.' as a man who had 'fresh and penetrating things to say' about all the major political issues between 1906 and 1928. Yet, as he admits, much that Birkenhead had to say was 'purest fantasy', 'magnificent emptiness', 'spurious nonsense', 'pure moonshine', 'crudest fustian', 'hollow emotion-alism' and 'wishful hot air'. It is rather difficult to know how to reconcile these views. 'The real F.E.' never actually stands up. Indeed, in certain guises, he would not have been able to. Cynthia Asquith thought him 'a magnificent bounder', whom she 'could not help' liking; and the same seems to go for Mr Campbell.

The fact that it takes some 140 pages to get the young F.E. into Parliament gives some idea of the soporific scale of this book. Of course, these were undeniably glittering years of promise and achievement: the open scholarship to Wadham; the brilliant col-leagues like Simon and C. E. Fry; the Presidency of the Oxford Union; the Vinerian Law Scholarship in which he defeated Holds-worth; the Merton Fellowship; the dazzling and lucrative career as a barrister on the Northern Circuit; the successful entry into Parliament in the 1906 general election; and the audacious and legendary maiden speech – all before he had reached his thirty-fourth birthday. Yet even at this early age, he was inclined to exaggerate both obstacles and achievements, and not everything went his way. His background was much less deprived than he liked to suppose, and the fact that his father died too young of too much drink was an ominous pointer to his own future fate. He bitterly resented his failure to win a scholarship to Harrow; he spent two years at Liverpool University before going up to Wadham; he had to eradicate his northern accent before he could become a Union swell; he only achieved a Second in Mods and the BCL; he had to wait a year for the Merton Fellowship; the maiden speech was little more than a lengthy cluster of impertinences; and for several years thereafter, he was still known in some parts of the Commons as 'single-speech Smith'.

Even so, between 1906 and 1914 he established himself as a coming man who might yet make it. He made a fortune at the Bar, took silk in 1908, and became a Privy Councillor in 1911, after only five years in Parliament and while still under forty. But his achievements were more pyrotechnic than substantive. As a lawyer, he was never involved in a really great case, had no outstanding interrogation to his credit, and was conspicuously worsted by Lady Sackville in the contest over the will of Sir John Murray Scott. And, when his political prospects conflicted with his professional obligations, as in the Lever libel case, he put political prospects first. As a politician, his searing assaults on the Liberals' Education, Licensing and Welsh Church Disestablishment Bills, as well as on the People's Budget and House of Lords reform, were too forced and frenzied to convince: clever advocacy rather than expressions of deeply held belief. He helped to shout down Asquith in the Commons in 1911, and his exhortations to Ulster Unionists in the years immediately before the First World War bordered on the treasonable. Yet, while publicly thus partisan to the point of excess, he was constantly in search of coalition with the Liberals from 1910; he founded the Other Club with Churchill in 1911; and he defended Liberal Ministers in the libel actions which resulted from the Marconi scandal. So, by 1914, he was hated by the Liberals for being too partisan, and distrusted by the Conservatives for not being partisan enough. For a man so obviously on the make, he was curiously unsure of what he wanted, and dangerously indifferent to what people thought of him.

On balance, his war was less good than bad. In 1915 he became Solicitor-General and then Attorney-General with a seat in the Cabinet, a post which he kept until the end of hostilities. But before the First Coalition came to his rescue, he had a disastrous spell as Press Censor; and his military service, although not evaded, was far from glorious. Cushily accommodated behind the lines, with ample supplies of cigars and brandy, he seemed to shirk the role of combatant he so strenuously pressed on others. And in the wartime governments of which he was subsequently a member, he was never a dominant figure. He played only a minor part in policy making; he was on the sidelines in the plotting to promote Lloyd George; he conspicuously misjudged both Kitchener and Asquith; and his tour of America was tactless and unsuccessful. The coalition meant an end to that partisan oratory essential to his style; he made few speeches inside or outside Parliament; as a law officer, unable to practise, his income was much reduced; and his prosecution of Casement brought him more notoriety than acclaim. By 1918, he had made little progress, and the knighthood and baronetcy that came his way signified lack of power rather than plenitude.

But in 1919, Lloyd George offered Smith the woolsack, a bauble so tempting that he could not refuse it, yet so tarnished that he would always regret it. Even by Birkenhead's standards of self-regard, it was a breathtaking prospect to be offered the Lord Chancellorship at forty-six, and in rapid succession he became Baron, Viscount and Earl, with a motto proudly and punningly proclaiming that he was 'smith of my own fortune'. But by dangling before him this irresistible prize, Lloyd George effectively thwarted him even as he promoted him. As a peer, the supreme political office was *de facto* closed to him; he was increasingly isolated from grass-roots, constituency opinion; and he would be unable to return to the bar to earn his living once he left the woolsack. Nor was his tenure of the office altogether happy. He hated the sitting and the ceremony associated with the job; he failed to reform the Divorce Law or the House of Lords; the 1923 Law of Property Act, which he regarded as his greatest triumph, was well advanced in the pipeline before he took office; and the Irish Treaty, in which he played a part, was more heroic than honourable. He was an irregular attender at cabinets, and once again was little involved in the making of government policy. His health began to trouble him; there was a long affair with Mona Dunn; and he began to drink not wisely but too well. By 1922, he was established in the public mind as the quintessential villain of the Lloyd George Coalition: arrogant, overbearing, boorish, hard-faced, bitter and contemptuous. As one contemporary put it, 'his brains had gone to his head'.

When the Coalition fell, Birkenhead fell along with it, and unlike Churchill and Austen Chamberlain, he never recovered. He failed to create a centre party of anti-socialist fanatics, and he was hated by the Tories – partly because of the Irish Treaty and his devotion to Lloyd George, partly because Conservatives (especially the women) found his lifestyle 'morally intolerable', partly because he called Lords Salisbury and Selborne 'the Dolly sisters', and partly because his 'glittering prizes' speech was an affront to Baldwin's new brand of emollient Tory democracy. Yet Baldwin brought him into his 1924 administration, probably thinking that F.E. would be less trouble inside the government than out. He was refused the woolsack again because he was so often drunk, and became Secretary of State for India, where he could do little harm and even less work. He knew nothing of India, never visited it, and cared not a rupee for its peoples, their thoughts or their aspirations. He played a great deal of golf; he was rude to visiting Indian deputations; he never mastered intricate matters to do with the country's economy; he advocated the cynical policy of divide and rule; and he only wished to hold on to India for the glory of the British crown. When he retired from politics in 1928, this was greeted more with relief than regret. As Laski put it: 'he has shot across politics like a meteor, and his disappearance leaves the sky unchanged'.

His last years were sorry in the extreme. He was surrounded by unsavoury characters and spongers like 'Buns' Cartwright and Maundy Gregory; it was rumoured that he was being black-mailed; he was often drunk in public, and saw the world through a glass, darkly, if he saw it at all. As his debts mounted, his style of life became only more irresponsibly extravagant, and he rowed publicly and indecorously over his Lord Chancellor's pension. To make some badly needed money, he wrote several dreadful books, whose titles (*Fifty Famous Fights in Fact and Fiction*, *The World in 2030*) were as bad as their contents. They were of minimal literary quality, amateurish, superficial, pompous and long winded, sometimes ghosted and occasionally plagiarized. In 1928, he had to resign from the government because his creditors would not wait, but he was unable to recoup his losses in the City, despite several lucrative directorships. He had neither knowledge nor experience of industry or finance, and he made no impact on the business world because he did not and could not try. He was disillusioned by his physical collapse, was unable to reconcile himself to his ultimate failure, and was appalled at the prospect of

his impending death. He had always believed in the survival of the
fittest and, when no longer fit, he could not survive. As his *Times*
obituary put it, he saw life primarily as a matter of getting on, and
having got on as far as he could, there was nothing left to do but to
get off.

In a shorter compass than nine hundred pages, this remains a
riveting story of flawed and fissured greatness. Like Lord Campbell's earlier Lord Chancellors, Birkenhead was undeniably distinguished and incontrovertibly interesting. But his ambition was
not reinforced by character and, although Beaverbrook called him
'the cleverest man in the kingdom', he was not clever enough to
understand that cleverness was not enough. He never lived down a
well-merited reputation as a superficial adventurer, who was so
fluent that he could parade platitudes as profundities or profanities
with equal ease. As a lawyer, he preferred advocacy to serious
legal argument, and as a politician he was always the partisan
rhetorician, never the statesman. He could ridicule his opponents'
proposals and witheringly expose inconsistencies in their arguments; but he left behind no major, positive achievement in law or
legislation, politics or government. He was high on invective,
impertinence and intolerance, but low on imagination, insight and
intuition. As a second-ranking political figure, his achievements
cannot compare with Butler's length of service to the state,
Curzon's devotion to Britain's imperial mission, or Bevin's massive contributions at the Ministry of Labour and the Foreign
Office. And even if he pandered to Churchill's vanity and vulgar-
ity, he lacked his charm, his stamina, his artistry, his magnanimity
and, above all, his greatness of mind and heart.

As a human being, he seems scarcely more winning. He was
selfishly indifferent to his family's immediate and future financial
needs, and left them only debts. As a father, he saw his children
entirely as an extension of himself. His only son was the repository
of all his dynastic hopes and, from an early age, was made to dress
like him and urged to do well, like him. He was forced to drink too
much too soon, and it did him no good. (The present Earl, F. E.'s
grandson, is understandably teetotal.) His attitude to women was

chauvinist in the extreme: they were conveniences, 'mere conduit pipes', ordained for men's use as relaxation and entertainment, to bolster their morale and massage their egos. But they were not intelligent, should not be given the vote, and must be kept out of the Lords at all costs. And, for a self-styled intellectual, he was singularly boorish and philistine about the life of the mind. He was not a true scholar, read little profound literature as an adult, and his much publicized library was more for bragging about than browsing in. He had no appreciation of the fine arts, and was completely tone deaf. And he had no time for introspection – which was a pity, but understandable.

At the end of this long book, Birkenhead's rise seems less attractive, and his decline more pathetic, than ever before. He may have been the architect of his own advance, but he was also smith of his own misfortune. Like Lord Campbell's earlier Lord Chancellors, there was 'a sort of romance' about him, and 'the strange vicissitudes' of his life were 'not exceeded by the fictions of novelists or dramatists', let alone the Savoy Operas. Throughout his life, John Campbell suggests, there was a constant tension between north and south, Birkenhead and Oxford, Liverpool and London, instinct and education, idleness and industry. Perhaps so. But it is difficult to avoid the conclusion that Lord Birkenhead's career, like Lord Randolph's, was 'mostly opportunism'. All in all, he must be just about the most lightweight figure in politics to have received the appropriately ambiguous accolade of such a heavyweight book.

(1984)

NOTE:
1. John Campbell, *F. E. Smith, First Earl of Birkenhead* (London, 1983).

# 28

# Neville Chamberlain

On Neville Chamberlain's death in November 1940, Winston Churchill delivered one of his most moving, majestic and magnanimous orations, which rightly takes its place among the Periclean peaks of his wartime speeches. It showed a rare and ready sympathy for disappointed hopes and upset calculations; it appealed to conscience and to history as the only sure judges of men's deeds; and it took the broadest possible view of Chamberlain's character and achievements. At the end of a year in which he had won immortality as the saviour of his country in its finest hour, Churchill could well afford to be generous to his vanquished contemporary, who had been, at one time or another, his colleague then his critic, his superior then his subordinate. And so he left a good deal unsaid, he dwelt on Chamberlain's undeniable virtues, and saluted him as one whom Disraeli would have called 'an English worthy': for his dedicated pursuit of peace, for his physical and moral toughness, for his precision of mind and aptitude for business, and for his firmness of spirit and fortitude in adversity. All this, Churchill declared, would stand Chamberlain 'in good stead so far as what is called the verdict of history is concerned'.

At that particular moment, when everything that Chamberlain had stood and worked for lay in ruins, even his nearest and dearest could only put their hope in the future judgment of the past, for the verdict of the present was, and nearly always had been, much less generous. In the late 1920s, when Minister of Health, and in the early 1930s, when Chancellor of the Exchequer, Chamberlain was varyingly described as having been 'a good mayor of Birmingham in a lean year', with 'a retail mind in a wholesale business', who looked 'at world affairs through the wrong end of a municipal drainpipe'. Nevertheless, he became Prime Minister in 1937, and in the following year went to see Hitler at Munich, dressed with inadvertent appropriateness like an undertaker, with his bowler hat, his February face, his Adam's apple, and his rolled umbrella. For a brief moment he was the most acclaimed man in the country, as he returned with 'peace in our time'. But peace and time soon ran out, as Hitler invaded Poland and, in quick succession, Chamberlain's policy, government, reputation and health all collapsed. By the time of his death, he was regarded and disregarded as the worst British Prime Minister since Lord North, the guiltiest of the 'guilty men' of the 1930s: provincial, arrogant, narrow-minded, inflexible and cold.

The verdict of contemporaries was harsh, and the verdict of history has been neither as crisp nor as compassionate as Churchill benevolently predicted. In 1946, the Oxford historian Keith Feiling mounted the first salvage operation, by producing a pioneering biography. It was brief; it was inevitably discreet; it was much influenced by Chamberlain's understandably partisan widow; and no one took much notice of it amid the drama and distraction of the war and its aftermath. In 1961, Iain Macleod, a Conservative Cabinet Minister, staged another rescue attempt, but again the result was not a success. Undeniably, he invested Chamberlain with a certain degree of pale and private warmth. But he had little real sympathy for his subject; he lacked any formal training as a historian or biographer; he was not prepared to work through the mass of relevant archival material; and the book reinforced Chamberlain's many critics at least as much as it consoled his few apologists. Twenty years after Chamberlain's death, the 'verdict of history' remained very largely adverse, and rehabilitating his reputation seemed about as forlorn an undertaking as raising the *Titanic*.

Now, twenty years further on, David Dilks has mounted the most massive relief expedition yet.[1] He brings to this formidable task formidable expertise in the history and politics of the twentieth century, having already been research assistant to Sir Anthony Eden, Lord Tedder and Harold Macmillan, the editor of the wartime Foreign Office diaries of Sir Alexander Cadogan, and the author of a two-volume study of Curzon in India. For this most recent undertaking, he has had free access to all the relevant Chamberlain papers and to the mass of official archival material that has recently become available; and, although he has benefited from the recollections and hospitality of Chamberlain's descendants, they have in no sense influenced his arguments or his writing. And so, after a decade's intensive labour, Dilks has produced the first instalment of what will surely be the most monumental life of Chamberlain ever to be written: six hundred pages, and the story has only reached 1929. What is more, its purpose is avowedly revisionist, as the author seeks to acquit Chamberlain from the long-held charges of being a 'gullible provincial administrator, of narrow sympathies, limited imagination, conventional background', which are at best 'misleading' and at worst 'a caricature'.

As Dilks rightly explains, Neville Chamberlain can only be understood with reference to his provincial family background, which he sees as a positive force rather than a negative constraint. Neville's father, Joseph, was one of those rare nineteenth-century figures who left London for the provinces to make his fortune – which he promptly did as a Birmingham screw manufacturer. By marriage he linked himself to the town's nonconformist élite; he entered local government and was a brilliant, reforming mayor; he moved on to national politics as an advanced radical; he differed from Gladstone and split the Liberal Party over Irish Home Rule; he committed further apostasy by becoming Colonial Secretary in Lord Salisbury's administration; and then split the Conservative Party in turn by taking up the issue of Tariff Reform. In his early years he was a man of deep nonconformist piety; he was the best-dressed public figure of his generation, always sporting an orchid in his buttonhole; and for two decades he was the most dynamic – and destructive – force in British politics. He was thrice married and twice widowed. By his first wife, he produced one daughter and a son, Austen; by his second, two more daughters and another son, Neville.

This tightly knit family group was self-sufficient and self-regarding, mutually devoted but highly reticent. Joseph Chamberlain could not talk to either of his sons about their respective mothers, and they, like their father, subdued their emotions all their lives. Having decided that Austen was to bear the family banner in politics, Joseph determined that Neville was to bear it in business. So, while Austen went to Cambridge University and on the grand tour, Neville took courses in metallurgy at the local college, and was articled to a firm of accountants. On his father's instructions, he then spent six years trying to grow sisal on the island of Andros in the Bahamas. The intention was to rehabilitate the family finances; but the result was a loss of £50,000. On his return, Neville became a Birmingham businessman, and established a reputation as a model employer. He married, became involved in local Unionist Party affairs, and did good works for hospitals, schools and the territorial army. Despite his determination to stay out of public life, he was elected a city councillor in 1911 at the age of forty-two, and became mayor four years later, like his father before him.

Thus far, his life and career had unfolded exactly as Joseph had planned and predicted. But the war proved a turning point. While serving his second term as Lord Mayor, he was summoned to Whitehall to become Director-General of National Service in Lloyd George's wartime administration. With no contacts or apprenticeship in government, no seat in the Commons or Cabinet, no support from the Prime Minister, and no clearly defined authority, there was little opportunity for Chamberlain to distinguish himself, and he resigned after six months. But there was now no going back to the Birmingham parish pump. He became an MP for a local constituency in 1918 when just under fifty, and did four years dutiful work as a Conservative back bencher. On the fall of the Lloyd George Coalition in 1922, he took office in Bonar Law's Conservative Government, serving successively as Postmaster General, Paymaster General and Minister of Health. When Baldwin succeeded Law unexpectedly in 1923 for his first brief administration, Chamberlain became, equally unexpectedly, his Chancellor of the Exchequer.

He had insufficient time to make any real mark in any of these posts, not even presenting a budget as Chancellor; but he established close relations with Baldwin, and became as influential in the national party organization as he already was locally in Birmingham. When the Conservatives regained power in 1924, Austen became Foreign Secretary, and Neville returned to the Ministry of Health, where he remained for the five years' life of the administration. It was a large department with varied responsibilities, including, housing, hospitals, pensions, the poor law and local government. Much of the work was trivial and routine, including such problems as the risk of death from Black Widow spiders and the danger of poisoning from cheap lipsticks. But there were also substantial achievements, such as the recasting of the rating system, the reform of pensions, and the abolition of the Poor Law. As the stock of many other ministers fell, that of Chamberlain rose remorselessly. By the time the Baldwin government was defeated at the 1929 general election, Neville Chamberlain was already being talked of as a future Prime Minister. And this after only ten years in Parliament.

There, for the moment, Dilks leaves his hero: fully established and on the brink of greater things. How good a case for the defence has he made out? Has Chamberlain been third time lucky in his biographer? Or has he been betrayed (or betrayed himself) again? Beyond doubt, Dilks tries hard to rehabilitate Chamberlain, seeking to present him as a more credible person and creditable politician than hitherto. He was well read in Shakespeare and the classics, well travelled in Europe and beyond, an accomplished shot and fisherman, and an expert on orchids, birds, insects and butterflies. He was an energetic administrator and formidable master of business, who only adopted a policy when he had weighed all the arguments and heard all the evidence. He took on tedious, unheroic chores which more self-regarding and self-seeking figures disdained, and despatched them efficiently and punctually. His experience in local government, his dominance of politics in Birmingham, his influential position in the party, and his reliability as a minister made him inconspicuously indispensable.

But although Dilks labours hard to make the most of Chamberlain's early life and worthy works, the book does not really succeed either as biography or as rehabilitation. In the first place, it is at once too long, yet too short. To lavish six hundred pages on a man who, whatever he later became, was in the first sixty years of his life at best a second-ranking figure, is indulgent in the extreme, and only achieves the self-defeating result of submerging its subject in a morass of material. There is far too much irrelevant information about the decoration of Neville's bathroom, the make of his car, and the variety of birds in his back garden. There are three chapters on Andros, three on National Service, and ten on his long stint as Minister of Health. And there are many episodes, like the succession of Baldwin to the Prime Ministership and the General Strike of 1926, with which Chamberlain was only tangentially connected, which receive excessively detailed treatment. In his introduction, Dilks approvingly quotes Sir Robert Menzies: 'a telling anecdote is of far more value than all the turgid minutes of those committees'. It is a pity he has not taken these words to heart.

Yet in other ways, for all its length, this book does not tell us enough. By wandering from subject to subject – from butterflies to business, from orchids to organization – we may get a full picture of Chamberlain's life, but the result is an unstructured and chronological treatment, in which no theme is ever satisfactorily explored. The picture of Joseph Chamberlain is too admiring, and the accounts of the family finances are fragmentary and contradictory. Time and again, we are told that Neville was a reluctant Conservative, yet their is no systematic account of his political views. Like his father, he was both the architect and beneficiary of a new-style, middle-class Tory Party; but this, too, is only thinly treated. And the author does not seem to have absorbed recent work on the politics of the interwar years, which sees Chamberlain as an important but highly controversial domestic reformer.

As biography, this book is not a success; and as rehabilitation, it is frequently unconvincing. For much of the evidence which is presented in such unstructured abundance suggests an interpretation very much at odds with that which Dilks himself puts forward. Take, for instance, Chamberlain's upbringing. Dilks presents it as quite idyllic, yet is this how it really was? The family was suffocatingly self-contained, so it is hardly surprising that in later life Neville found people hard to get on with, and was so conspicuously lacking in the gifts and graces of friendship. All the young Chamberlains were dwarfed and scorched by the towering inferno of their father's personality: Austen and Neville were shy to a pathological degree, even with each other; both married very late in life, and Neville lived as a bachelor under his father's roof until he did; while three of their sisters never married, and two clucked away in their later years like Arsenic and Old Lace. For Neville himself, the failures at Andros and at National Service clearly cut deep, and it can hardly have been a boost to his understandably low self-esteem to be so obviously inferior in his father's eyes to his elder half-brother.

Although Dilks does not discuss this, it is clear from the evidence that for most of his life, Neville was dominated by somebody: as a boy by his father, whom he idolized to excess; as a man by Austen, whose early career was so much more glittering than his own; and as a husband by his wife, who cherished political ambitions for him which he was too reticent or realistic to admit for himself. As a result, Neville was such a late developer, both psychologically and politically, that there was not very much to develop when the opportunities finally and unexpectedly came. Dilks claims that his marriage showed him 'a passionate man, with intense feelings and humour'; but there is little corroborating evidence presented. The First World War seems to have made curiously little impact on him, either experentially or emotionally. His hobbies were solitary or cerebral or both. The only time he became really cross was when his umbrella was broken. Not surprisingly, his wife suffered from recurrent depression and breakdowns. Life with Neville was hardly a revel.

Likewise, as a public figure, he emerges as being, at best, a poor man's Peel. He disliked speech-making, was in many ways out of sympathy with the Conservative Party, and never enjoyed politics, as his father had done, for the great game it was. As a personality, even Austen spotted that it was 'his coldness which kills'; he was never capable of crossing a political or intellectual gap by an act of imaginative understanding; and he had all the distrust of intuition, imagination, originality, cleverness and panache which those who lack these qualities often display. He owed his rapid advance in the early 1920s entirely to the absence of senior figures in the Tory Party; he was outrageously patronizing and sneering to Labour MPs in the House of Commons; and his appraisals of such flawed but gifted men as Churchill and Lloyd George are little more than smug catalogues of prime and priggish disparagement. By 1929, Chamberlain had no major, imaginative achievement to his credit, but was indispensably and unstoppably second-rate. As such, he was set in a rut of self-righteous narrow-mindedness which hardly equipped him to cope at an even higher level with the crowded and tumultuous decade that was to come. As a person and a politician, he was just like his umbrella: drab, stiff, and rolled up tight.

The Chamberlain who stands forth from Dilks's pages is a man of limited talents and ruthlessly subdued emotions, who was powerfully driven, sometimes by the need to emancipate himself from the domination of others, sometimes by the need to meet up to the expectations they entertained of him, sometimes by the need to prove himself to himself in the light of past failures, and sometimes by the need to show that being a non-university provincial didn't matter. His aloofness was thus born more of insecurity than of arrogance, and the ease with which he criticized others was but a way of protecting himself. So, despite Dilks's revisionist intentions, the Chamberlain who emerges from the evidence is a man of familiar faults and failings: it is only the explanation of them which he has really changed. If Austen was born to a greatness which he could not fulfil, and Joseph achieved a greatness which he could not handle, then Neville had greatness thrust upon him – and, in trying to prove that he could bear it, collapsed under its weight.

Comfortingly, if disappointingly, there is really remarkably little discrepancy between Joseph's assessment of Neville's future prospects, Churchill's account of his past achievements, and Dilks's picture of his pioneering and reforming activities. Joseph envisaged him as a sound man of business, but nothing more. In his perceptive valediction, Churchill acclaimed exactly the same solid virtues, and drew a discreet veil over Chamberlain's limitations of mind and heart. In his admirable desire to do full justice to his subject, Dilks suffers from no such inhibitions. But, as President Nixon learned to his cost, making all the evidence available is no guarantee of vindication. At worst, this book offers much reinforcement to the view that Chamberlain was indeed 'a gullible provincial administrator, of narrow sympathies, limited imagination, conventional background'. And at best, it wearingly exemplifies those very sober and stultifying characteristics by which Chamberlain himself significantly set so much store: untiring industry, mastery of detail, inexorable competence, and remorseless information. They no more made Chamberlain a great man than they make this a great biography.

(1985)

NOTE:
1. David Dilks, *Neville Chamberlain*, volume I, *Pioneering and Reform, 1869–1929* (Cambridge, 1985).

# 29

# Sir Anthony Eden

On 4th April 1955, Sir Winston Churchill gave a dinner at 10 Downing Street on the eve of his retirement as Prime Minister. For him, it was the definitive end to an Olympian career. For Sir Anthony Eden, his chosen and cherished successor, it meant that the long-awaited promised land was now finally in sight. Yet although Churchill claimed that 'no two men have ever changed guard more smoothly', relations between them had recently been strained almost to breaking point. Eden had been so enraged by Churchill's procrastination and obstructiveness that he had sometimes come to hate the man he most admired. And Churchill was so distressed by Eden's hunger for power and hostility to his policies that he had even come to doubt the fitness of his own protegé for his own job. At the end of the evening, when all the guests had departed, the Prime Minister turned to his Private Secretary, John Colville, and observed with vehemence, 'I don't believe Anthony can do it.'

Throughout his life, opinion about Eden was always sharply divided. His admirers acclaimed him as the golden boy of British politics, who was handsome, glamorous and debonair, and whose courage in war and integrity in peace were beyond question. Abroad, he was a statesman of world stature, while at home, his appeal to people of all classes and parties was uniquely strong. Indeed, according to this interpretation, it was only the megalomania of Nasser and the perfidy of the Americans which tragically ruined a prime ministership of which the greatest hopes had quite rightly been entertained. But to his enemies, Eden's glitter was entirely superficial: he was a 'charm-school' politician with a 'screen-star' image, whose reputation was based on style rather than on substance. He never coined a memorable phrase nor begat an original idea, but was always bland, aloof and indecisive. Accordingly, the day of reckoning was bound to come. Suez may have been unexpected; but nemesis was inevitable.

Since Eden's death, his critics have been emphatically in the ascendant, and their case against him has recently been greatly strengthened by David Carlton's much-praised and highly-critical biography. By contrast, Robert Rhodes James's book is intended as an eloquent and moving case for the defence. It is the first biography to be based on Eden's own papers, and has been written with the support and encouragement of his widow, Clarissa. It specifically sets out to rebut the 'consistent and mystifyingly hostile' portrait painted by Carlton. And it does so by depicting Eden as 'an English worthy', whose 'brand of humane, liberal and progressive Conservatism' Rhodes James – himself a Tory MP – believes to be the only appealing political creed. Yet ironically, he is so successful in producing a book which is 'sympathetic, but not uncritical, and, above all, fair', that he lends almost as much support to Eden's detractors as to his admirers. The result is a rivetingly paradoxical biography: well-disposed in intention, but ultimately damning in content.

Rhodes James's argument is that there were indeed two Edens, the one attractive, accomplished and successful, the other unappealing, inadequate and unfathomable, and that it is the tension between them which provides the key to understanding his career. He was born in 1897, the younger son of a County Durham baronet, and remained an aristocrat all his life. The family home, Windlestone Hall, was secure and civilized, and Eden grew up to love books and pictures, trees and flowers. He was educated at Eton and Christ Church, Oxford, where he took a First in Oriental Languages, without apparent effort. Between school and university, he served in the First World War. He was a brave and brilliant soldier, won the Military Cross, and became one of the youngest Brigade Majors in the army. At twenty-six, he was elected MP for one of the safest Tory seats in the country, and he soon established a reputation in the Commons as an expert in international affairs. Within three years, he was given junior office under Austen Chamberlain, the Foreign Secretary, and by the early 1930s he was widely acclaimed as the rising star of his political generation.

But as Rhodes James amply demonstrates, there was another side to this success story. Despite the undeniably idyllic surroundings, Eden's childhood was lonely and difficult: his father was eccentric, tyrannical, and given to furious outbursts; his mother was financially irresponsible beyond the point of profligacy; and Eden himself may well have been the illegitimate offspring of her affair with George Wyndham. He was a physically delicate boy, further afflicted with poor eyesight, and he grew up to be exceptionally sensitive, highly strung, and inclined to bad temper. During the First World War, two of his brothers were killed, his father died, and the family fortune was dissipated. As a younger son, Eden himself had very little money, and was obliged to augment his meagre inheritance with journalism. In 1923, he married the beautiful Beatrice Beckett; but almost from the outset, it was an ill-fated union. Eden was increasingly wrapped up in his work, whereas she loathed politics and diplomacy. By the late 1920s, the marriage was already failing, and the combined pressures of private sadness and public success brought on Eden's first ulcer.

This was an ominously insecure base from which to launch a major political career. But during the 1930s, Eden's rise was meteoric, as he seemed the glamorous survivor of the lost generation, nobly striving to build a better world. In 1931, on the formation of the National Government, Baldwin sent him to the Foreign Office as Parliamentary Under-Secretary, where he won golden opinions for his work in Geneva at the Disarmament Conference, and for his shuttle diplomacy between the European capitals. He was soon promoted to full ministerial rank, and his reputation was further enhanced when he sought – albeit unavailingly – to thwart Mussolini's invasion of Abyssinia. Late in 1935, he became the youngest Foreign Secretary of modern times, and waged a courageous campaign from inside the Cabinet against Chamberlain's policy of appeasement, which culminated in his sensational resignation in February 1938. In a depressing decade, Eden seemed, in Churchill's words, 'the one strong young figure standing up against the long, dismal, drawling tides of drift and surrender'.

Once again, however, this was only part of the picture. Tense, lonely and unhappy, Eden was already driving himself too hard. His many absences abroad, and his dislike of political infighting, meant that he made few friends in the Commons or the Cabinet. Even in the realm of foreign policy, his attitudes were neither clear nor consistent. Initially, he was a strong supporter of disarmament and was well-disposed to Hitler. As Foreign Secretary, he was more preoccupied with the Italian than the German menace. And his resignation was astonishingly maladroit: he was outman-oeuvred by Chamberlain in the battle for political advantage in the Cabinet; the specific issue on which he left the government was vague and trivial; and his speech in self-justification impressed no one. The rumours put about at the time – that he was on the verge of physical and nervous collapse – may well have been the malicious whisperings of his enemies. But there was already some evidence that he did not hold up well in a crisis. Thereafter, he failed conspicuously to exploit his position: he refused to join with Churchill in attacking the government wholeheartedly, his speech against the Munich settlement was feeble, and even in early 1939, he was still unsure as to precisely what policy to adopt towards Germany.

Nevertheless, on the outbreak of the Second World War, Eden returned to power as Dominions Secretary, and on the fall of Chamberlain's government, he became Secretary of State for War. He organized the Home Guard, he promoted gifted com-manders like Dill and Brooke, his orders to hold the Channel ports made the Dunkirk evacuation possible, and he rightly took much of the credit for Wavell's early victories against the Italians in Africa. When Halifax was exiled to Washington as Ambassador on the death of Lord Lothian, Eden took over the Foreign Office again. He established close contacts with exiled leaders like de Gaulle and Sikorski; he scored notable diplomatic triumphs on two visits to Russia; he was the first major western figure to divine

Stalin's expansionist intentions; and he was a significant influence in the preparation and agreement of the United Nations Charter. In 1942, on the eve of one of his foreign visits, Churchill advised the King to send for Eden in the event of his own death. Thereafter, his position as Crown Prince was assured and unassailable.

Yet even these were tainted triumphs. His health and his marriage were further undermined by the burdens of office, and his eldest son was killed in the very last stages of the war. While in charge of the Dominions Office he was inevitably a marginal and insignificant figure. Even as Secretary for War, he did not sit in the inner War Cabinet. And at the Foreign Office, he played no more than a peripheral part in the crucial meetings between Churchill, Stalin and Roosevelt. Throughout the war, diplomacy was subordinated to strategy and, on the British side, Churchill was emphatically in charge of both. While Eden consolidated his reputation as an accomplished and highly professional negotiator, who was outstanding at settling problems and working out agreements, he was implementing policy rather than formulating it. On more than one occasion, he considered abandoning his subordinate position for 'a real job'. In 1943, he was strongly tempted to go to India as Viceroy, and at the end of the war, he longed to be appointed the first Secretary-General of the United Nations. But after the massive defeat of the Conservatives in 1945, he stayed on, in the forlorn hope that Churchill would soon retire.

As Deputy Leader of the Opposition, he encouraged young, progressive, liberal conservatives, who were seeking to update the party's image and programme. He divorced his first wife, and married Clarissa Churchill, who was not only his leader's niece, but also brought him happiness and companionship hitherto unknown. When the Conservatives returned to power in 1951, he resumed the Foreign Office a third time, and as Churchill aged, Eden became correspondingly more assertive. In 1954, he pulled off a spectacular string of diplomatic coups: he brought about a cease fire in Indo-China and held back America and Russia from the brink of nuclear war; he successfully negotiated the withdrawal of British forces from the Suez Canal Base; he stabilized the precarious situation in Iran to Britain's financial advantage; and he brought West Germany into NATO and established the Western European Union. Appropriately enough, he received the Order of the Garter from the Queen, and the Wateler Peace Prize from the Carnegie Foundation. When he finally succeeded Churchill as Prime Minister in 1955, it was to widespread welcome, and within a month, he had increased his party's majority at a general election, the first occasion on which this had been accomplished in peacetime since 1900.

But as Rhodes James admits, the signs were not all this encouraging. Although more assiduous than his leader, he was ill at ease in opposition, and Churchill invariably stole the limelight on great occasions. In foreign affairs, Eden was deeply hostile to the cause of European unity, did not get on well with the Americans, whose overwhelming power he resented, and was unable to come to terms with the diminished role which Britain was now constrained to play in the world. On the home front, he was understandably unsure, and the one speech Rhodes James quotes as evidence of his domestic interests is as boring as it is banal. As Foreign Secretary, he was constantly at loggerheads with Churchill, was appalled by the Prime Minister's idea of a top-level summit with the Russians and Americans, and was stung by right-wing criticism within his own party that he was appeasing the Egyptians and the Communists. When Churchill suffered a stroke in 1953, Eden would almost undoubtedly have succeeded him, but for the fact that he was himself gravely ill at the time. Thereafter, his health was more suspect than ever, while the strain of waiting for Churchill to make up his mind when to go was, for a man of his nervous temperament, almost unendurable.

Nor, as Prime Minister and Conservative Party Leader, did Eden begin auspiciously. His shyness and aloofness meant that his parliamentary power base was dangerously narrow, and the fact that he had never passed a single piece of domestic legislation was now exposed as a grave weakness. He never really stamped his identity on his administration, his first Cabinet reshuffle was a mistake, and his second a disaster. He interfered too much in the day to day running of departments, he drove himself too hard in his evident desire to succeed, and the strain showed in frequent outbursts of petulance and bad temper. He was excessively sensitive to press criticism, and was noticeably maladroit in handling the media. At the general election, he offered no firm lead on policy, and despite his victory at the polls, the total Tory vote actually fell. Even worse, Churchill's Indian Summer was followed by Eden's cold spring: at home, the economy went into recession, and there were rows about security, immigration and the death penalty; while in foreign affairs, there was a crisis in Cyprus, humiliation in Jordan, and the visit of the new Russian leaders – Bulganin and Khrushchev – was a public relations disaster.

It is in this context – of a government and prime minister visibly losing grip and ground – that the Suez crisis occurred, provoked by Nasser's nationalisation of the Canal after the British and the Americans had refused to finance the Aswan High Dam project. In defence of Eden, Rhodes James argues that his appraisal of Nasser was essentially correct: an international pirate, another Mussolini, who constituted a major threat to world peace. In addition, Eden was clearly let down by the Chiefs of Staff, who were too cautious and indecisive in their planning, and especially by Mountbatten, who did grave disservice by refusing to make his doubts about the enterprise known. Moreover, Eden was badly served by his Cabinet colleagues: Butler was ineffectual, and gave no opinion one way or the other; Selwyn Lloyd as Foreign Secretary was simply not up to the job; Monckton as Minister of Defence declined to make his reservations public; and Macmillan as Chancellor of the Exchequer was conspicuously inconsistent. Above all, Eden was deceived and defeated by the Americans: partly because Dulles gave ambiguous signals which encouraged Eden to expect US support when none was ever intended; and partly because Eisenhower coerced the British into halting their military operations by refusing to rescue sterling until they did.

Yet despite these extenuating circumstances, the fact remains that Eden, ostensibly the great international statesman, was broken by his mishandling of a great international crisis. For much of the time, he was clearly unwell, and his judgment was distorted by his violent personal animosity to Nasser, whom he wanted destroyed at any cost. He showed a lack of firmness in dealing with the Chiefs of Staff, and simply ignored the unequivocal messages from Eisenhower declaring that under no circumstances would the United States give military support. He failed to carry opinion with him, in Britain, in America, in the Commonwealth, and at the United Nations. Even Rhodes James cannot understand why he accepted the plan whereby the French and British would intervene after an Israeli attack on Egypt, since it was clear to all that its real intention was to topple Nasser rather than to divide the combatants. By ordering the cease fire when he did, Eden ensured that the British troops in Egypt incurred the maximum of odium and the minimum of advantage. In denying in the Commons that there had been collusion between the British, the French and the Israelis, Eden undoubtedly misled the House. And his decision to leave for Jamaica when his health finally broke down was an act of catastrophic political folly.

Whether Eden finally resigned on grounds of ill health (as Rhodes James insists), or because he feared that evidence of collusion would leak out (as Carlton claims) remains unclear. But for whatever reason, his career was finished: the youngest Foreign Secretary of modern times had become the youngest Prime Ministerial casualty since Lord Rosebery. Only when dealing with this last phase of Eden's life does Rhodes James's wish to be sympathetic triumph over his desire to be fair. In a chapter implausibly entitled 'Victory, 1957–77', he deploys all his rhetorical skills to argue that in the aftermath of Suez, Eden 'rebuilt' his shattered reputation. But the evidence does not support such a happy ending. His memoirs were predictably boring, and their theme, 'the lessons of the 'thirties and their application to the 'fifties', suggested that he had learned no lessons at all. Like many a former Prime Minister, he dreamed of making a Commons comeback; but his health would not permit it, and when he finally took a peerage, he made almost no impact on the House of Lords. At best, he was a forlorn, forgotten figure; at worst, he was a failed man of peace, an ineffectual man of war, a self-styled prima donna whose brief solo performance had been disastrously second-rate.

*

Beyond doubt, Rhodes James paints a more sensitive and sympathetic picture of Eden than that drawn by David Carlton. In part, this is because he is more well-disposed to his subject. In part, it is because he draws so heavily on both personal and official papers to which Carlton did not have access. But inevitably, the result is an individual portrait rather than a richly contextualized historical study. Much recent writing, especially on the politics of the 'thirties and the policy of appeasement, seems to have passed the author by, and he does not appear to have consulted any major manuscript collection beyond Eden's own papers. One such important source is the diary of Evelyn Shuckburgh, who was Private Secretary to Eden between 1951 and 1954, and in charge of Middle Eastern Affairs at the Foreign Office from 1954 to 1956. At the time, he was highly critical of Eden, both as Foreign Secretary and as Prime Minister, and his cogent and damning comments were extensively quoted by David Carlton. But Rhodes James – for quite unaccountable reasons – deliberately did not seek access to them. All too often, indeed, his attitude to Eden's contemporary and scholarly critics is little more than one of querulous and disdainful dismissal.

How are we to explain and to reconcile the two Edens which Rhodes James depicts so vividly? The author's own answer is that Eden was quite extraordinarily unlucky – in his temperament and his first marriage, in his health and his doctors, in the long years of waiting for Churchill to retire, and in the colleagues at home and abroad who misled and betrayed him over Suez. To the extent that this is correct, it prompts the remark that no one so vulnerable or so accident prone should ever have been so prominent in English public life. And this in turn suggests that Eden's greatest misfortune was not that he was dogged throughout his career by bad luck, but that, on the contrary, he was in many ways far too fortunate for his own and for his country's good. Promoted too soon and too far for his abilities, his career then acquired an inexorable momentum of its own. And as a result, he became the object of extravagant and unrealistic expectations which he lacked the ability to meet. Despite Rhodes James's disclaimers, it is difficult to resist the conclusion that at Suez he was making a despairing attempt to prove that he really was up to the job. But as Churchill had predicted, when the crunch came, Eden could not do it.

Undeniably, there is much in Eden's career which may be explained in terms of luck (both good and bad) and personality (both his own and other people's). But to understand his successes and his failures more fully, his life needs to be set in a broader historical perspective than this biographical treatment allows. It is important to remember that Eden was born in 1897, the year of Queen Victoria's Diamond Jubilee, but died in 1977, the year of Queen Elizabeth II's Silver Jubilee. Between those two dates, the world, and Britain's place in it, was transformed almost beyond recognition. At his birth, gentlemen still ruled Britain, and Britain still ruled much of the globe. Even during his apprentice years at the Foreign Office, Europe remained in many ways the hub of the universe. But by the time of his maturity and pre-eminence, the British Empire was in dissolution and Europe was in disarray, and in the resulting retreat from greatness, Eden was his nation's foremost casualty. Unable to defy, like Churchill, or to dissemble, like Mountbatten and Macmillan, he possessed neither the firmness nor the flexibility to survive in such demanding and difficult times.

Moreover, even in the heyday of British greatness, expertise in international affairs was rarely the route to the very top in politics. Among nineteenth-century figures, only Palmerston and Salisbury of outstanding Prime Ministers made their reputations in that realm, and both were much more tough and robust than Eden. But thereafter, almost every British Prime Minister, including Churchill himself, spent the majority of his (or her) ministerial career in home rather than overseas affairs. Eden apart, the only exception is Sir Alec Douglas-Home, and he is surely the exception who proves the rule. Seen in this light, Eden was never really Prime Ministerial material, and never served the appropriate Prime Ministerial apprenticeship. On the contrary, his place was among those patrician Foreign Secretaries who have held office in Britain for so much of the twentieth century: Lansdowne, Grey, Curzon, Halifax, Home and Carrington. All were aristocrats, ill at ease amid the infighting of politics; most of them provided a dignified façade while the Prime Minister was in charge of foreign policy; none of them was really fitted by temperament or by training for the supreme office. In this sense, Eden was indeed unlucky, not in waiting so long to succeed Churchill, but in the fact that he succeeded him at all.

So how, exactly, did this happen? In part, it was because Eden's pre-eminence in foreign affairs was itself largely accidental. He only obtained junior office in 1931 because Baldwin pressed his claims with uncharacteristic vigour; he only became Foreign Secretary in 1935 because Hoare was forced to resign and there was no one else available; and he only returned to power in 1939 on Churchill's coat tails. During the Second World War, the domestic jobs in Churchill's coalition were virtually monopolized by the Labour Party, and the Prime Minister's preference for cronies like Beaverbrook and Linderman meant that few younger Tory politicians were promoted. The result was a post-war Conservative Party with a missing generation, which meant that Eden was faced with no serious rival, except possibly Oliver Stanley, who died in 1950. And this in turn meant that in Churchill's last government, most of the ministers were elder statesmen devoid of political ambitions (like Salisbury, Lyttelton, Alexander and Monckton), while the two who had did have their sights set on the top job (Butler and Macmillan) were much too young.

Under these unusual circumstances, Eden's rise was as unavoidable as it was unfortunate. For the truth is that it would not have mattered when he took over. Regardless of the timing, Eden would invariably have seemed a lame-duck leader by comparison with the Churchillian golden eagle, the village fiddler after Paganini, Mr Pooter following the Duke of Omnium. Indeed, modern British history is littered with similar instances of lesser men succeeding greater, who then went down to defeat: Rosebery after Gladstone, Balfour after Salisbury, Home after Macmillan, Callaghan after Wilson. In each case, it may have been bad luck to have succeeded in such unfavourable circumstances; but it may also be that the circumstances only appeared unfavourable because of the very limitations of the successors who inherited them.

Viewed in this broader perspective, the most remarkable feature of Eden's career was not that he was a great man tragically destroyed, but rather that he was a mediocre figure who had got too far. In many ways, he was a thoroughly decent fellow. But as Rhodes James admits, 'he lacked hardness and ruthlessness'. Then, as now, decency alone is rarely, if ever, enough.

(1987)

NOTE:
1. Robert Rhodes James, *Anthony Eden* (London, 1986).

# R. A. Butler

It is a cliché of American history that the inscription on Thomas Jefferson's tomb at Monticello carries understatement almost to the point of self-indulgence. There is no mention of the great offices of state which he held and adorned: instead he is remembered as the author of the Declaration of Independence and as the architect of the University of Virginia. The same disdain for government endeavour may be seen in the words on the gravestone of R. A. Butler in Saffron Walden churchyard. There is no allusion to his long and illustrious ministerial career: all that is recorded is that he was Member of Parliament for the constituency for thirty-six years, and Master of Trinity College, Cambridge, for a further thirteen. There, however, the similarities end. In Jefferson's case, the indifference to worldly distinction was that of a man whose public career had been triumphantly successful; whereas with Butler, it coyly concealed the fact that he had never actually made it to the very top. For while the sage of Monticello was twice elected President of the United States, the squire of Saffron Walden twice failed to become Prime Minister of England.

To his supporters, who insisted on calling him the best Prime Minister Britain never had, this was an unmitigated disaster – for Butler, for his party, and for his country. His ministerial career, lasting from the early 1930s to the mid 1960s, was among the longest and most distinguished of twentieth-century statesmen. The Education Act which he passed in 1944 established the modern system of secondary schooling, and is one of the few pieces of legislation known by the name of its promoter. As the leading figure in post-war Tory policy-making, he reconciled the party to the Welfare State, and was the chief architect of its long spell of power between 1951 and 1964. As Chancellor of the Exchequer in the early 1950s, he came close to presiding over an economic miracle, and as Home Secretary at the end of the decade, he was notably reformist, civilized and humane. Viewed in this light, his claims to lead the Conservative Party were beyond dispute, and it was only the towering ambition and vindictive cunning of Harold Macmillan which denied him the supreme office, in 1957 and again in 1963.

But to his enemies – and, significantly, they seem to have been more inside his own party than without – this was a wildly distorted picture, of a man who was well fitted to be a permanent understudy, but who lacked the essential qualities for the starring role. Throughout his career, Butler was indecisive, accommodating, inclined to give way. He lacked mettle, toughness, determination. He had no rhetoric, no panache, no charisma. In foreign affairs, he was an incorrigible appeaser. During the 1930s, he surrendered over India and Germany; in the 1940s his commitment to total victory was distinctly lukewarm; in the 1950s he was soft and supine over Suez; and in the 1960s he was in charge of another scuttle operation when he wound up the Central African Federation of Rhodesia and Nyasaland. On the home front, he was no more robust. His belief in the mixed economy and the Welfare State marked him out as a socialist fellow traveller; as Chancellor of the Exchequer his policies were all but indistinguishable from those of Hugh Gaitskell, his Labour predecessor; and as Home Secretary he was too eager to compromise on law and order and immigration. In all these ways, his critics asserted, he was quite unfitted to lead the Tory Party, and in keeping him down and out, Macmillan was merely doing his duty.

Throughout his long career, these conflicting and competing views of Butler regularly re-surfaced, and they came to the fore once more on the publication, in 1971, of his memoirs *The Art of the Possible*. Written in his sunset years as Master of Trinity College, and in an elegant tone of ironic and irreverent detachment, they were widely praised as a minor masterpiece. As a short, slim work, his autobiography was a most effective riposte to the ponderous, multi-volume memoirs which Harold Macmillan was simultaneously producing. Admirers like Edward Boyle and Enoch Powell greeted it with rapturous acclaim, seeing in its pages the quintessence of those liberal and humane qualities which had always made him the last best hope of the Tory party. But his critics were unrepentant. One reviewer in particular argued that Butler's memoirs were complacent and self-serving auto-hagiography; that they left undiscussed the many 'mistakes and blunders' of his career; and that the real reason he had failed to gain the supreme office was that, for most of his life, he had never had to fight for anything, and so he lacked the killer instinct. This young, dismissive and perceptive writer was at the time the deputy editor of the *New Statesman*. And his name was Anthony Howard.

Only a politician with so well developed a sense of irony as Butler would have appointed the critical reviewer of his autobiography to be the author of his official life.[1] And, in 1980, that is precisely what he did. At first glance, Howard's qualifications for the post were at best non-existent, and at worst quite inappropriate. He was a political journalist, not a political historian, who had never undertaken a large work based on serious scholarly research. And, as befitted a man who later became the editor of the *New Statesman*, he was a supporter of the Labour Party, expressed a 'wary admiration' for Harold Wilson, and greatly admired maverick iconoclasts of the left like Richard Crossman. Yet, as Butler himself may have hoped, Howard has in fact produced an enthralling book. It is certainly not the last word on the subject; but it is indeed a fascinating and surprisingly sympathetic account of one of the major figures in twentieth-century British politics. And it would surely have given Lord Butler great satisfaction that it provides ample support for his critics and his champions alike.

Butler was born in India in 1902, the child of academe and of the Raj. He was descended from a long line of Cambridge dons, who had been Fellows – and occasionally Masters – of their colleges since the mid-eighteenth century, and who were thus firmly ensconced among the intellectual aristocracy of late Victorian Britain. By that time, they had also branched out into public life, and Butler's father was a member of the Indian Civil Service, who ended his career as Governor of the Central Provinces. The young Richard Austen (who was given those names to provide him with the soubriquet 'Rab', by which he was known throughout his life), followed the conventional upbringing of his class. He returned to England for preparatory and public schooling, but it was at Cambridge that his career blossomed. He obtained Firsts in History and Modern Languages; he was elected President of the Union; and he became a Fellow of Corpus Christi College on graduation. Shortly after, he married Sydney Courtauld, one of the richest heiresses of her generation. This brought Rab wealth, country houses and fine pictures in abundance. And in 1929 it also propelled him into politics, when he was elected for the Courtauld-controlled constituency of Saffron Walden, at the tender age of twenty-seven.

Beyond any doubt, this was a formidable and fortunate foundation from which to launch a career in public life, as brains, money, youth and connection were so impressively allied. Yet in many ways, despite these unusual advantages, Butler's background did not fit him ideally for the rough and tumble of politics. The twin traditions of academic detachment and government service were not easily reconciled with the loyalty, passion and partisanship rightly demanded of a party politician. As a child of empire, he was often separated from his parents, and this engendered a sense of isolation and melancholy bordering on fatalism and self-pity which was to prove another major disadvantage throughout his public career. There was no martial blood in his veins, and a riding accident in Indian meant he was bad at games, unfit for military service, and generally hostile to both – not the soundest of views for a Tory MP to hold. And even as a young man, he seemed weak and uncertain in a crisis: he apparently suffered a major nervous breakdown in his third year at Cambridge, about which it would have been instructive to know more.

Nevertheless, during the 1930s, Butler's career continued its seemingly effortless and inexorable advance. He was by now fully established as an Essex country gentleman with an impressive London town house in Smith Square, and he was rapidly taken up by the three most powerful figures in the Tory Party: Stanley Baldwin, Lord Halifax and Neville Chamberlain. Within two years of entering Parliament, he was given minor preferment, and he was soon appointed a junior minister at the India Office. He was conspicuously accomplished in piloting through the Commons the complex and controversial Government of India Act of 1935, and in so doing won golden opinions from friend and foe alike (Churchill included). Having established himself as a sound, safe, reliable company man, he was moved to the Foreign Office in February 1938, where he was deputy to Lord Halifax. Since this obliged him to represent his department in the Commons, he came into close contact with Neville Chamberlain, whose protégé he now became, and whose policy of appeasement he wholeheartedly supported.

But as the clouds darkened in Europe, it was clear that Butler's identification with the men of Munich was excessive and potentially damaging. Already, in the early 'thirties, he had clashed with a young, radical, dissenting Tory named Harold Macmillan. Throughout 1938, and until the outbreak of war and beyond, he was totally committed to appeasement to a far greater extent than he was later prepared to admit in his memoirs, where he took great pains to conceal the active, energetic part that he had played, and to defend the policy on the grounds that the later Britain went to war with Hitler, the better. But as Howard candidly demonstrates, no such considerations seem to have occupied the mind of the younger Rab at the time. In private and in public, he favoured appeasement, not because it won precious time for Britain to complete its military preparations, but simply because he believed in Anglo-German friendship, thought Hitler could be trusted, and felt that German demands should be met. So, when Chamberlain's government and policy crashed in ruins in May 1940, Butler was understandably dismayed at the prospect that he, too, might be a victim.

Yet for all his dislike of Churchill as a buccaneering 'half-breed', Butler's luck, astonishingly, held. While most of the appeasers were cast out, Rab found himself the unexpected – and still largely the unexplained – beneficiary of Churchillian magnanimity. He was soon promoted to be President of the Board of Education, and piloted through the measure which bears his name. Even the electoral defeat of 1945 worked out greatly to his advantage. As the only major Tory figure with recent experience of domestic – as distinct from foreign or military – affairs, he was put in charge of the Conservative Research Department, and soon produced the first of the 'Charters' which reconciled the party to the Welfare State. The death of Oliver Stanley in 1950 meant that when the Conservatives returned to power in the following year, and Rab became Chancellor of the Exchequer, he was the undisputed number three figure in government. The next five years saw him at the peak of his power and influence; when Churchill and Eden were both incapacitated in the summer of 1953, it was Butler who took over as acting head of government; and on Eden's assumption of the Prime Ministership two years later, there seemed no doubt as to whom his ultimate successor would be.

But even during these fifteen years of unimpeded progress, culminating in a series of brilliant budgets, Butler continued to make mistakes. In 1940, even after the fall of France, he was still pressing for a negotiated peace with Germany, to the embarrassment and outrage of many of his colleagues. His handling of the Education Bill was less successful and determined than it might have been, and he missed a unique opportunity to bring the public schools into a fully-integrated national system. By espousing the mixed economy and the Welfare State so enthusiastically when in opposition, he cut himself off from many right-wing Conservatives, and was accused of being a milk and water socialist. And even in Churchill's government, his power-base was less strong than it should have been. He made influential enemies within the Party hierarchy, like Lord Woolton; he underestimated the growing challenge to his position that was being mounted by Harold Macmillan; and he made no effort to conceal the fact that he did not take Eden entirely seriously.

In retrospect at least, Butler's career definitely passed its zenith in 1955. His wife Sydney died of a particularly gruesome form of facial cancer, and thereafter, Rab was never quite the same man again. To make matters worse, he was himself soon afflicted by a severe viral infection, which further diminished his decisiveness and effectiveness. In Eden's Cabinet reshuffle following Churchill's retirement, Butler grudgingly gave up the Exchequer, and let himself be fobbed off with the posts of Lord Privy Seal and Leader of the House of Commons, without a department, and without a real role in government. Meanwhile, Harold Macmillan advanced inexorably, first to the Foreign Secretaryship, and then to the Exchequer. Then came Suez, where Butler's touch was noticeably maladroit. Throughout the crisis, he seemed aloof, distant and uncertain. Yet when Eden's health collapsed, it fell to Rab to bring home the troops, restore the pound, and repair the Anglo-American alliance. But while all this was well accomplished, there was no glory in it. And so, as Butler played the part of the loyal and dutiful caretaker once more, it was the more flamboyant and adventurous Macmillan who battled and intrigued his way to the very top.

Beyond doubt, his first failure to obtain the supreme office hit Butler very hard. And thereafter, he was subjected to a succession of sustained humiliations at Macmillan's hands which, even twenty years on, do not make edifying reading. By giving Rab the Home Office rather than making him Foreign Secretary, Macmillan satisfied his hankering to return to a major department, but ensured that he would only do himself further damage with the right wing of the party. Thereafter, he was loaded with more offices, including the Chairmanship of the Conservative Party, and became a veritable Poo-Bah. But since these party and government jobs were fundamentally incompatible, they only diminished his effectiveness while increasing his labours. Eventually, he attained the even dizzier heights of First Secretary of State and Deputy Prime Minister. But in practice, this meant he became an increasingly marginal figure. He was obliged to give up the Home Office, and subsequently spent much of his time abroad, dealing efficiently but unobtrusively with the dissolution of the Central African Federation.

Nevertheless, despite the real decline in Butler's position

between 1957 and 1963, the very great trouble taken by Macmillan to place him at every conceivable disadvantage was the surest possible indication that even the Prime Minister was obliged to recognize him as the man most likely to be his successor. Since he was nine years Macmillan's junior, and since many in the party believed he had been badly treated in 1957, he was still clearly in with a second chance. His marriage to Mollie Courtauld – the widow of Sydney's cousin – brought him renewed happiness, and she had absolutely no doubt that her husband should be the next Prime Minister. As Chairman of the Party and of its Research Organization, Butler remained a formidable figure. His work as Home Secretary, though controversial, meant he was constantly in the news. His unrivalled experience in government, his undoubted expertise in administration, and his publicly acknowledged position as the second man in the Cabinet, meant that he was generally regarded as being as much the natural successor to Macmillan in 1963 as he had been to Eden in 1957.

But again, it did not come off. While Butler once more took over the government in the aftermath of the Prime Minister's illness, Macmillan did everything he could, even from his hospital bed, to prevent the succession going Rab's way, including making the fourteenth Earl of Home the next Prime Minister. Thwarted a second time, Butler's career soon collapsed. He became Foreign Secretary for a brief period, but his heart was no longer in it. He played almost no part in the 1964 election campaign, except to give a catastrophically indiscreet interview in which he predicted the Conservatives' defeat. Thereafter, it seems that everyone wanted to be rid of him. Sir Alec Douglas-Home tried to remove him from the opposition front bench by offering him an Earldom in the dissolution honours. More successfully, the new Prime Minister, Harold Wilson, urged on him a life peerage and the Mastership of Trinity College. He accepted, reigned in dignified grandeur, and wrote his memoirs. In 1980, he made a brief return to the political fray to lead a revolt in the Lords against the Thatcher government's proposals for educational reform. But after this final fling, the Saffron Walden churchyard soon beckoned.

★

It may be precisely because this biography is written from such an unusual – albeit 'official' – standpoint, that admirers and opponents of Lord Butler will both find it much to their taste. For if anything, this account accentuates, rather than resolves, the contradictory views which are held about him. Indeed, in some ways, it makes him more of an enigma, not less. After four hundred pages, his temperament remains elusive, the reasons for his ultimate failure unclear, and his place in history uncertain. Perhaps the key to his unfathomable character lies in the unsure and contradictory nature of his own circumstances. He was too worldly to be an academic, but too detached to be a partisan. He was middle-class by origins, and plutocratic by marriage, yet he lived the life of a country squire. He was a child of the empire who spent much of his adult life helping to give it away, a patriot who would go to any lengths to accommodate Hitler. Despite the Cambridge Firsts, the Courtauld money and the safe Saffron Walden majority, it is difficult to resist the conclusion that for most of his life, Rab never really quite knew who he was, what he was doing, or where he was going.

Put another way, this means we need to know more than we are told in this biography about the life of Rab's mind. That he was donnish, sceptical, detached, intellectual, is true but trite: no attempt is made here to explore what he was actually thinking, nor to describe how his views changed – which they did, very dramatically. In the 1930s, his opinions seem to have been conventional Tory platitudes about religion, the countryside and the national community: Baldwin without the pipe, Halifax minus the elephants. Unlike his more radical rival Harold Macmillan, he seems to have shown little interest in contemporary social or economic problems. Yet somehow, sometime, in the 1940s, he became a convert to Keynesian economics and Welfare State policies. How the champion of rustic decency became transformed into the apostle of full employment and the mixed economy is not explored. Whether Butler worked this out for himself, or whether he merely absorbed unthinkingly the conventional wisdoms of the time, is left unexplained.

Nor is it altogether clear from this account quite why it was that

Butler never got to the very top. As befits his essentially journal-istic approach, Howard puts a great deal of it down to luck. Throughout his book, he is very sensitive – and often rightly so – to the importance of sheer accident, the unpredictability of events and the quirks of personality, which so powerfully influence political life, even though professional historians are sometimes embarrassed to admit it. And in Rab's case, it is clear that the luck was distributed very unevenly, and ultimately very disadvan-tageously. Until the mid 1950s, he was quite astonishingly fortun-ate: in the Courtauld marriage, in his progress during the 'thirties, in his survival in 1940, in the Tory defeat of 1945, and in Oliver Stanley's premature death. But thereafter, the luck ran very much against him, while it ran very favourably for Macmillan. Yet explanations such as this do not go very deep. To see Rab's career in particular, and politics in general, as little more than a battle between 'artistry', 'instinct' and 'antennae' on the one side, and 'traps', 'blunders' and 'banana skins' on the other, hardly seems sufficient.

The author's more penetrating explanation is that Butler was defeated by the 'blue blood and thunder group' of the Conserva-tive Party, the aristocratic and military element exemplified by the Cecils, the Cavendishes and the Churchills, who had reasserted themselves in 1940, and who still, according to Howard, wielded great weight in the upper echelons of the party twenty years later. In their eyes, Rab was wholly unacceptable: partly because he was middle class, and partly because he was an appeaser. As the careers of Macmillan (a publisher's boy) and Lord Home (another Chamberlain acolyte) both showed, it was quite possible to be one or the other and still get to the very top. But unlike these two men, Rab was doubly damned. And that, combined with his irrever-ence and his indiscretions meant that the magic inner circle were determined to do him down, come what may. Ever since 1963, this explanation has received wide currency: but the amount of evidence which can actually be marshalled in its support still seems decidedly thin, even in this book.

Indeed, as Howard emphatically insisted in his *New Statesman* review, and as he more reluctantly concedes in his biography, the person who bears the greatest responsibility for Rab's ultimate failure is in fact Rab himself. In his early years, everything had gone too easily for him, with the result that he came to expect events to go his way, and never learned the arts of private intrigue or of public theatre to which any ambitious politician must eventually have recourse if he (or she) is to make it to the very top. And Butler not only lacked the means to fight: he also lacked the will. He had no instinct or relish for the jugular. He would not stoop to conquer. Had he chosen to exert himself in 1957, or again in 1963, it seems likely that he would in fact have prevailed. But as Macmillan rightly and ruthlessly calculated, Butler always held back and gave way. It does Macmillan little credit that he treated Rab as he did between 1957 and 1963. But it does Butler even less that he acquiesced so passively and supinely in his own emasculation. Like another academic turned statesman, but even more so, Rab was simply too proud to fight.

By definition, the publication of an official biography transforms its subject from being a recently deceased contemporary into an authentic historical figure. Yet in Butler's case, this process was well under way even before Howard's book appeared. As the first (and last) great Tory 'wet', he was a waning force even in the era of Macmillan; but in the age of Thatcher he seems at best an anachronism and at worst plain irrelevant. With a Conservative Government exploiting the Falklands factor and proclaiming its commitment to the free market economy, Butler's supposedly solid achievements – turning the Tory Party away from its delight in untrammelled competition and imperial hubris – now look decidedly more ephemeral than they did only twenty years ago. In death, as in life, Rab seems fated to occupy a subordinate role. Although he relished ironies, it is difficult to believe he would have appreciated this particular one.

(1987)

NOTE:
1. Anthony Howard, *Rab: The Life of R. A. Butler* (London, 1987).

# Acknowledgements

I am grateful for permission to use revised versions of essays that originally appeared in the following publications:

Chapter 1: *New York Review of Books*, vol. xxxiii, 12 June 1986.

Chapter 2: *New York Review of Books*, vol. xxxi, 8 November 1984.

Chapter 3: *New York Review of Books*, vol. xxxiv, 23 April 1987.

Chapter 4: *London Review of Books*, vol. v, 15 September 1983.

Chapter 5: *London Review of Books*, vol. iv, 2 December 1982.

Chapter 6: *New York Review of Books*, vol. xxxii, 9 May 1985.

Chapter 7: *Times Literary Supplement*, 20 September 1985.

Chapter 8: *London Review of Books*, vol. v, 4 August 1983.

Chapter 9: *London Review of Books*, vol. iii, 2 April 1981.

Chapter 10: *London Review of Books*, vol. iii, 2 July 1981; vol. v, 17 March 1983.

Chapter 11: *London Review of Books*, vol. iv, 21 January 1982.

Chapter 12: *London Review of Books*, vol. vii, 21 March 1985.

Chapter 13: *Encounter*, vol. lxi (1983); *Times Literary Supplement*, 13 April 1984.

Chapter 14: *London Review of Books*, vol. iv, 15 April 1982.

Chapter 15: *History*, vol. lxviii (1983).

Chapter 16: *London Review of Books*, vol. vii, 6 June 1985.

Chapter 17: *London Review of Books*, vol. iii, 16 July 1981.

Chapter 18: *New York Review of Books*, vol. xxxi, 20 December 1984.

Chapter 19: *London Review of Books*, vol. vi, 19 July 1984.

Chapter 20: *New York Review of Books*, vol. xxxi, 2 February 1984.

## ACKNOWLEDGEMENTS

Chapter 21: *New Society*, vol. lxx, 20/27 December 1984.

Chapter 22: *London Review of Books*, vol. vii, 24 January 1985.

Chapter 23: *New York Review of Books*, vol. xxxiii, 27 March 1986.

Chapter 24: *New York Review of Books*, vol. xxxii, 19 December 1985.

Chapter 25: *London Review of Books*, vol. iii, 3 December 1981.

Chapter 26: *London Review of Books*, vol. iv, 21 October 1982.

Chapter 27: *London Review of Books*, vol. vi, 19 January 1984.

Chapter 28: *New York Review of Books*, vol. xxxii, 28 March 1985.

Chapter 29: *New York Review of Books*, vol. xxxiv, 22 October 1987.

Chapter 30: *New York Review of Books*, vol. xxxiv, 17 December 1987.